HOW TO BECOME AN IAS

HOW TO BECOME AN IAS

DR. VIJAY AGRAWAL

BENTEN

Published in India by

Benten Books

MIG A-121, 1st floor, P and T Rd,
Near Sharda Vidya Mandir Foundation School, Kotra Sultanabad,
Bhopal, Madhya Pradesh 462003
Phone- 0755-4245626
E-mail : bentenbooks@gmail.com
Website : www.bentenbooks.com

First Published : 2015
This edition : 2026

ISBN : 978-93-82419-58-7

Translated and edited by : Ruchika Uniyal

Cover design by : Pooja Agrawal

Printed & bound in India by : Thomson Press India Private Ltd.

Price : Rs. 395/-

Index

PREFACE

I understand your impatience to become an IAS officer because I have been through this. I also know the social and parental pressure you are facing because I have felt it too. I am also aware of the obstacles and challenges you are going to meet during your IAS preparation because I myself have dealt with them, but in the end, achieved what I had toiled for.

My young friends, I feel much satisfaction in telling you that I did not stop after accomplishing my goal, instead I set up a new goal. My new goal was to help and guide other IAS aspirants. And I started doing it at a personal level and at various institutes right after the completion of my two year training. And I'm proud that I succeeded in this.

This book stems from these experiences. I assure you that if you are honest with this book, it will guide you like the light from a light house. So remember this is not a book you read once and pass on. It is a book that should be on your study table until you are no longer in the IAS battlefield.

This book will answer all your queries. You may need an answer anytime so you will need to keep the book with you.

Nothing would give me more pleasure than making a tiny contribution to your success. This book is such an effort. I pray to God that he gives you enough strength and wisdom so that your dreams can come true.

With best wishes,

Dr Vijay Agrawal

Email -vkagrawal57@gmail.com

Website-www.vijayagrawal.com

www.afeias.com

Chapter 1

Why have you decided to become an IAS?

If you have decided to be an IAS officer, let me welcome you to our country's largest, and quite difficult, competition. I give you my blessings and pray to God that he provides you with the patience, confidence and enthusiasm that should last you a long time, because these things are very important for what you have set out to achieve.

Still, before I tell you how to become an IAS, allow me to ask you a very important question. The reason I'm asking you this question is that in my long experience of guiding civil service aspirants, I have found that most of the young men get so excited that they enter the competition without giving it a careful thought, and after few years of repeated failures they leave tired and exhausted. This is why I feel that every participant who wants to enter this race should ask himself the question that I'm going to ask you. I'm not going to ask you 'Why do you want to become an IAS officer?' My ears have lost patience listening to the same old, clichéd answers. In any case, whether you want to be an IAS for power, for social status or for the prestige and a car with a red beacon on top, it has nothing to do with your preparation. Take any job that you want to do; it would have something that attracts you towards it. That is why you would want to do the job in the first place? Unless doing it is some kind of an obligation.

Of course, IAS is different than other jobs in the sense that it has multiple attractions. It has so many attractions that I do not think it is wrong that majority of the students in the country want to pursue it. But, yes, if you think of it in the context of our country, a doctor or an engineer opting for IAS is damaging to our nation. The country could not benefit from the resources that were spent on producing that particular doctor or engineer. Anybody can become an IAS but not everybody can become a doctor or an engineer. However, as long as UPSC (the body that conducts IAS examinations) has allowed it, even the doctors and engineers are welcome in this competition.

Let me now go back to the question I wanted to ask you. Answer me with all sincerity and think carefully before you reply. What did you see in yourself that made you think that you can be an IAS officer? This is the small question I want to ask.

Before you read the book further, you need to find your answer. Another person's answer will not work for you. To walk ahead in the path of becoming an IAS you need your own answer.

When I put up this question to students who seek my guidance over phone or in person, at first, they simply do not understand the question. Actually they get dumbstruck after hearing this question because nobody has ever asked them such a weird thing! Until now, all they have heard is that they can do anything they want. Anyone can do anything is an ideal thing to say, but it can sometimes be misleading. I do not believe that anyone can do anything. What I do believe is that there is nobody who can do nothing. Everyone has the capability to do something or the other, but no one can do everything. I asked you this question so that you do not remain in such illusion.

Here are some answers to my question that were given by student immediately and others that were given after a careful thought.

- ☑ I have always stood first in my class, so I think I can do this.
- ☑ I can do this because I can work hard.
- ☑ People tell me that I have a strong memory, I can be an IAS officer.
- ☑ I have to do this because my parents want me to do so, and I can't disappoint them, so I have to do this, no matter what.
- ☑ I can learn everything by rote, even math.
- ☑ I have vowed that I'm going to do this.

Friends, these are the answers that keep repeating themselves in different words. It is with regret that I'm telling you that none of them can satisfy me and I have to tell my young fellows, "Go and think about your goals once more." This is because none of the above mentioned reasons will make you an IAS, and the lack of any of them is not going to keep you from becoming one.

Do not get bothered by my comment. In a short while, you will know what exactly is required of you to become an IAS. Now, I'm going to present you with some real-life examples so that before you embark on your journey - and in case you have already started your journey, before you end it - you can evaluate yourself accurately to see what kind of traveller you are to walk the path of IAS. This evaluation will help you clear your mind and make you firm by presenting you with the truth. Ultimately, this will benefit you.

A young boy once came to me. He was smart, enthusiastic and had a decent academic record. He had come to ask me how he could become an IAS. While I was giving him some tips on how to prepare for IAS, he was constantly repeating, "Sir, I will do whatever I have to do for this. I can get myself beheaded but I have to do this."

I asked him to come to me after a month. When he came after a month, his first question to me was, "Sir, I have heard that IAS officers do not get paid very much?" "Yes, you have heard correctly," I told him. He asked me another question, "Sir, I have also heard that they get transferred quite frequently because of which their kids may face some difficulty in studies?" This was also true. He was hesitant to ask me the third question, "Sir, is it true that MPs and MLAs can scold collectors and walk away?" I told him that this does not happen every time but I could not say that it never happens.

Now you should hear the final answer of this IAS aspirant who was so passionate about being an officer that he was ready to be beheaded for it. "Sir, I'm thinking that if even after becoming an IAS there are so many difficulties, what is the point of becoming one?" he said. I respected his decision and got rid of him because it was impossible to make him an IAS officer.

I knew a girl who was in her final year of MBBS. She claimed that she would not only qualify in her first attempt but also bag a place within the top ten. I tried hard to get her out of this delusion but it was of no use. Unfortunately (as expected), after three failed attempts, she decided not to give the last one. The worst part is that she could not even qualify the preliminary examinations!

A boy had passed all his examinations until his bachelor's degree with compartment. Still, he thought he could become an IAS because he had heard that anybody could do this. What was even more amusing is that he not only believed what he heard but also took that path. Thankfully, he wasted only two years of his life before he realised the truth and changed his direction.

There are students who do not know language and whatever they do know is not totally correct. They are graduates but they do not have knowledge about any subject. In fact, they do not even know the procedure and the syllabus of IAS exams and yet they decide that they will become an IAS officer. The saddest part about this is that they waste precious three to four years of their lives in this delusion.

You can be deserving if...

I have guided so many people in becoming an IAS officer, but I can't tell you how many of them were really deserving of it. It is of no use arguing it either. What is useful to know is how many of them 'worked' to make themselves worthy of it. I believe nobody is deserving of anything, you have to work to make yourself worthy of something. What harms the first-class performers is that they make the mistake of thinking themselves 'already worthy' of the job. While sometimes the second and third division holders succeed because they know that "I am not worthy of it, and I have to become so." The movie '12th Fail', based on the success story of an IPS officer, beautifully portrays this inspiring truth.

Yes, I can tell you what percentage of those people made themselves worthy of achieving their goal. But my answer is only going to disappoint you because it is less than even a percent. Yes, out of every 500 candidates who appear for the exam, only one student.

I know you may not believe my statistics and even assume that I'm merely saying it to support my stand, because even the rate of success is around these figures. But you should believe me. For example, I believe that the biggest challenge in the IAS exam is to write an accurate answer. After I taught boys and girls how to understand a question and write the correct answer, I told them to write the answers for me, and also stressed upon its importance when they did not do so. I did this so I could evaluate their answers and guide them properly. Would you believe that the success percentage here was even less than half a percent? The students would not bother to write the answers. They knew that their answers were lacking yet they believed that they would be able to do well in the exam. I don't think they even know what led them to this conclusion, but they chose not to practice and lost the chance to learn from their follies.

I ask my students to listen to the news on radio daily. But the maximum that they have followed my instructions is for one and a half month. They have some excuse up their sleeve to avoid listening to the news. It is the same case when it comes to reading newspapers. I tell them that devoting 30 minutes daily to newspapers would suffice. They could read the important news and then analyse it from different angles. But they are one step ahead of me. They spend more than two hours on newspapers and when I ask them what they have read they have nothing substantial to tell. This is because they read bits of all news items rather than focusing on one important item. As a result, they end up reading nothing.

Overall, they ask how they should prepare and they are told how to go about it. They listen; they like it and even get impressed. But they still end up doing what they have always been doing. Even if they take my advice for some time, they return to their old ways after a while. This is not the case with just one or two people. In fact, there are hardly one or two people with whom this may not be the case. Now what can you do with such people!

I have observed this, and quite rightly so, that preparing for IAS nowadays is not so much a career option as it is a fashionable lifestyle choice - and a respected one at that. When someone asks, "What are you doing these days?" a person takes great pride in replying that he is preparing for IAS. This is the case even though most people are just whiling away their time under the pretext of studying for IAS; they don't even know how they should be preparing in the first place. Even if these people are told how to do it, they will listen to everyone but do what they wish in the end.

So friends, my advice is that in response to the question

'What is it in me that I can become an IAS?' you should search inside yourself, and find out whether you will be able to adapt yourself to the needs and demands of IAS preparation. You are what you are. It is possible that your mettle is even stronger than what is required for IAS. But you must know that there is no use for a sword where a needle is required. You have to acclimatize yourself according to what is needed to be an IAS.

You can do this if...

It will require a solid mentality, undeterred thoughts and a tendency to keep your promises with yourself. It is easy for many to resolve that they would do something but very few have the ability to stick to it. I believe that the one who vows to do something and follows it through can achieve anything- even if he is a third-division holder.

If you approach IAS preparation without mental strength, it will either remain just a dream or a very difficult feat- if not an impossible one. Without mental strength, your mind will start seeding excuses and you will end up putting off all the work that you must do.

For instance, a girl asked me, "Sir, where do you give your classes?" After I answered her she told me that she would not be able to join. Do you know why she said this? It was not because the classes were expensive or she didn't have enough time or even because she didn't need them. The reason was that her house was three kilometres away from where the classes were held. Now what would you call this?

I used to hold three-day workshops in New Delhi on a monthly basis. I would guide young minds on how they should prepare for IAS. Students from around the country would come to attend it. Some would even call and ask when my next class would be. Even though I knew my next class would be the following month, I would tell them 'I don't know'. I knew that even next month, they will ask me again, "Sir when will your next class be?" There is no end to these questions.

Now you need to identify what is making you talk like the girl who was making excuses or like the boys who keep asking such questions. You need to identify the culprit behind all this. Otherwise you will think that you are doing everything that should be done. But instead you are just doing what you want to do.

There is a huge difference between 'what should happen' and 'what I wish should happen' and it is this difference that is the deciding factor between your victory and defeat. The IAS exam doesn't care about what you want; it only cares about what it wants.

So there is not just a gap between what you want and what the UPSC wants, but there is also a clash.

You can only bridge this gap and end this clash through mental strength. There is no other way.

Once you acquire mental strength, you will feel some changes inside you that will make you feel as if you are closer to your goal. What really happens is that the principle of 'The Secret' starts working and you will feel that your environment is favourable to you. Author Paulo Coelho mentions this in his novel 'The Alchemist' when he writes, "When you want something, the entire universe conspires in helping you to achieve it." With less or no mental strength, usually you get frustrated and feel that the whole world is against you and nothing is moving in the right direction.

So let me tell you what will happen to you once you have decided to do something and you are determined about it, especially if you have decided to prepare for IAS (not decided to become one):

(1) The most important thing that will happen is that your mind will stop making excuses. The only thing that will remain in your mind is the determination- "I have to do this." IAS preparation will top your priority list and become the first thing in your schedule as opposed to something you put off. IAS preparation is not something that you can do part-time or in your extra time. If you think so, it is better you stop wasting your time.

(2) Within few days of IAS preparation, students start complaining about boredom, exhaustion and drowsiness when they sit down to study. They, perhaps, actually experience these symptoms and they may not be mere excuses. If you are mentally weak and IAS preparation is some sort of fashion statement, then these things are bound to happen. When these complaints cease to exist, you can be assured that you are mentally fit to prepare for the exam. You would still get tired even if you are mentally strong but it would be only for two reasons. Either you have studied too much, or you could not study for some reason or the other and are feeling guilty about it.

(3) Your understanding of your subjects will get deeper and deeper, and the speed at which you memorise things will gradually improve. There is scientific evidence for it. Your determination and mental strength will lead you to take more

interest in your studies. Comparatively, we are better able to learn and understand the things that interest us. Also, things that we understand, we remember them for a long time. This is the reason you remember the plot of your favourite movie and can recall it for longer.

(4) Suddenly you find yourself being highly active and alive because the mental strength inside you switches on and activates all four channels of your energy. You will find yourself physically fit and happy at a mental level. Your mind gets flooded by positive thoughts and they continually boost your confidence. You get emotionally involved with your goal, so much so that your emotional energy keeps inspiring you to do something. When you get the combined support from all the three energies, they form a fourth energy which I would like to call spiritual energy. This spiritual energy generates a nice feeling inside you and makes you feel light. It even creates such situations and coincidences that will take you closer to your goal. Do not doubt this. You will experience it yourself at a later stage.

(5) Undoubtedly, becoming an IAS is no child's play. The exam is difficult and there is always a doubt of not clearing it. This is not happening only with you, it happens with everyone out there. To your face, people will tell you, "Work hard, you will make the cut." But behind your back, they will say, "Now that he is in deep waters, he will realise what it really takes to be an IAS". I mean to say you are going to be surrounded by such invisible negative energies. This negative energy will hurt your being and you may fall into depression. You may also feel shattered under the pressure. But mental strength has the power to turn the negative energy into a challenge and this ultimately

becomes your power. The power that fights the challenge has to be even stronger than its opponent. This will happen with you as well.

I want to tell you that you would require mental strength not just in IAS but in every sphere of life. It is most important, essential almost, when the goal is important and difficult- and the ambition of IAS is an important and difficult goal.

Keep in mind that the mental strength I'm talking about does not mean a passionate decision taken in a moment that "I want to be an IAS." Most people take such passionate decisions that fizzle out with time. This is a tide that settles down after a while. You can't do anything just by saying it. You have to calmly think about it. Once you have decided something, then you have to stay firm on that decision and work to achieve your goals.

I have often heard people say that they took the 'wrong' decision. Decisions are not wrong; it is just that the steps taken to fulfil them are not the correct ones. If you do not have the strength to know the correct process (it will be told a little later) and follow it, it is better you refrain from taking such decisions.

If you never take a decision to take the IAS exam, no one is going to point at you and say, "Oh look, what kind of a person he is, he never sat in the IAS exam!" But if you decide to give the exam and are unable to prepare accordingly, obviously you will fail. Then people might smugly proclaim, "Oh yeah, serves him right, what was he thinking, trying to become an IAS." This is why I believe you have to think very carefully before you take this decision or else you can stay happy in your present situation. Only a well-thought decision can give you mental strength.

So now the question arises- how to take a 'well-thought' decision? I would like to discuss some things regarding this with you. These are based on my observation, experience and analysis, and hence I can claim them to be practical and genuine:

(1) Inner need

You need to scrutinise very carefully if becoming an IAS is just a show-off to you or it is an inner requirement. Look at it this way- 'are you in love or is it just infatuation?' If it is your inner need, if you really love somebody then you will enjoy everything associated with it, even things that most people dislike. Then you become restless to meet him/her, to get closer to him/her. You suddenly start thinking that life would be incomplete if he/she is not yours. And you would be ready to do anything to bring him/her into your life. Isn't it?

(2) Interest in academics

You need to be a graduate to be eligible to sit in the IAS exam. So before you start preparing for IAS, you have already been studying for 14 years. You have the wealth of this experience. You know whether you enjoy studying or not. If you find studies a burden, then IAS is not for you. You should enjoy studying at least till you are preparing for IAS.

When I say you need to enjoy studying, I do not mean that you should study for 14-15 hours every day for three to four years. All I'm asking you is whether, at present, you enjoy studying or not. You can spend the rest of your life without even glancing at a book, but you need to be in love with them at this stage. You should enjoy studying because this is what you have to mostly do for IAS. The ladder to IAS includes studying and writing down what you have studied.

It is not at all necessary for you to study endlessly. This is useless advice and people who say so just want to create panic in the minds of students. If a student studies with full concentration and sincerity for five hours a day, I believe it would suffice. But this bit of studying should be with complete interest, not as fulfilling an obligation. If you wish to know the correct way to study you can read my book 'The Art of studying.'

(3) Consistency

You must have heard the tale about the hare and the tortoise. The crawling tortoise defeats the hare in a race. The tortoise's win underlies the importance of consistency in our lives. The tortoise won the race because he never stopped running- even if the pace was slow.

In IAS preparation too, consistency is essential. The nature of the preparation and the subjects is such that without consistency, not much would be achieved. The strategy you employed during your university exams will not work here. You can't study two months before the exam and get first division.

For example, general knowledge plays a crucial role in IAS exam. It is in the syllabus in the preliminary examinations and the mains. It is even asked in the interview. You can't prepare for this without reading the newspapers and magazines to keep up to date. It is obvious, then, that you need to take out time for this daily reading. You need to do it anyhow. UPSC does not care for your excuses.

You can only answer the questions you are asked in the mains perfectly if you have in-depth knowledge of your subjects. For this knowledge, you can't just memorise your lessons, your brain needs to digest them. This is possible only when you study daily and also analyse the topics.

Also, the race for IAS is not a 100m race, it is a marathon. A sprint racer would tire out very easily. The race has to be completed with a medium pace as the success depends on the principle of continuity.

(4) Mental capability

This competition is primarily mental. The country's best minds will compete and register their wins depending on their abilities. So obviously your aptitude has to match a certain standard. Even if you do not possess it, you need the strength to be determined to boost your capacities and work hard. What will you achieve if you do not understand this and act like the man who went to Delhi and stayed there preparing for IAS for five years, even after I advised him not to do so. His poor younger brother sold fruit juice to send him money. God took five years to show mercy and finally he returned home.

So what do I mean by mental capacity? It is this-

(a) You should have the ability to understand your subjects.

(b) After you have understood a topic, you shall be able to discuss it with others and even teach it to them if need be.

(c) You can put forward your opinion on a subject.

(d) Your memory may be nothing to boast about, but it should not even be extremely ordinary. You should be able to remember facts for some time and should be able to quickly recall them when repeated.

(e) Your grasp on language should also be decent. You should be able to speak and write well. To achieve fluency, you should start practising.

(5) Outside support

Since the process of becoming an IAS is a time-taking one, I believe you should have some outside support. Girls especially need this support because they have to adjust according to the wishes of their parents and also the parents get worried about their marriage.

A good thing here is that outside support does not need to be in terms of money whereas if you do a professional course, you would need money. Thank God that currently there is no professional course required for IAS. All you need is a little money for books and hundred bucks for some monthly newspapers and magazines. As far as coaching is concerned, it is not something that UPSC has asked or deemed necessary. It is totally up to you whether you need it or not.

However, it is necessary that you know how to prepare. You know how to study and how to write correct answers.

Even though outside support is not mandatory, it still directly or indirectly boosts our abilities to help us succeed. The outside support can come from following sources -

(a) A supporting and cooperating family can make a big difference. It takes away mental stress and you can prepare with patience. They also support you financially.

(b) If you are working, you can benefit from the support of your employer.

(c) You can benefit from the experiences of your college professors and those who have cleared the civil services. The SP and collector in every district belong from civil services, you can seek their help. In state capitals, officers are appointed in various sectors, you can meet them. Believe me; most of the officers would love to help you out.

(d) The support of your friends can help you discuss topics with them and it will also encourage you.

If you feel you can satisfy all these conditions or if you do not fulfil the requirements but believe you could adapt to them in the future, let me welcome you once again in this competition called IAS.

Chapter 2

Understand the nature of the exam

According to Hindu mythology, Vishnu is God and so is Shiva. According to botanical science, lotus is a flower and so is jimson weed (dhatura). Now I want to ask you a simple but very important question underlying social behaviour. Can you offer jimsonweed while praying to Lord Vishnu because it is also a flower? Our ancestors have answered this with a simple idiom- 'To each God His own prayer.' Jimsonweed can be offered to Lord Shiva but not to Lord Vishnu.

You can apply this to the context of exams and competitive exams. Even though they are both exams, they are not similar. If they were similar, then there would have been no need to use 'competitive' before exam. So before you start preparing for IAS, or any other competitive exam for that matter, you should understand the nature and character of the exam in depth.

This is like the time when you visit a new place and gather information about the weather there beforehand, so you can prepare accordingly. You need to pack clothes depending on the weather. If you plan a trip to the hill station of Mussorie, even in summers, you have to keep an umbrella with you.

I feel sad when I see many enthusiastic young men preparing for IAS continuously for years. In fact, an area called Old Rajinder Nagar in New Delhi is famous for this. Old Rajinder Nagar is now like an island full of IAS aspirants. They study night and day. Their eyesight may be weakening, their cheeks are probably sunken and their faces have lost all glow. They still did not taste success and even their eyes are not shining with hope as they did when they first started out. But why does this happen? Is this exam really so difficult that it seems impossible to conquer this fort? Or did we fail to come up with the right strategy which make the fort seem stronger than it actually is?

If you need to pass a long thing through a crisscross-shaped pipe, a steel rod won't work. What you would require is something flexible - like a string - that can mould its shape according to the pipe.

This is the case with competitive exams and it applies very strongly to the IAS exam. If you know how to jump across this IAS wall, which looks like it has the strength of steel, you can stop beating your head against it while trying to break it. After all, your purpose is not to break the wall but to reach the other side, and this you can achieve by jumping across it. In this context, it would benefit you a lot to understand the personality of the exam so you can prepare with that mindset.

There is a lot of evidence to back what I'm going to say here. There is no bigger evidence than the statistics of the exam which show that 50 percent of the selected students are those who do not have a first division. After looking at these statistics, a question arises in the mind- 'could it be that out of

10-12 lakh students who apply for the preliminary IAS exam, there are not even thousand candidates who are toppers or first-division holders?' Actually, their number amounts to a few thousands. Then, why is it so that these toppers and PHD holders do not make it while the second and third division-holders do?

It is not a co-incidence. Clearing IAS is not a fluke, and even if it was a fluke, it could not possibly be a coincidence for 50 percent students.

This proves the fact that these second and third-division holders were those who moulded their studies according to the competitive IAS exam. The toppers and first-divisioners, which could not make it, were those who studied for IAS according to university exam pattern.

The biggest challenge that I have faced when mentoring students to prepare for IAS is that they refused to turn their solid being into a liquid form that could fit into the IAS scaffold. I was limited by the fact that I could explain things to them, but not change them. Of course, I could not change the UPSC exam, either. So in the end, it was the students who suffered. They could not change their university-style studying and answering questions. The only change they incorporated was to study lots of books on a particular subject, even reading some very good authors. In fact, they were not just reading them but memorising them.

However, civil services require neither of these things. The thing that it actually requires is lacking in these aspirants. This is why both cannot adjust to each other and this leads to them getting a divorce without even marrying!

This has been a sad and bitter experience for me and I have discussed it before. I do not know why students come to believe that only studying is sufficient to clear IAS exam. If you start giving them tips about other important IAS requirements, they will yawn and start looking around, which shows their disinterest. They wonder how this information is related to their preparation. I would like to share with you something that was said by former American President Abraham Lincoln and which I find to be relevant here. He said, "If someone were to give me six hours to chop wood, I would spend four hours sharpening my axe." This is a very important saying which you should try to understand. What Lincoln is trying to say here is that it is not just important to do as much work as possible but also to do it efficiently. If your axe is sharpened enough you can chop as much wood with it in two hours as you would in six hours. Therefore, there are things apart from studying that are equally important for you to achieve your goal.

So now let us see what actually makes competitive exams different from other exams:

Selection criteria

I consider this an important characteristic of a competitive exam which renders it different from all university exams. College exams are based on the principle of passing or failing. Even if you score minimum passing marks, your year will be justified and you will move on to the next class. Thus, you will be able to drag your way to a degree in the end.

But competitive exams do not work on the principle of

passing or failing, they work on the theory of selection. In competitive exams, the total number of candidates that will be selected is already declared. The exam is conducted and in the final result, which is prepared on merit basis, students are declared selected according to the number of administrators that are needed. In this scenario, it is highly possible that even though you secured 60 percent marks, you could not qualify the exam.

This means that those who got selected scored higher marks than you. You will now have to take the exam again. You will get no leverage next year because of what you scored in this exam. Also, you will get no certificate that you have achieved such and such level of success.

This is essentially an examination based on competition where everybody is in opposition to one another. Here, your success could mean somebody's failure while your failure would ensure someone else's success. Thus, what we actually need to surpass others is a killer instinct.

This is why the style of preparation for this exam changes. Your selection depends not only on how good your preparation is but also on how well others have prepared. It is possible that this year you score 60 percent marks and not get selected but next year you score only 55 percent marks and are able to make the cut. This is why competitive exams demand the best from you. The tactic of reading the syllabus just to pass would not work here. Here you are not limited by just what you are doing. If I'm allowed some cruel words, then over here, the strategy of vanquishing others works. You need enough power to defeat others. Don't you think that if these things are necessary then you would need to change your method of preparing?

Before a student sits for competitive exams, he has already been exposed to at least 15 years of yearly exams. Giving these exams on a yearly basis moulds the student's studying, writing and thinking style in a certain fashion. This may work for state civil services, but it will not work for IAS exams at all. To tell you the truth, this method has no value in this exam. It is a big challenge for any student to get rid of these old habits.

Up against students from various streams

All the exams that you have given until now were homogenous in nature. If you were an arts student, then the other students giving the exam were also from arts background. The engineering students gave exams with engineering students only while commerce students gave exams with commerce students. Since the syllabus is the same for everyone, the books and the question papers are also the same, everything appears simple and straightforward.

However, the IAS exam is neither straight nor simple. The exam is like a huge sea where many streams such as arts, commerce, science, engineering, medical, CA, management, law etc. merge. Anybody who has done a graduation can appear for the exam.

If you want to see your name in the selection list, you have to think carefully. So many streams and all of them have various subjects! In the preliminary exams you won't face any challenge because of this, but it may pose a problem in the mains where you have to choose an optional subject. Some papers are high scoring while some are not. Although UPSC has a scaling method to tackle this, you still have a fear about other people's scores.

It is also not completely true that such kind of problem is faced only with optional papers. For example, students from different study backgrounds have distinct advantages and disadvantages during the general knowledge paper also- arts students get an obvious advantage here, while science students may naturally be at a slight disadvantage. But when it comes to CSAT, it's the engineering students who benefit. However, a lot of space is given to science also so that science students do not lose out. All in all, though UPSC has tried its best to maintain a balance between all streams, it has not been totally successful.

Now, the challenge you face depends on which stream you have studied. To overcome this challenge, you need to focus on things that are holding you back. UPSC is not concerned with your academic background. It will only see the marks you have scored and announce your result. In this competition, you are up against students from various streams and this may pose new challenges.

Pan- India exam

Students in the state civil services, however, do not have to worry about this. Although, students from other states can give the exam in any state, their number is very less. But IAS is different, students from all over the country, the ones who believe themselves to be good students, take the exam.

Here states do not matter but state education does. Every state has a different level of education. The medium of instruction and the amount of exposure also differs. In this context, some states are considered advanced while others are backward. States have their own education board and the syllabus is thus different. However, private state schools have the option of following CBSE pattern of studying if they wish to do so. Many schools have adopted this.

It need not be debated that the level of syllabus and exams in many state boards is not at par with that of CBSE. Students from state boards may be at a slight disadvantage because the level of IAS, its syllabus and the pattern of questions asked is somewhat similar to the CBSE pattern.

A similar difference exists in universities. Some universities are considered very good and it is a feeling of pride to get admission in them. Universities also have different syllabi and different questions are asked in their respective exams. For example, the syllabi and questions asked in exams of Delhi University and Jawaharlal Nehru University match the IAS syllabus.It is obvious then, that a student who has graduated from either of these universities has an advantage.

When we are talking of geographical differences, we have to consider the difference between a village, town and a metro. A student from a rural background is often unaware of the modern experiences and lingo. Even his body language is different. He also lacks study material, proper guidance and friends to have an intellectual discussion with. While students living in metro cities do not have to struggle for any of this if they are smart.

So there can be numerous situations which depending on a student's location can become their strength or weakness. However, UPSC is not concerned with which university you have studied from, which state you belong to or whether you are from a village or a metro. It only tests you for the mettle it requires. Now, this situation may pose a great challenge which you have to overcome yourself.

Power of experience

I find this to be the biggest challenge. When I was preparing, there were two things that I was afraid of. Firstly, since I had studied as a private student after eighth grade, I was insecure that students who have studied from regular colleges must be much better than me. My other fear was that how I would compete with students who have been preparing for years and have sat for numerous exams- after all, experiences have their own importance.

During our times, there were only three attempts allowed for students belonging to general category. I got through in my second attempt. Now this challenge has slightly risen. Statistics show that most selections happen during second and third attempts. Still, no attempt should be underestimated. When a candidate gives his first attempt, he is also competing with a candidate who is giving his fourth attempt. That student not only has the experience of three attempts but it is also clear that he has been preparing for the exam for a long time. Do you think it would be easy to compete with such students? I'm not scaring you here, just warning you. And let me tell you another truth, most of these students who have given number of attempts are unable to gain anything from the experience. So neither should you feel pressurised because of it nor should you take it lightly. In the end, the time will also come when you are giving your second, third or fourth attempt. Although, I pray that this doesn't happen to you.

There is another aspect to the power of experience which is connected with various other competitive exams. While you are preparing for IAS, you should take other competitive exams as well. This will help you mature. Just remember, a person competing with you who only has the experience of this exam will find himself a little weak in front of you. I'm telling you these things so that you do not consider the student who has started preparation with you to be your main competition, but your actual competition is the student who has been preparing for a long time.

Questions asked

The questions asked in university examinations are not like the ones asked in IAS. I feel disheartened even with the CBSE question papers because they also pose questions which have straight-forward answers. It is the same case with state civil services. You are asked a clear-cut question and you can give a straight-forward reply. You will get marks for it. I have no hesitation in saying that in state civil services, they don't really care how much an aspirant actually knows. That's why in state civil services, there is always a possibility of ordinary students surpassing genuine and brilliant students. If a crammed answer is the benchmark to get marks then it is an easy task. Most students are good at cramming.

However, this learning by rote is not going to work in UPSC. This is the main reason why collage and university toppers often do not find a place in UPSC. This is the Mt Everest-like challenge of UPSC which only genuine students can climb.

You pick out any UPSC paper from general knowledge in preliminary exams to general knowledge in the mains. You can even take a look at a paper for an optional subject. When you read the questions, you will feel that they are from topics included in the syllabus. You will also get the feeling that you have read about it and know a few things about it. But when you start writing down your answer, either your pen will stop writing after 2-3 lines or start repeating the things you have already written in different words. This becomes not just the biggest but the sole reason for many students' failure. I consider this to be the biggest challenge posed by civil services.

Now the question is how to face this challenge. If you don't address this issue, you can't succeed no matter what you do. You should take my warning very seriously. Your university exams-style of answering questions (with which you may have scored well in college exams) will not work here. It is not your fault. You kept writing in this style. And you kept scoring good marks. So why would you think that you are wrong and need to write in a different manner. Well, our purpose here is not to fix blame. Our objective is to understand and evaluate the challenges you may face, because when you understand the challenges, your methodology of preparing for IAS will change.

Chapter 3

What is UPSC looking for in you?

Okay, so let me tell you the secrets to being successful in IAS by revealing what UPSC is looking for in the candidates. It is but quite natural that there has to be some criteria to choose. It is not just UPSC but all countries have come up with their own methods to select candidates for administrative services. Nearly all of these mcthods include exams and interviews. UPSC has also modified the selection criteria according to its needs and settled upon a three-stage selection process. You already know about this.

You must ask this question now- how will UPSC assess you for everything that is required in an administrative officer through this exam? If this question is occurring to you then it is a good sign that you have the potential to be an IAS officer.

It is obvious that if you opt for history and become a district collector you will not be asked to write a history of the district. If you take geography, you will not have to produce a map of the district when you are the District Magistrate. Your vast reserves of general knowledge will not be of much use once you start working as an administrative officer. So if all this is not required later, why does UPSC make us toil over it?

The answer is simple- it is through these methods only that UPSC tests your mind, thoughts and character. This is similar to how before buying a new pot you tap it with your fingers to check it. If you do not like the UPSC pattern, then I would like you to suggest another improved pattern which is fool-proof with no errors. This is not just difficult but almost impossible. You may hold any opinion about the UPSC selection process but as of now you have to say that whatever it is, howsoever it is, you have to tackle the current scenario and prove that you are IAS material.

Therefore, it is good for you to learn what exactly UPSC is expecting from you in this three-stage exam. It will help you better understand what is expected of you in the preliminary exam, in the mains and in the interview. Believe me this is going to help you prepare better.

Preliminary exam

First of all, you must realise that it is a kind of entrance test and not the actual exam. UPSC has made a provision for it so that candidates for mains exam can be shortlisted. You must know that unlike preliminary exam, the basic nature of main exam is descriptive. Its papers cannot be evaluated by a computer as is done in the case of preliminary exam papers. I am saying this for those students who do not take this into account and think that preparing for and clearing the preliminary exam is enough in itself.

So let us study its structure first :

(a) It includes a general knowledge paper.

(b) It includes a CSAT paper.

(c) It asks objective-type questions.

(d) The given options are complex, long and difficult.

(e) You have to solve 100 and 80 questions in 120 minutes.

You must be aware that for the first time since 1979, in 2011 i.e. thirty-two years later, it was decided to change the nature of the preliminary exam. I personally believe it was a delayed move. The change should have happened sooner, by 2001 at least, because in these 32 years, the nature of Indian democracy, administration and economy has undergone tremendous change. But it is better late than never. UPSC deserves praise for it anyway.

But why am I telling this to you? I had to mention this to explain to you that this change will benefit the country and the society. So, of course, it would benefit you too. This will help you decide how to do your preparation because if you link your preparation to the benefit of the nation and the society it'll not only change the way you prepare but also make it easier. You should also be aware of this so you do not find yourself in an awkward position when you start your job or face difficulties in performing your role. This way you'll be able to enjoy whatever you do. And this way you will be working for the betterment of yourself and of all.

As I mentioned that in the last 32 years, the country and the world have faced major changes. I would divide them into two categories. The first aspect is changes in the administrative structure. With the expansion of democracy, there is a decentralisation of power and the nature of administration has turned more into organisation. The difference between the two is that whereas 'orders' are used in an administration, 'request' is used in an organisational structure. Administration has some scope for dictatorship but organisation depends on your skills as a leader. So the country needs now more of a manager than an administrator. This means the person should be able to fulfil his duties using motivation, not punishment. Now a manager is required, not an administrator. Students of public administration will be able to understand what I mean. I would like to refer to the present administrative structure as the 'new public administration'.

The next big change has occurred due to globalisation. Geographical boundaries may still exist but social, economical and cultural boundaries in the world have been blurred. Now our own nation shall not suffice. Our feet should be on the ground but our arms above the entire world. Of course, we can't do this literally but we can do this mentally. In other words, we need a mind that is logical, broad and highly receptive. Only such a mind can bring about this amalgamation of the self with the world.

It's simple. When an organisation hires someone, their sole purpose is that the person should be able to do the work that is need to be done. Hospitals do hire people who are capable of treating patients, educational institutes look for people who can teach, research institutes want scientists whereas industries need engineers and managers. But when it comes to civil services, it is not so specific.

There are two kinds of administrators that are required in public administration- specialists and general. When you start the job you fall under the latter category. By 'general', I mean students with all the basic qualities that can be moulded as per the need. For example, Indian Administrative Service is a general service. Administrative work, while being very important, does not require specialisation. However, Indian Police Service, Indian Foreign Service and some other services demand specialisation. But UPSC, so far, hasn't come up with an idea of different entrance procedures to different services. It has a single exam for all services. In these circumstances, it is a real challenge for the UPSC to choose young people who fit the requirements of all the services. There are mainly two bases for which service you will get. First, your ranking. And second, preferences given by you for the services. This is why UPSC has to adopt a 'general entrance exam' approach for civil services.

In other words, for civil services, such a metal is required that can be moulded into anything- plate, bowl, glass etc. It does not matter much to UPSC what you wish to be at a personal level. It is only interested in determining whether you are a deserving candidate or not.

Now the question is- how do you know whether an individual has that metal or not? To decide this, two things will be taken into consideration- the person's mind and his personality. The individual takes a decision and his personality implements it. In other words, decisions are shaped by personality and the individual follows them. So mind and personality are connected. For instance, I have decided to oversee the law and order situation- this decision has been made by my mind. Now there are many ways to implement it. I could take strict measures to achieve my goal. I can also ask people to coordinate with me. I can implement my decision at once or do it step by step. This will depend on my personality. It is evident then that if I don't have the ability to take a decision, I can't have the ability to implement it. Therefore, Civil services candidates are tested for an appropriate mind, practical thinking and effective personality. All the systems and mechanisms adopted by the UPSC are meant to achieve this very objective. The preliminary exams, the mains and interview are meant to test these characteristics only. Everything from deciding on to the subjects to the style of forming questions is intended towards that goal.

I decided to talk about this because I have seen young students study for up to twelve hours, year after year. They have this misconception that the more they will study; the more likely they are to pass the exam. This reasoning stems from their 'successful' experience of university exams. However, the requirements of civil services and the university are different. University exams test one's knowledge, not personality. But knowledge is not required for civil services. Knowledge is only the means to test the analytical ability of the mind. If you do not develop the ability to critically analyse the knowledge you have gained, it will be difficult to qualify the civil services exam, even if you have memorised the entire syllabus. Civil services require a strong personality and the way you analyse your knowledge can give clues to your personality.

Another thing I would like to mention here is that UPSC is not bothered whether you get IPS or IRS or any other service. If you have proven that you have the desired metal in you, the UPSC will recommend you. That's it. It is your personal preference which service you want to be in. But please do not let this preference influence your preparation. You just have to prove your mettle that you deserve to be a civil servant.

All the ministries have their own training institutes. You will be trained according to the service you get. And this training will last for almost a year and a half. So, the UPSC is only evaluating whether you deserve to be trained in these institutes. It is not meant to evaluate whether you are eligible especially for IAS or IPS or any other specific service. You are to remember this. If you have the mettle for it, the training institutes will handle everything themselves. Your job is only to follow instructions.

I hope you are now clearer about how to do your IAS preparation. Trust me and absorb everything I have to say now. You will then realise that the way you were preparing has changed and this would be the correct way to go about it.

Ask the old people in your house, they will tell you the difference between today's collector and SP and the ones during their time. Earlier, when these officers would roam the city's streets in their jeeps, life would come to a standstill, and people would longingly stare at them. But today, the public does not care. Earlier, it was extremely difficult to meet these officials. Now the officers find it necessary to hold meetings with the general public on a regular basis. All in all the administration has, thus, gone through many changes.

Now let us see the qualities that UPSC tests you for in the entrance exam.

Clarity of mind

If you have ever taken the UPSC exam (if you haven't,

I strongly suggest you go through the unsolved papers of the preliminary exam before reading any further) you must have felt 'I have read about this somewhere' while attempting the questions. 'I know the question, I'm familiar with it' this is what you think but still answer incorrectly. This is the biggest challenge posed by the preliminary exam. You read a question and you feel you have read this somewhere. But when you read the options, you have to choose from to answer, you get confused. In most cases, all the options contain some truth in them, they all seem correct. The options evaluate how clear you are about your subject. They are written in such a manner so as to confuse you.

So what do you do in this situation? You will read an entire chapter on this in coming pages. Here, I would just like to mention that if your hold on the subject is not strong enough, then you will have great difficulty in choosing the correct answer from the given options. It is obvious then that if your mind is clear about the subject, you will be able to choose the answer faster and accurately. Do you not think that someone who the government is entrusting with the responsibility of the society should have a mind which is very clear on its thoughts? If the administrator has a muddled mind how will he take a just and lucid decision?

A related issue here is the 'solidity' of the mind. When you start solving CSAT or general knowledge questions, you will be fine initially, but after solving half the questions you will feel like your mind is wandering and stumbling. The given options start messing in your mind in the same way that woollen balls get entangled with each other. The time limit is fixed at two hours which pressurises the mind. Half the questions remain unsolved, but time is running out. These thoughts also stress your mind. If you mind is not strong and solid, you will panic. If this happens then your chances of answering incorrectly will increase and you will have to exit in the first stage of the competition. To answer the questions in a balanced manner, it is necessary that you have a strong and solid mind.

Speed of mind

As you are well aware, you get 120 minutes to solve round 100 questions of general reasoning and another 80 of CSAT. This means you have approximately one and a half minute for each question. I have a theory that may not be applicable to general reasoning but it is definitely valid for CSAT. The theory is that students can increase their scores by fifty percent compared to their previous scores if instead of two hours, they were given three to four hours to write the exam. If they get more time to think and calculate they will be able to get more correct answers.

But if such a thing is done how a good mind would be selected? If there is ample time, then it will bring all minds to the same level. A mind that answers fast and calculates with speed is considered great. The question asked for entry in 'Kaun Banega Crorepati' is so easy that nine out of 10 people can answer it correctly. But they choose the one who answers before all others.

An administrator has to take big decisions. In fact, in some situations, they have to take important decisions immediately. There is no time to think and evaluate. If a weak mind is appointed in this position, he will take slow decisions. You must have heard the adage, 'what's the use of rain after the crops have dried.'

The CSAT exam includes questions related to mathematics and logical reasoning, some questions are about relationships, and some are about locations and directions. These questions are written in a way that after reading them your mind is in a state of chaos. You wonder what you have read, what the question is asking and how you should begin answering it. The time limit also looms large like a threat. But there are brains that are fast enough to catch the answer immediately. They know the tricks and the formulas. They apply the required trick and formula to the question and come to the answer. It is believed that faster a mind can calculate, the greater it is. Therefore, this was one reason to start CSAT exam.

Memory

A country's memory is etched in its history and a person's memory of the past is stored in his brain. How well you know your subject is very important, especially when it comes to the general reasoning paper. You have to go deeper than the information and knowledge of the subject and understand its very essence. Nobody can deny this fact, this importance of understanding. But at the same time, you will have to realize the importance of memorizing things also. Your memory also plays an important role here. Around one-third of questions are those that you won't be able to solve if you do not have a strong memory. This is especially true of current events.

But let me tell you that the memory required here is far

beyond the average memory. The kind of memory required here should be as strong as a footballer who is surrounded by five rivals but still manages to score a goal. So the memory that you need should be able to sort out what it requires even in the foggiest situations.

Focus

CSAT paper includes comprehension questions. Truly speaking, looking at the level of civil services exam, these questions seem sort of amusing. I have seen many students take these questions lightly. But if you take it seriously, you will realise what a challenge these comprehensions pose to your mind. The biggest challenge is that of focus.

You read the comprehension and you are asked three to four multiple choice questions based on it. When you read the options, you face two major issues. The first is that most of the options you have to choose from seem to be correct. They are correct. But the question is which option is related to what you have studied in the comprehension. You will only be able to choose the correct answer if you have remained focused while reading the comprehension.

The second problem is how much of your mind could you control. You will notice that most of the answers that are given are correct if viewed from the perspective of general knowledge. In fact, if it is not compulsory to answer keeping the comprehension in mind, the option you decided on the basis of general knowledge is probably a better match. So when you are deciding upon an answer based on the comprehension, your general knowledge will invade your mind. So you face the challenge of ignoring this invasion and keep your mind from drifting.

Concentration is the speciality of a high-ranking officer's mind. If he reads something and understands something else, then such a mind will also do something completely different. Just imagine as a collector, you read a two-page note in a file. You have to inform your senior, a commissioner or a minister about it. And simply channelizing the information as it is may not work here. You may have to sum up the two-page information in just a paragraph. Do you think a mind which is not focused can do so?

Decision-making ability

The challenge of choosing the correct answer from so many confusing ones is also linked to your decision-making power. An administrator's success depends on how many correct decisions he could take in his life. Although every person's success depends on the decisions he took, in the case of an administrator, this becomes even more important. This is because a common man's decision will only affect him personally but an administrator's decision can affect the country and its people. Keeping this in mind, the CSAT syllabus has topic on decision-making.

Awareness and Alertness

The questions asked in the general knowledge paper in the preliminary exam are related to current events which may have happened in the previous year or up to a month ago. I know some of you would be thinking 'what is the need for knowing about these current events as they are not directly related to the administrator?'

Actually this is a wrong belief. It is very important that an administrator is aware of all the current events. If an administrator is not aware of the times, the requirements of the times, and the technology and means available, he will not be able to make a good decision. If you need to make a financial decision, you should be aware of the current economic scenario. If you have to make a developmental decision, you should know about the wants and needs of the society. You also need to know how all this would be possible. This is the reason that not just preliminary exams but even mains have four question papers related to general knowledge. It would not be wrong to say that general knowledge is the backbone of IAS preparation. It is not just the responsibility of an administrator but also that of a citizen to be well-informed of his times. If someone is not doing so, he does not deserve to be an IAS. He also does not have a right to be called a responsible and educated citizen.

There is another thing here, a good knowledge of current events shows that your mind is sharp and stable. It shows that you absorb things that happen around you and retain them. Undoubtedly, such a mind would have a store of information and knowledge that he could use as raw material while taking a decision. Such a mind would definitely have power and a unique viewpoint. Such a mind would definitely be far more efficient in taking appropriate decisions than those who are not so aware and alert.

An awareness of your times signifies that your mind is continuously working and it is progressive. It is a psychological fact that a mind which is progressive can better interpret and analyse situations and incidents. Such a mind is rational and being rational, it is also prudent. For an administrator, it is not just necessary to possess such a mind, but it is also his greatest asset.

Mains exam

I have no hesitation in saying this and I want to convince you too that the true IAS potential of yours is judged by the main exam. It is true that you would not reach this level without clearing the preliminary exam but the true assessment of your knowledge, understanding, wit etc. is at this level only. It has been observed that sometimes students who clear the preliminary exam cannot even score 25 percent in the main exam. On the other hand, there are students who fear the preliminary exam but are well-prepared for the main exam. I'm discussing this fact here so that you can understand the difference between the two exams. This will help you approach your studies in a scientific manner and you can mould your brain and personality accordingly. Now we shall see what expectations UPSC has from you in the main paper.

We can perhaps conclude that while the preliminary exam tests for qualified minds, the main paper tests for qualified thoughts. To find the correct option in the given amount of time is the most difficult challenge posed by the preliminary exam. This requires a clear and stable mind. In the mains, there are no multiple-choice questions, whatever you write here is the content of your own mind. There are no ready-made answers. You have to write your own answers. When you write your answers some of your qualities and thoughts will subconsciously enter your answer sheet and will represent you in front of the examiner to see.

The nature of the main exam is as follows

(1) There are four question papers on general studies. Out of these four, there is a paper on ethics, integrity and aptitude.

There are two optional papers too.

(2) There is a paper on essay-writing.

(3) There is a paper on General English and a paper on General language.

(4) All the questions are descriptive.

(5) The questions are such that they allow you to express your thoughts on the matter.

(6) There is a word limit on questions on general studies.

Now, based on the nature and structure of these questions we will highlight the qualities UPSC expects you to possess:

Analytical ability

Your ability to memorise will not work here. The questions asked in the exam are such that you can't write a memorised answer. The facts you have memorised will be useful so far as to provide content for your analysis. Whatever you have studied will be the raw material to feed your answer just like you need potatoes, cabbage, chillies, salt and spices to make vegetable curry. You cannot make a curry simply by mixing the vegetables; you also have to cook them. This applies to the mains too.

I would again insist that before you read any further, you should go through the unsolved papers of the main exam. When you see the questions, you will realise that every question requires an analysis. The questions will test how well you understood the things you have studied and how well you can analyse them.

The hallmark of a good mind is that it can better analyse things and such a mind is more productive. Your mind is exercising when it is analysing things. Just like exercise can make your body fit and healthy, analysis can make your mind healthy and useful. We need administrators with such minds.

Originality

An analytical ability alone is not enough. You read the questions in the unsolved papers again. You will notice that most questions end with 'give a critical analysis' or 'what steps should be taken' etc. You have read the subject and you have the general knowledge. It's fine. You can also analyse what you have read. Fine again. Whatever you have studied and absorbed indicates the awareness and alertness of your mind. An ability to analyse what have been studied and absorbed hints at the brightness and productivity of your mind. But when you express your thoughts about the subject it reveals what exactly your productive mind has produced. This tests the originality of your mind. This shows what and how your mind thinks on a certain subject. Do not forget that when we think of something which is original and present our thoughts, it unveils our entire personality.

Many students dismiss the part of the question which

says 'you'. They think it is just a small part of the question so it is not important. Also, they discover that it is not an easy thing to answer this. They do not want to spend time brainstorming over it. Since they had formed no opinions on the topic, they find it difficult to write anything here. And it proves to be a big mistake of theirs. Consequently, UPSC finds the originality of the mind needed to be a good administrator is missing.

Society continues to exist like it always has and things keep repeating themselves. But a change is brought about when someone driven by original thoughts decides to do something new. Doing something new is the contribution (in a true sense) of an administrator to the society and the country. If he is unable to do so, he is simply confined to the role of the manager who only keeps on organising things. Originality is an important thing in every aspect of life.

Language proficiency

Civil services included an essay-writing paper before 1979. It was discontinued for a decade. It was then re-introduced for various reasons. First was to test a student's thoughts on any given topic. Secondly, it tested the language proficiency and style of the candidate. Essay-writing is a paper that you can't really prepare for. It is sort of a self-writing exercise and there is no student who does not attempt the essay. They may choose their topics and write differently, but all students write the essay.

It is the simplest paper but also full of challenges. The challenge is that this paper is more of an art and less science. It is clear that when a subject comes under the category of art, its boundaries get blurred and the outcome depends on the person. When you need to answer a general knowledge question, the facts are clear and in front of you. And to answer questions on optional subjects, you have books. But these things are not available for the essay-writing paper. Here, the role of a writer is that of a bee which has to suck nectar from many flowers to create honey. Similarly, to write an essay, the writer collects his wisdom from many sources. This reveals how vast the ocean of writer's knowledge is, how well his understanding of facts is and how well he uses the facts to reach a desired conclusion.

The most important of all is the presentation and expression. Remember, essays are not written for intellectuals, they are for average readers. So the challenge while writing an essay is how to write a piece that the common reader can understand, even if the topic of the essay is tough or related to science. If the essay is too intellectual, it will come across as an article and not an essay. If it is too loosely written, instead of an essay, it will come across as general talk. So the question is how should the essay be presented? Remember, if the strings of a sitar are pulled too tight, it will break and if they are left loose there would not be good music.

Now, let us address the question of language. As an administrator, you will deal with all kinds of people. Some of them may be illiterate. They will come from different backgrounds. Whichever department you belong to, your role will be that of a leader who guides others. If your language is not simple, not fluent, not relevant, and if it lacks sympathy, it will fail to make an impression and you will not be able to govern people effectively. The essay you write reveals whether you have this quality.

Brevity

I feel that if the word limit is removed from the questions asked in general studies paper, it would become much easier for students to answer it. But something which is easy for one person would become easy for everyone else too. It will then become difficult to select the best. The purpose of word limit is to test which brain has the ability to control and express its thoughts within the limits that it has been asked to. This ability can prove how efficiently we can control our thoughts.

To follow the word limit and give the best possible answer is not easy unless the person has thoroughly imbibed the subject. This strategy helps eliminate those who just memorise everything. It also proves that you have understood the topic you are writing on.

Your ability to say what you need to within the word limit reveals your unique style of expression. It is like the ability to drive safely in the narrow, winding roads in the hills. You are in total control of the steering of your car because you know that one mistake will cause the car to fall in the gorge.

There is a practical aspect of it too. When you actually get into civil services, you will have to orally inform your superiors about many things every day. You will also have to submit files with your comments. Too much talk and long comments are the products of a weak and disillusioned mind. A man who can say and write what he intends to in brief is considered to be an able administrator because he says or writes only that what is really needed. This is what the word limit on questions tries to test.

Besides informing your superiors or writing comments on files you also have to deal with press and reporters or brief the public on so many occasions. As an administrator you need to be as precise with them as possible. On these occasions people naturally cross-question you, so it is better not to say anything out of agenda. Less you talk more you succeed. Violate this thumb rule and you will find yourself in deep waters. And remember, you are the representative of the government. Any slip of tongue on your part would make the government pay the penalty.

Test of Integrity

Whether we talk about an administrator, a politician, a farmer, a labourer or an average citizen, the quantity and the quality of their gross effect on their surroundings depends on their 'integrity'. You may have heard the name of ENRON, a big MNC that was in the process of setting up an ambitious power project in India. But suddenly it got bankrupt. Nobody could believe it. 'How can this be possible' people were asking each other. Specialists in the trade tried to find out the exact reasons behind this breakdown. Do you know what their findings were? They concluded that though ENRON succeeded in hiring the best engineers in trade, they probably could not hire the best people! Don't you think if every citizen of India promises to hold his/her integrity, we can change the fate of our country? We have never been short on resources. We can claim to have the best brains in the world. The only thing we are lacking is the integrity that should be an essential part of our character.

Keeping this in mind, a voluntary paper on ethics, integrity and aptitude was introduced in 2013. And I consider it as a very positive move. Though we keep improving upon these aspects while interacting with elders or teachers or with wise people in our community, we simply lack a well arranged knowledge in this regard. I think this paper would serve the purpose of giving a practical knowledge of this to people whom the government would be handing over some of the most crucial tasks in the country.

And marks obtained in this paper would give a clear cut indication of morality, integrity and aptitude present in various aspirants.

Approximately half of this paper is based on case studies. In the paper, you are given a situation and your viewpoint towards it is judged. There are many ways to tackle a situation and your approach is revealed in your answer and you get marks accordingly. Consequently, there is a greater chance of selection of candidates as officers who potentially possess more integrity and a positive attitude.

Therefore, books are of little use while preparing for this paper. They can give you general guidelines and nothing more. In order to be fully prepared for this paper, you have to grasp the core values of life, you need to understand how to maintain these values while fulfilling your duty as an administrator. In other words, you have to learn how to be practical without being unethical. Or I should say how to be an effective administrator without compromising your integrity. Only then will you be able to present yourself effectively to the evaluator through your answer sheet.

Interview

This is a selection criterion that is used in most services and employed worldwide. It is possible that there would be no written test for entry into some services but it is not possible that there would be no interview. Mostly, candidates for top posts are selected just on the basis of interviews. You can understand the importance of interviews from this.

In the first two stages of civil services your assessment is sort of oblique. In the written exam, many people get eliminated so only the best minds get to the interview stage. It is a proven fact that it is not necessary that a person who possesses a stable and clear mind, lucid and prudent thoughts, and whose integrity is beyond doubt, would also have a dynamic personality. A dynamic personality means someone who has leadership qualities. Such a personality can inspire people, and one who harbours a desire to change himself and displays polite and exemplary behaviour. You can categorise these as behavioural qualities as they are revealed from how you behave with other people.

An interview tests you for these qualities. Even though an interview lasts maximum for half an hour, the time is enough for the experienced and alert interviewers to see through you as if they are X-raying you. Your body language, the way you talk, the way you stand and sit, your debating skills, the liveliness of your replies to questions asked, how you put forth your views and opinions can reveal whether you should be made an administrator. If your personality fails to make an impression, it does not matter how intelligent you are, you will not be successful.

My friends, in this chapter I have discussed with you in great detail the qualities UPSC is searching for in a candidate. This has not just been my experience but many other candidates have gone through this. These experiences have helped me lead many students to success. That's why I am putting so much emphasis on them. It is my belief that IAS preparation is not such that only books would suffice. Books are required but they are not sufficient. This is a psychological journey; you need to be mentally prepared. So when you understand these psychological facts, your style of writing answers and the way you study will change for the better.

I know that this chapter has not made you very happy because it contained no information about what could be asked in the exam. Maybe, you are accusing me of rambling and are angry with me. But honestly, it is not my fault, this is how the preparation is supposed to be done and I can do nothing about it. But know this that after a year when you re-consider this book, and especially this chapter, you will not think the way you are thinking right now. Your style of studying and thinking would have changed gradually.

Chapter 4

The truth about some common exam-related beliefs

Since IAS is the top-most exam of the country, students from all parts of the country studying all sorts of subjects take the examination in large numbers. This is one reason a lot of exaggerated theories about IAS preparation are floating around. These overstated things seem true given the stature of the exam. People tend to think that because it is such an important exam, these things must be true. Let us separate myths from facts so you can develop the right strategy to prepare for the exam.

(A) Chances of selection are few

If you see the available data, then you are 100 percent correct in assuming that the odds of being selected are few. On average, every year, 10 to 12 lakh students fill the form but the final list of successful candidates hardly exceeds 1000 names. Now if you calculate the ratio of those who sit for the exam to those who get selected, it would indeed be frightening. So it is better we do not do it here.

The statistics above are true but the truth is not what we have come to accept. So let us learn the actual truth so you can be free from needless fears.

Let's assume that for 1000 vacancies, 10-12 lakh candidates have applied for the preliminary exam. These many students saw the advertisement and felt they should take the exam. But it is not just about applying; it is also about taking the exam. We should not be concerned with how many have applied, but with how many actually sat for the exam.

You will be glad to hear that every year 50 to 60 percent of applicants do not actually take the exam. I believe these people are intelligent because there is no point in taking the examination without preparation. So the truth behind the figure of 10 to 12 lakh comes down to around 4.5 lakh. Now let us take a deeper look at this figure too.

(1) Out of this new figure of 4.5 lakh, half of the students are not at all prepared and just take the exam because it is convenient for them. These are 'on-the-fence' students. They keep wondering whether they should take the exam and end up sitting for it. You should not consider them your competition.

(2) For those belonging to SC/ST there is no restriction on number of attempts, while the attempts are limited to 9 for OBCs. So some students can take the preliminary exam and not worry about wasting their attempts.

(3) Some students prepare and take the examination. However, their preparation is not intensive. They consider hard work as preparation enough and thus fall behind.

(4) Some students sit just for the experience. I find it surprising that they want to experience the exam without having undergone any preparation.

Friends, believe me, the crowd you see during preliminary

examination is not the genuine crowd. This horde is just for show, it includes few people who have prepared and the numbers for those who did prepare correctly are even lower. To be true, the numbers of students well prepared never exceed fifty thousand to sixty thousand. To sum it up all, the odds of an individual's selection here are 1 in 7. Around 12-13 times more of the total advertised posts are declared successful in the preliminary exams.

The real deal about the mains is also quite different. Out of the total number of students declared successful in preliminary round, around 25 to 30 percent are those who start preparing for the mains after qualifying the preliminary exams. You can remove them from the competition. Also remove 10 percent of those students who can't focus on their preparation for some reason or the other, such as lack of time. But they still sit for mains because they qualified. Around 15 to 20 percent are students who clear the mains but their marks are so little that they never make it to the list. So you can see that in the mains also, which I consider the real exam, half the students belong to the category which I would shy away from labelling as valid competitors. I consider them players that give a walkover in the field.

Whether you believe it or not, the odds of success in the mains are 1 in every 4 students. I do agree, though, that it is not that easy either to get better than those four because they are all very bright. This is not a cricket match between India and Kenya or Bangladesh. This is India playing against Australia and South Africa, where unless you are an excellent performer, you won't last.

In the interview, the chances of success are one in every two and a half students. If you reach the interview stage, you have already won 40 percent success. But the problem is that there is no such thing as 40 percent success. Success is either 100 percent or it is not there at all.

So I want to free your mind of this terror of the masses, this wrong belief. Indeed, there is a lot of crowd, but it is not genuine and won't stand a chance against you if you are fully prepared.

(B) It is a very tough exam

There may be many aspects to why the exam can be classified as a hard nut to crack. For example, because of the competition (but I have already told you the truth about it), because the syllabus is vast, because the difficulty level of the exam is too high... so on and so forth. Let us examine them in detail.

First let us discuss the syllabus. The minimum requirement for IAS is graduation. So if you opt for the subjects you have studied in graduation, it means you must have studied them much already. Actually the syllabus for IAS includes a little more than what you have studied in graduation and less than what you have studied in post graduation. Its level is at par with that of Honours. In any case, by the time you complete your graduation, you are not yet 21, which is the minimum age to sit for the exam, so most people do a post graduation. Even if you are not doing a post graduation, you still have a year or so to be 21. According to the maturity that you will gain in the year that you have left, should not the syllabus be a little more?

This is how it should be and this is how it is.

You may feel that the syllabus is too much in the following cases -

(1) You chose subjects that are new to you, i.e. you opted for subjects that you neither studied in your graduation nor in your post graduation.

(2) You chose the subject of your graduation but you have passed exams by cramming at the last minute so you have forgotten everything by now.

(3) You cannot develop an interest towards the subject.

(4) You compare IAS to state civil services, or

(5) You do not view the syllabus as a whole but instead you see it as paper 1 and paper 2.

The syllabus is not that huge otherwise. Also, if you have decided to enter the top-most service in the country, the prestige of the service has to be protected. It is only possible when the syllabus is according to it.

Now let me address the gripe that the difficulty level of the exam is too high. I completely agree with the fact that the kind of questions asked in the exam and the kind of answers that are expected raise the difficulty level quite high. But, this is, both the beauty and the challenge of the exam.

The level of the exam is high and so is the status of the job. If this is reduced to the level of state civil services, then instead of 4 lakh, 40 lakh students will apply. However, the worst thing to happen will be that it will be difficult to spot more talented people. I have met so many people from the civil services and I cannot say that even one of them was not knowledgeable.

Whether the level of the exam is high or low, is also subjective. It could be that my own level is so low that I find the level of the exam too high. Otherwise there is nothing like this. For a student who is in the habit of studying and understanding his subject in depth, this exam will be like any other. If you also start doing this, you will feel that the exam is at your level.

Competitive exams do not work on the principle of pass or fail. They work on the principle of selection. The exam selects as many candidates as it needs from the top, their scores do not matter. The questions whether the paper was easy or difficult and whether the difficulty level was high or low do not matter here. This is so because if the paper is difficult, it is so for everybody, and if something affects everyone equally, then it also influences the results in a similar manner.

If the paper is difficult then selection is based on fewer marks but if the paper is easy, the cut-off will go high.

(C) The exam demands too much hard work

If you fear hard work, then this exam is not for you. However, it does not mean that the exam demands so much of hard work that you would soon be wearing spectacles and would not even have time to shave. You must have read terrifying accounts in interviews of successful students in which they claim, "I studied 15 hours a day, for four years." Somewhere, I read this narration of a girl, "I did not even step down from the first floor in three years of my preparation". These are ridiculous statements and even if they are true, then I pity their intelligence, their ability and their method of preparation. I'm wondering how foolish these people must be. What really worries me though is what these bookworms would do in the administrative services. They would be a better fit in the university.

These are people who want to create a larger-than-life image of them. To glamorise themselves they come up with these half-truths. They may have studied for 15 hours at a stretch for two or three days, but they talk as if it applies to the entire duration of their studies. Beware of falling into their trap.

The truth is that you should devote at least 5 to 6 hours to studies. This amount of time should suffice. The mind can also only grasp things up to a limit at a given time. Clothes that are already wet will not soak anymore water in the tub.

You need 5 to 6 hours every day for the initial year of your study because this is just the beginning. Once the preparation is complete you can limit your studies to 4-5 hours and eventually only 3-4. Now, if you believe that even this is hard work, then only God can save you.

I wish to tell you one more thing here. People who say IAS requires extreme work are those who study many writers, almost all available ones, for a particular topic. These people study 4 to 5 newspapers a day, and they study everything in it. They try to read as many magazines as possible too. If this is the approach, and it is not a very feasible one, then doing all these things obviously will take time.

Actually, there is no need to study this much. Doing something like this is not just unproductive, but also counter-productive- your brain becomes a dust-bin where all sorts of useless information get stored in. This will make you lose focus. Instead of concentrating on important points, this overload will make you waste time on futile points. The rule that works in IAS preparation is that 'read less, but whatever you read, read it completely and meticulously.' Rather than knowing little of everything, it is better to know everything about something. The thing here is that you should know what this 'something' should be.

(D) Lack of a first-class Academic Record

This question is asked to me by almost every second-division holder and third-division holder who is now preparing for IAS. They believe that since during interviews a candidate's entire bio data is in front of the interviewers, their second and third division will have a negative effect and they will not be shortlisted.

Let me reason with you about this. If a first-division was important for UPSC then it would have been added in the eligibility requirement like it is if you are applying for lectureship. If this is not a requirement, it is because it is a well-thought decision. UPSC knows its job is to select those who can be good administrators. That's it. And it also knows that to be a good administrator, one does not need a first-class examinations record. Akbar was one of India's top-most administrators, and he was illiterate.

When you are in front of board members for an interview, they are aware that you have reached this stage after qualifying the preliminary exams and the mains. There is no direct entry to reach where you are. You have proven that you deserve to be there. This is why your past does not matter, what matters is your present.

Similarly, if you are a first division holder, topper or doctorate, do not be in the illusion that you will get some additional benefit. This is not the case. What will matter is your performance there. So, instead of thinking about your past, focus on your present. UPSC is very generous about this.

(E) Family Background

Just like lack of fluency in English language and inferiority complex about not holding a first division can create doubts in some candidates and dampen their enthusiasm, so can family background. Some young people worry "I'm from a village. My father is a labourer, farmer. My family is illiterate, I'm not smart. My family income is too little, leaving me with no hope against resourceful candidates. My family conditions may hamper my progress."

To address these concerns, I would like to say the same thing I mentioned above. The job of UPSC is to select candidates that have the potential to be administrators and hand them over to the government. That's it. All the ministries and departments of the government have their own training institutes where they train the selected candidates for not less than one and a half to two years. Needless to say that this training is to get rid of all the deficits an administrator should not have and to instil all the good qualities he should have.

I do, however, admit that if you had had these doubts before 1980, I would not have had the nerve to discard them with so much certainty as I do now. In fact I don't even need to gather my courage because this is the truth. Family background may have played a role in older times (when 'English effect' was pre-dominant and the upper class was given the priority) but given the present political scenario (decentralisation of the power) of the country; it is a thing of the past.

You will be pleasantly surprised to know that since the last 20-25 years, the number of youth from rural backgrounds who have cleared IAS is rapidly increasing. If you do not believe me, you could visit UPSC's website to verify this.

(F) Coaching

This is an important question. Students often wonder whether they should attend coaching classes. I want to address your dilemma in great detail. That's why I have devoted an entire chapter (chapter 6) in the book to this. You can read it if it is applicable to you.

In a nutshell -

(1) If you have a query, trivial or important, right or wrong, you should find answers.

(2) When the purpose of a journey is clear, when the roadmap of the journey is already in your hand it is easier to ensure its success.

Chapter 5

The roadmap to IAS Success

There are two ways of going to a place. You buy a ticket, reach your destination and start exploring. The other way is to know everything about the place you are going to visit beforehand. You take a map with you and already know which places you should go to. While you can visit the place following either of the methods, the output of the trip differs. It is obvious that one who adopts the second method will not only save his time, money and energy but also enjoy the trip more since it has been planned systematically.

This can be applied to the IAS exam too. A lot of young people impulsively decide to take the exam and start wasting their attempts. Unfortunately, we don't have the culture of planning ahead for something. This approach is okay when it comes to trivial matters, but not when it is something important. Of course, it need not be mentioned that passing the civil services exam is no easy feat.

You know the three stages of selection- preliminary exams, mains and the interview. You need to clear all three rounds and that too in the same attempt. If you pass this year's preliminary exams, you will not be allowed to skip it next year and sit for the mains directly. So if you flunk at any level, even if you have reached the interview stage, you have to start from square one.

There is another challenge associated with civil services that the candidate only gets to know when he takes the exam. Maybe you will have trouble believing what I am going to tell you, but that does not change the fact that it is the truth. You should absorb this truth well and prepare accordingly. Sometimes, it has happened that a candidate has been selected in the civil services but he wants to improve his ranking. So he takes the exam next year, but he can't even qualify the preliminary exam. Some candidates score less marks in the interview, or they get decent marks, but it is not enough to change their ranking. So they have to take the exam again if they have an attempt left. You can face this challenge only if you have a roadmap for your exam preparation.

There is yet another challenge that is linked to the optional paper. Until you take the mains exam, it is difficult for you to assess whether the subject is the best choice for you. However, once you have opted for a particular subject, try not to doubt your choice. Also, do not change the subject unless it is absolutely necessary to do so. Sometimes, though, it becomes necessary to rethink about your first choice. If you prepare well and still do not score well in the optional paper, it indicates that you should change your subject. If you do this it would render your previous attempts to be trial attempts. There is no guarantee, however, that the next one is not going to be a trial attempt too. Basically, what I'm trying to say is that the challenges in the exam make it a 20-20 over cricket match, not a five-day one. Here, the number of balls is limited, the wickets are limited, and the target that has to be achieved is huge. Every ball and every wicket is precious. A single limitation can throw the game away. But obviously everyone has drawbacks, so when it comes to getting selected it evens out. Still we should strive towards perfection so that we not only succeed but do so in the manner that would please us. So let us now talk about the planning part of the process.

Elements of planning

This is not free-style wrestling. There are lot of rules and regulations that you have to follow in order to be eligible to play, and to achieve your goal. How much success a candidate does achieve will depend on the fact how well he/she adjusts himself/herself to these rules and regulations. So what are these rules and limitations?

(a) A candidate from General category has six attempts. Candidates belonging to Other Backward Classes (OBCs) have nine attempts. For those from the Scheduled Castes (SC) and Scheduled Tribes (ST), there is no limit to the number of attempts- they can attempt until they cross the maximum age-limit. This is the first limitation of the game.

(b) The next limitation is that of age. You can take the exam from the age of 21 to 32. For OBC and, SC and ST candidates, the age limit is 35 and 37 respectively.

(c) There are three levels of the exam and a candidate has to qualify all three in the same year. This is the third limitation.

(d) These are the rules laid down by UPSC. But other

than these there are social and situational limitations that people may face. For example, it is not very easy for women to keep trying to clear the civil services exam till the age of 30. The pressure to get married from the family may control their plans to a certain extent. It is not wrong for parents to think this way either. It becomes very difficult to marry girls who have crossed a certain age. Although, if they do get selected in the civil services, in most cases, they are allowed to choose their own life partners. In case of men, marriage is not the primary concern. The issue is to get settled. Thirty is not a young age. If you get selected then it is all good, but if you don't then what? And don't forget, the chances of your selection are not very high according to the theory of probability. But the problem is that if you don't try, you have no chances of selection at all. As you age, not only do your attempts decline, you also feel the pressure to get settled. Past failures and frustrations also weigh you down.

These are the facts you should keep in mind while coming up with a 'complete and long-term' plan on how to prepare for the exam. It should be 'complete' in the sense that you not only succeed but get the service of your choice. It should be 'long-term' in the sense that you should have a plan for all the years or attempts you have left. You may get selected and not even require all this planning, and I wish you luck for that, but you need to plan ahead until your last breath.

Now let us discuss some facts that will help you plan.

Planning should be long-term

Firstly, if you are in a hurry and want quick success,

then I would suggest this field is not for you. A genuine IAS preparation is like running a marathon; it is not a 100 metre sprint. Cloudbursts will not work here, even though a lot of water may pour down. Here a steady downpour is needed, where each droplet is absorbed by the soil and becomes an integral part of it. The knowledge you need for your preparation should similarly be absorbed by the brain so deeply that it ceases to exist outside of it. The candidates who employ this to a higher degree are more likely to succeed. So this career path is not for impatient people.

Some people get so worked up, they declare, "I will grab a position among the top ten in my first attempt." When I look at them sceptically, they mock my suspicions. They also justify this by giving me examples of people who have achieved this feat. They are not wrong. However, this is not the whole truth. The students are not able to understand the other facts behind this truth. The truth is that those who achieved this success did so because they were preparing for a long time for the exam. They probably started their preparation when they were in the first year of graduation or even before. It is true that it was their first attempt, but it is not true that they only prepared for a year or so. But the attempt is not the concern here, it is the preparation. You can prove your preparation in the first attempt itself or not be able to prove it till your last. It is important that you understand this fact about civil services before you make your plan. You need to be rational about this preparation, just like you can't win a cricket match without the right strategy.

If you had decided in tenth grade that you want to get into civil services, it would have been very easy for you to achieve success. Even if you decide this in twelfth grade it is good because you can opt for a subject in graduation which you can take in civil services too. You could not only opt for the subject but even study it better than others. Also if you had decided your aim this early in life, preparation for general knowledge would have been a lot easier for you than it is proving to be now.

Today, when you are reading this book on how to become an IAS, I don't know which grade you are in. If this applies to you, it is a positive coincidence and you should take this as a hint from nature that it is telling you to think about IAS. If you are doing your graduation, then also it is fine- better late, than never. You will just have to work a little harder. And in any case, IAS is not for those who shy away from hard work. If you are thinking about IAS after graduation, you are a little late but all hope is not lost. Take heart from this psychological fact- as your brain matures, you take 50 minutes to understand the things that took you 5 hours to comprehend.

To be honest, you have no reason to worry until you have four attempts left. Although most of the people get selected in their second attempt, a third attempt should not dishearten you. Yes, the risk is high if it is your fourth attempt. But you can still taste success. Many matches have been won in the last ball.

You should understand it well that in the first attempt, people don't even clear the preliminary exams, except in some cases. I think of this attempt as an attempt to gain experience, just like an amateur cricketer plays safe and dodges the first ball. After the first attempt, you are in a position to evaluate your preparation. According to statistics, even if you do qualify the preliminary exam in your first attempt, it is very hard to crack the mains. One reason behind this is that due to lack of experience, the students only focus on the preliminary exams. Some students even say that they will prepare for mains after the preliminary exams. How impractical they are! This is not possible.

So it is very likely that your second attempt proves to be your final attempt- no matter if you had not been able to qualify the preliminary exam in your first attempt. Yes, there are chances of missing out on a good rank though. Students take the exam again because they do not have a good rank. So it may happen that your second attempt is successful but still not satisfactory. I'm only mentioning the usual scenario here; there are of course exceptions to this rule.

I would suggest you do not give your second attempt in the next consecutive year if your preparation is not up to the mark. When I'm talking of preparation here I mean the preliminary exam, mains and even the interview to some level- preparing only for preliminary means nothing. If after taking the exam once you feel that you need a longer time to prepare, do so. Do not hurry. But you cannot repeat this in between your second and third attempt and between your third and remaining attempts. Ideally, after your second attempt, you should continue giving the exam- if it's needed any more. Otherwise some stagnancy may creep into your preparation and this may hamper it. And you won't be able to help it. Once we have prepared well, we do not need to work so hard next time. After this, the focus is on enhancing your knowledge about the subject and understanding it in depth. To accomplish this you need to think more and study less and you do not need as much time to think as you need to study. There is a psychology behind preparing for an exam. Studying the same thing over and over again can get boring and frustrating. If we study with this frame of mind, it will not be of any use.

Do not take time to get involved

Do not forget that as we age, our enthusiasm to study fizzles out. People also come under a lot of pressure due to increased age. So you should at least start studying at 21 years of age and aim to finish your preparation by the age of 26. If you take too much liberty, you can stretch it to the age of 27, but no more. Forget the fact that you can actually give the exam until the age of 32. Initially the age limit was 26, then it was increased to 28 and now it is 32. It would be good if the age limit is again reduced to 26. The increase in age limit can keep you in an illusion because you think that there is a lot of time left. But this is actually an indication of weakness. If you want to achieve something, why not work for it now? Why don't you pledge that 'I will work hard and whatever has to happen will happen by the time I am 26-27. If this happens fine, otherwise I will try my hand at something else'. When you start thinking this way, your brain cannot play tricks on you anymore. This will maximise your efficiency.

Many students, especially those from rural backgrounds overlook an important fact about the civil services. During preparation, the students' main focus is to get selected. And they are not wrong either. However, they do not realise that if they get selected at a young age, their career will be better.

They can retire from a higher post. For example, in a given year, two men are selected in the same service. One man is 22 years old while the other is 29. While they are from the same batch, there is a 7 year age difference. The 22-year-old has 38 years of service left in him, but the 29-year-old has 31 years only. It is obvious then that the older man will not be able to reach the peak of his career that is means so much in the later half of the life.

There is another thing. Let us assume that the younger man has a better ranking than the 29-year-old. In this case, even though they belong to the same batch, the younger man will be considered senior. When the post of a superior falls vacant, it will be offered to the younger man. You may not realise it now but once you are in the service, you may have these bitter experiences. So while planning your preparation do not focus on the maximum age, instead focus on how to achieve your goal as soon as possible.

Sit for other competitive exams

I told you to plan long-term. This long-term planning includes taking other competitive exams simultaneously. Most of the students are found ignorant about it, but who follow this do find success somewhere. Some people get egoistic and think that since I'm preparing for civil services why I should take state civil services exams, banking exams, or staff selection commission exams. This way, they are only harming themselves.

You should not see various exams as undermining each other. In any case, in any exam whether banking or state civil services, they have one general knowledge paper. Since you are preparing for IAS, you do not have to do special studies for these exams. Yes, for state civil services, you have to read up on the state and this is something you should not avoid.

Even if you do not want to enter these services, you should take the exam for the experience. It will hone your skills and provide continuity to your preparation. It will also boost your confidence if you get selected in any of the exams. So your planning should include taking these exams even if it is not the focal point of your preparation.

Now I have a question for you. What will you do if while preparing for IAS you get selected in some other service? Many students are faced with this dilemma and they worry that if they take up a job, they will not be able to study for IAS. Some worry that if they start working, it would dampen their enthusiasm for IAS. That's why many of them eventually decide not to join the service at all.

Here is my advice to those who are wondering whether to take up a job or not. If you get a job offer, take it- without giving it a second thought. My dear friend, IAS exam is tough and there is no guarantee of success. Even he who has been selected once cannot claim he can do it again. Yes, people do get selected, so why cannot you. If you think so I appreciate your confidence. You should definitely be thinking like that- but without losing the practical viewpoint associated with it. What practical viewpoint? 'What if I, by chance, do not make it?'

So don't reject the job; just see how you can manage work as well as studies. For example, if it is possible to delay the joining, do so. You can take a long break (if you are allowed to) after you have started working. This also depends on how much time you actually need for your preparation.

You will be pleasantly surprised to know that most people who get selected for civil services are those who already have a job. Job is not an obstruction to your civil services aspiration. Why don't you work on honing your skills instead? Reduce your sleeping hours, cut down on entertainment, say no to aimless outings and spend every minute preparing for it. It is better you figure out a way to juggle both things rather than sit around thinking this is impossible.

Manage preparation with regular studies

Let us assume you are done with your graduation and want to become an IAS. You are not 21 yet. What should you do in this case? Most students focus only on IAS preparation assuming that once they are 21, they can sit for the exam. They are not wrong. But if they modify this thinking a bit they could utilise their time better. The subject that you want to opt for in IAS mains, you should choose that subject and do the post graduation. You do not have to be a regular college student for that. Indira Gandhi National Open University (IGNOU) has standard notes and it could be a good idea to do a post graduation from IGNOU through correspondence.

This will not only help you prepare for IAS but you will get a post graduate degree as well. Anything can happen in the future. If you don't get selected you will still have a degree. There is one more thing related to the interview that I must mention. It has been observed that if you have done your post graduation in a subject or conducted research on a subject, you are generally asked questions about it. This way you are also preparing for the interview because it is easier to answer questions on topics that you are aware of.

Benefit from experience

One last piece of advice- we can only benefit from experience in future if we employ it in our daily lives. Imagine that you took the preliminary exams for the first time and did not get selected. As I said earlier this is an attempt to gain experience. But you will only gain experience from it if you use it efficiently. You need to evaluate the attempt, understand your weaknesses and strong points. It is only after understanding things that you can strengthen your strong points and eliminate your weaknesses. I will explain to you how you should achieve this.

As soon as the preliminary exam is over, immediately or the next day, evaluate the paper and note down the points. Do not be lazy and think that you will remember everything. You will forget these things and then you will not be able to make the best use of your experience. So please write them down. You can evaluate yourself on the following points-

(a) How many questions did you answer correctly?

(b) How many questions have a 50 percent chance of being correctly answered?

(c) What confused you about these questions? Why couldn't you be 100 percent sure about the answers to these questions? This analysis is important to help you understand your weak points. You will notice that you get baffled by a question because you did not study the topic seriously. This evaluation will help you do better next time.

(d) How many questions could you not answer at all? Try to understand why you could not answer these questions. It could be that you did not study the topic or did not take it seriously enough. It could be that you read the topic but it did not include the particular question that was asked. Try to figure out which book you should have read to be able to answer the questions correctly.

(e) Also write down how long it took you to finish the exam and what did you do with the remaining time. It is seen on numerous occasions that students do not use this surplus wisely. Ideally, they should use this time to solve questions they haven't been able to answer at first. You should keep in mind that in competitive exams each mark matters.

The most important thing here is not whether you cleared the exam in your first attempt. It has been seen that since the age limit for taking IAS exam has been raised, along with an increase in the number of attempts, the number of students who cleared the exam in their first attempt has gone down to 8-10 percent. Now students taking the exam for the second, third or fourth time are more likely to be successful. This shows that experience plays an important role in success.

However, experience does not come from merely taking an exam. It is important that you jot down your experiences, analyse them and give it a serious thought. Try to get rid of your weaknesses with the help of this critical analysis. Otherwise your destiny will be similar to a car which has been started on jack stands so its wheels are turning but it hasn't moved forward even an inch.

Chapter 6

Is Coaching Essential ?

When I was providing guidance to students for IAS preparation, I met three types of students or rather I should say students who had predominantly three different kinds of beliefs about coaching. The first category of students believed that joining coaching classes to become an IAS was a must. To them, this is a fact which is beyond doubt. This is similar to a situation where none of the parents ever question whether their kids should go to middle school. These students have the resources and they start their journey to become an IAS by joining coaching classes. I welcome their decision.

The second category of students includes those who have no doubts about the importance of coaching classes but unfortunately their financial situation does not allow them to join the classes. They have to do their own preparation.

Then there are students who are not able to decide whether they should take coaching or not. Such students ask me, 'Sir, is it compulsory to take coaching?' But I find myself unable to give them a satisfactory answer. I tell them, 'you have to decide whether you need coaching or not'. Am I saying something wrong?

I know how the students are conditioned to hold one of the three views mentioned above. Before 1980, there were only a handful of coaching institutes. After 1979, students from not just English, but all national languages were allowed to take the exam. After this revolutionary step taken by the UPSC, the number of those taking the exam increased manifold and so did the institutes offering coaching for IAS. This happened not just because there was a market for it, but also the need. Now, whether these institutes are able to fulfil this need is an entirely different matter.

Today, institutes that provide coaching for cracking the entrance to IIT or Medical courses are running like corporate businesses. There will not be any exaggeration in saying that they have established such a strong and parallel system that even school studies seem dull in comparison. There will hardly be any student who is not taking coaching for one reason or the other.

All this has affected today's youth. In any exam, where there is competition, there are coaching institutes to help you prepare for the competition. Everyone is afraid- the ones who are good students and the ones who don't consider themselves to be good. This fear has rendered coaching institutes indispensable.

Today, when students get selected in any competitive exam, there are advertisements that reveal the coaching institutes they attended. Actually, these advertisements are part of the business strategy of the coaching institutes, and they have been successful in making students believe that they can't make it without coaching.

But the coaching institutes that are doing a decent job demand such high fees that those belonging to middle and low income groups cannot afford it. Students are, thus, in a tight spot. They face a dilemma because they believe that coaching is essential but they are unable to pay for it. If the money is arranged it would solve their problem, then there would be no dilemma at all. But technology has reduced your concerns by providing the facility of online coaching for this. It is relatively much cheaper and can be done while sitting at home.

Students who are preparing for IAS should not be stuck in such dilemmas. I'm going to share some things with you to help you in this.

Is coaching essential ?

The keywords here are 'coaching' and 'essential'. I would define coaching as guidance. Now IAS exam is not an average exam. In fact, in a way it is a very technical exam. The exam has its own science and the student who understands the science behind the exam ensures his success. Even if you are a top student and you try to employ the style of studying you did at university, the chances of your success would stay slim. You need to change yourself and adopt the method of studying that UPSC requires.

Now the question arises - how do you do all this? The answer to this also explains what is 'essential'. You need coaching means you need guidance. Now it is up to you how you fulfil this need. Following are the ways you could do so-

(1) You already know about the IAS process like I did. I was fortunate enough to complete my studies as a private

student. If this was not the case, I have no doubts I would not be a civil servant. I'm not boasting, but there is logic behind what I'm saying. I could not learn by rote. Memorising something was impossible for me. In this situation, I only had one option- to understand every topic very well. There was no one in my village and town to guide me so I had to understand everything on my own. As a result, answering the questions in IAS exams became easier for me because it required a deep understanding.

This can happen with you as well. If you are in the habit of understanding a subject, then you are ready for IAS. You don't need guidance from anyone.

(2) If your college professors are willing to help you- if they are good enough to aid you. I am very particular about 'good enough'. Just because they are lecturers and professors, it does not mean they will be able to help you touch a subject in depth. It is not enough that they teach the subject, they should be able to help you understand it in depth. If you have someone like that take his help.

(3) The best personal guidance you can get is from someone who has qualified civil services. It is not important whether he got IAS or any other service. It is just a matter of few numbers. It is enough that he cracked an exam as tough as civil services. This person knows very well how the preparation is to be done, what to read, and what not to read and how particular questions need to be answered. And these are the only things you need to know in order to become an IAS.

However, it is very difficult to find such a person. Those who get selected do not teach; they do an administrative job.

So what can you do now? Let me give you a solution. In every district, there are one or more young officers who have just qualified the civil services exam. In state capitals, you will find many such officers. You can go to them and request their guidance. I'm not saying that they will have much time to spend with you, but whatever time that they give you would be as precious as 24 carat gold. Grab it. Do not hesitate. Believe me that even they would love to help you. But before you approach them have a clear picture in your head about what you are going to ask them.

(4) Discussion plays a major role in IAS preparation. If you have friends with whom you can discuss things, then they can compensate for any lack of guidance whatsoever. But these should be open discussions where you are ready to listen to the other person and understand their viewpoint. It has been observed that often these discussions are less about learning and more about winning and losing. This will result in nothing but a false sense of satisfaction.

(5) Let us talk about coaching institutes now. If you are unable to do any of these, then you are left with only two options- join a coaching institute or do self-coaching.

So the question here is not whether one should join coaching or not but how should they get what they need to prepare for IAS. How beneficial coaching would be to you and how to make the most of it is something I would discuss further. Right now I will tell you how to do some self-coaching.

Self-coaching

The first thing you have to do is to stand up against

yourself. This is a psychological truth. Your mind is accustomed to the same pattern of studying, writing and thinking due to your studies till now. To change this, you have to be mentally prepared and accept that your method is not correct. But it is easier said than done. In the beginning, you have to repeat this thought many times a day so that it gets imbibed into your subconscious and you get accustomed of it.

But it will not be as easy as it does sound. Your mind will not accept this change easily. It will revert to the old ways again and again and try to reason with you that they were better. You have to fight this illusion created by your mind.

The second stage of self-coaching will show you that the best professor is an unsolved paper. Take an unsolved question paper and analyse the kind of questions that are asked. You will see very few questions that are plain or direct. With every question will be attached 'criticise', 'analyse', 'do you agree?' Some questions would be so twisted that you would not know what to answer. You should understand the questions, in fact, you should memorise them. These will act as a lighthouse for you, guiding you to the right path.

After you are done with the unsolved papers, start studying. While studying, keep in mind that you should be able to answer the questions you read in the unsolved papers. Your way of studying should be the way to answer those questions. In the beginning, you will see that you have read the topic but you are unable to answer the questions. Don't worry. This is your biggest challenge and it is present because of the old mind. So in the beginning, you have to hit your mind with ideas of change just like a rock is hammered- cracks will appear soon if not immediately.

Read the topic again and again. Think about it. It might be difficult initially but thoughts will soon pour in. And remember, your ability to think like this will take you closer to your goal of being an IAS.

I have to warn you that this may get boring and even frustrating for you. You may even think that it is useless advice. But it is not, believe me. This is what you need to do at the moment. And if you keep doing it, and if you do not quit halfway, you will start seeing such underlying facts in the same topic that were not visible earlier. This is called 'reading between the lines.' Everyone can read what is written in black and white, but to interpret what is being said in between the lines is possible only for great thinkers. After practicing this for a while, you will start having various questions in mind about the topic. You will also get your answers. When this happens, you will know that you are on the right track.

The last stage would include writing down the answers to the unsolved papers. After you have written down your answers, you yourself have to judge them. You should judge your answers on two things-

(a) First, you read your answer and then figure out if it answers the question that was asked. Imagine you are the one asking the question and someone else is writing the answer. Now ask yourself, are you happy with the answer? Have all the aspects of your question been addressed fully? Or you still have some unresolved things in your mind? If you do have, then it means your answer lacks something. Find out and then address the issue.

(b) Another way you can judge your answer is by taking help of a book. After writing the answer, read the topic again. See the points that are missing, and that you should have included in your answer in order to make it more meaningful. Let your answers be updated accordingly.

You have another option; you can ask someone who knows about the subject to judge your answer. But make sure to choose the right person. Wrong advice is like a wrong diagnosis. You get treated for something you don't have. As a result, the actual condition does not get treated and side effects of the wrong medicine may create other problems. It's better not to take any advice at all, then to take wrong advice.

Friends, I have told you about the process of self-coaching that I do believe in. My belief is grounded in the experiments I have been doing with it since long. Having been successful with it myself, I recommended it to various people. And I am glad to tell you that they benefitted from it. You are also welcome to adopt it and be successful- if you wish to.

Now let us come back to the talk of coaching institutes. You have to decide whether you want to join coaching. And you have to find out whether this institute or that. It depends on your need, comfort and resources. My advice is that no matter what the teaching methodology of an institute is, you can still benefit from it- provided that you are aware what benefit to take and how it can be taken. There are many students who never took coaching, but achieved their dream. So the question here is that of your need, it is not a necessity.

Now, I will tell you how coaching can be beneficial for you and how to make the most of it.

(1) Coaching would prove beneficial to a science student who has picked up an arts subject. Such a student would not know anything about the subject. Listening to the lectures in the institutes and taking notes would provide knowledge about the subject. There is a difference when a student studies from books and when he listens to the lectures and then reads from the books. Classrooms also give you the opportunity to clear your doubts on the spot. Now this does not apply to someone who is an arts student and is already familiar with the subject.

(2) The importance of General knowledge for civil services has increased through the years. I doubt how well students know General knowledge and how well they can prepare for it on their own. Coaching institutes have a long experience of teaching. They know the kind of questions that are asked and how to get the material for them. This way these institutes can help you prepare for the general knowledge.

But I want to clarify here that you should not take your coaching to be the end of all your study. You should look upon it as raw material but don't be totally dependent on them.

(3) I take coaching to be a forum where people with the same purpose gather. It is not possible for an aspirant to form a study group of his own. But in coaching you can select your companions and form a group. This group will help you during group discussions. So please don't miss out on it.

(4) I have seen that coaching institutes have libraries but students are not using them. You can find many books concerning your subject here. Reading them will make you mentally strong. So take full advantage of it.

(5) If you are alert and open to all the possibilities,

coaching can help you develop your personality- provided you don't just go there, attend the lecture and come back to your room. You should interact with as many people as possible. This will help you get rid of any hesitation you might have. It will improve your social skills, your language, and help hone your leadership qualities. Do not put all your efforts only into studying.

(6) Discipline is important when you are doing something big. Coaching can help you with this. Every institute has its own set of conducts and a time-table that are bound to be followed by the students. It will help you live according to a fixed routine. And as soon as you start living in a disciplined way it will start reflecting on your preparations as well.

Friends, let me tell you that a weapon does not matter, what matters is who is using it. If you keep the brave warrior Maharana Pratap's strong and sharp sword on the shelf in your living room, what use will it be? It can't win battles for you until you learn to use it efficiently. When preparing for IAS, do not forget this truth that no book and no institute can help you on its own, it is you who can get juice out of them. Remember, you have the power and the ability to increase or decrease the value of something with your touch.

Chapter 7

Some Important Facts about Civil Services

I have often heard students say, "I'm preparing for IAS exam". People know what IAS is so they understand what the student is trying to say. But technically, it is incorrect. I wish students aspiring to be an IAS officer do not make these kinds of silly mistakes.

IAS stands for Indian Administrative Service. It is not the name of some exam but the name of one of the services you join if you crack a particular exam. The name of the exam is Indian Civil Services Examination. This includes more than 20 services, one of them is Indian Administrative Service (IAS). The other popular ones are Indian Police Service (IPS), Indian Foreign Service (IFS), Indian Revenue Service (this includes two services- income tax as well as custom and excise service), Indian audit and account service, Indian Railway Service etc.

There is no doubt that Indian Administrative Service is the most sought-after service among all. You hardly find an aspirant who is willing to aim for anything less than IAS. However, everyone cannot realise their dream so they have to join other services. But this does not mean that the other services are not good. It's truly a misconception.

When students are taking the exam they are not well-informed about the services offered by the UPSC. So they just decide their preference on hearsay. But the truth is no service is meant for everyone and no person is meant for every service. This depends on a person's nature, desire, need and circumstances.

No job is complete. There is something lacking in every job. So it is better if you know some fundamental truths about the services being offered. It will help you in deciding the service that is right for you.

Civil Services exam allows entry to three main services-

(1) Top Indian services

(2) Group 'A' services

(3) Group 'B' services

(1) Top Indian services

IAS

Indian Administrative Service was started by the British more than 150 years ago. Prior to 1950, this service was known as ICS (Indian Civil Service). Initially, during the British rule in India, only the British were allowed to take the exam. This was because this service was the most important service of the British administration and the foreign government did not trust Indians. After a while Indians were allowed entry into Indian Civil Service. During the British rule, all those who joined the service held important positions in the administration. They also yielded a lot of power. These were the actual rulers who allowed British to rule over India. They were known as the king of the district and steel frame of the government.

After independence, in 1950, the name of the service was changed to Indian Administrative Service but the role, power and benefits of the job remained the same. But as democracy spread its roots in India, administration was decentralised. The concept of Panchayati Raj was strengthened and this service lost its lustre. Now the situation has changed from the ruler to that of an administrator. And it's a good thing from the point of view of democracy. However, the service still has its sheen and status- as they say 'a dead elephant is worth more than a live one'. Most young people today still dream of becoming an IAS officer. And they have all the reasons for it. Let us see some of those reasons closely:

(1) IAS officers are generalists, not specialists. If we still want to call them specialists, we can call them specialists in administration. Since every department needs administration, IAS officers hold positions of power across all departments of administration. This way they exert a direct or indirect control over all departments and ministries. For example, let us study the Indian Revenue service. All the officers of this service will head their departments but in the ministries, the secretary, the upper secretary and joint secretary are IAS officers. This way they control the service.

So is the case with the departments of the state governments. All the important departments of the state governments are generally headed by the IAS officers.

(2) These officers have the collective benefit of working in all the services. Police Service, Foreign Service and other services have officers who are specialists and have

thorough knowledge of their field. So they usually hold different posts in their own departments only. Their work changes a bit when they are deputed to a ministry of the Central government. But IAS officers have a dynamic job.

(3) IAS officers have a direct role to play in the policies that are formed.

(4) They have the experience at both grassroots level and at the top administration level. In the initial 8 to 10 years of their careers, they get introduced to developmental problems and issues faced by the locals in the districts and tehsils. This is considered a difficult posting but an adventurous one which provides immense experience.

(5) All the rights of administration lie with these officers.

(6) The cadre management of this service is strong. Once you enter the service the chances of your promotion are strong. The promotions you get here are frequent and at high levels. There is hardly any service that can match this.

(7) The officers get a lot of respect from society because they have the power to get work done.

(8) As far as material things such as house, vehicles etc. go, all of this is received as soon as you enter the service and remain till you retire.

(9) If someone wants, along with a routine job, to do something big that he enjoys doing and always wanted to do, it is possible to do so in this service. Other services won't give you this much liberty.

(10) This is the country's oldest and most well-organised

service so as soon as you become a member of it, you become a part of a wide network. There are almost 6,000 IAS officers in the country, and you will become one of them. There is no part of this country that doesn't fall under the administrative control of an IAS officer. You can assume that you can reach this area through your colleague.

(11) And last but not the least, a lot of problems associated with daily life will no longer pose an issue because you are an IAS officer. People will respect you and give priority to your work.

These are some of the facts associated with this service, so if young people give IAS as their first preference, they aren't doing anything wrong. There is more than mere luxury and power that is on offer.

But you have not seen the other side of the coin, my friend, which is equally important. There is nothing free in this world, or as they say 'no lunch is free'. If IAS offers so many benefits, it also makes demands of you. Isn't it better if you are aware of the costs beforehand? Let us have a look:

(1) If you prefer a peaceful and routine life, if you want to go to work at 10 and leave at 6 then IAS is not the job for you. Initially when you are posted in districts, you may be responsible for not just the development of people but also their life. This will not allow you to follow the principle of office time. In fact a civil servant is bound to be available for work all 24 hours.

(2) If you shy away from struggles of daily life this is not the job for you. Wherever there is public, there will be

problems and you will have to take part in this struggle.

(3) If you dislike politicians, this job is not meant for you. A politician is the representative of the people in a democracy while you as an IAS officer represent the government. The politicians will obviously come to you to get the work of their people done. You cannot escape them and why would you want to? You simply need to find ways of tackling them well. After all, how you handle these situations shows how good an administrator you are.

(4) If you are very 'choosy', then also you will face problems. The biggest problem you face may be that of cadre. There are two services under civil services that are known as All Indian services- Indian Administrative Service and Indian Police Service. A third All-India service is Indian Forest Service for which UPSC conducts another exam.

One of the main features of the All Indian service is that it allots you a cadre and you have to work in that cadre for a lifetime. For instance, if you get Madhya Pradesh cadre, you will always work there- except in the case of deputation, and that too if you opt for it.

After passing the preliminary exam, when you fill the application for mains, you are asked your preference for the states. If you do not give any preference, the government will decide for you.

There is a formula for cadre allotment. According to this formula, if you are allotted the cadre of your choice well and good, if not then you will have to go to the state that you have been allotted. You may get a cadre you do not want. In this situation, you will have to live your whole life (till retirement) at a place that doesn't seem favourable to you. Now it's up to you whether you can adjust with this very nature of the job.

(5) If you are in favour of working at one place, this job will disappoint you. In the initial ten years, you should be prepared to work in different parts (including remote areas) of the state. After this, you may be posted in the state capital for a while, but your department will keep changing. This does not happen because of a rule but out of tradition and administrative convenience.

(6) If you want a very high salary package, the service will not be able to provide you with that- not even in the later years. While you will not be in want of anything and all your needs will be met, you can bid goodbye to your dreams of living a luxurious lifestyle.

Now I have shown you both aspects of IAS. The decision is yours. I would advise you decide on your own and only take suggestions from others.

IFS

There was a time when a candidate would get Indian Foreign Service only if he ranked among the top ten. After the liberalisation in the 1990s, it became easy to go abroad. Consequently, the craze of the service was reduced.

Indian Foreign Service is one of the most prestigious services in the country. The officers spend most of their lives posted in Indian embassies in foreign countries. There is not too much work pressure in this service and there is only a slight chance that you would stay in India. There are good possibilities of promotions. When the officers are posted in foreign countries, they are paid allowances which put them in a strong financial position. The only problem these officers face is that of staying abroad. Still it is in demand.

IPS

Just like IAS, this is also a popular and respected service. IAS officers work closely with the common people, so is the case with IPS officers. This is also a service which has its roots in the British era. Since the service takes care of law and order, it is considered a sensitive service.

The service requires a different temperament. The majority of their time is spent investigating crimes and dealing with the criminals. An officer has to be alert 24 hours. So obviously, you cannot expect a routine job and sometimes even your family has to pay the price. Let us not overlook the fact that there is definitely some risk involved. But the risk is not big enough that it should scare you away from the service. There are some who enjoy adventure and challenges. Some are attracted by the glamour of the uniform. And yes, the cadre aspect applies to this service, just like IAS.

This is a professional service. Officers for this service are also hired from institutions such as BSF, CRPF, RAW, Intelligence Bureau and CBI. They get there on deputation.

2. Group A services

Account Services

Civil services exam also gives jobs in services such as audit and account, civil account and defence account. An account job is a very comfortable job and it does not pose many challenges compared to other jobs. Officers are not required to communicate with the common people. Among all the account services, the audit and account service is desired the most because it has good chances of promotion.

Revenue Services

This includes income tax and Customs & Indirect Taxes services. These services are also quite popular. This service also gives you the opportunity to connect with the masses but not like IAS and IPS. These services are connected to issues related to wealthy people and industrialists, so they test an officer's honesty. And so, many young men are found eager to get their honesty tested. In terms of preference, this service is ranked highly.

Indian Postal Service

This service is not very sought-after anymore. It does not offer many challenges and promotions are also not great. But there are various facilities available.

3. Group B service

Group B services can be equated with state civil services. Officers for Delhi as well as union territories are appointed through this service. The careers of officers in Group A service is equivalent to those in the top Indian services- they do not enjoy that much power though. IAS is the strongest service when it comes to powers the officers hold. But this is not the case with Group B service. There is a major difference in the careers of officers from Group A service and those from Group B service. But this service is still preferred because it is considered better than other government jobs.

Friends, I have tried to give you a brief but essential description of all the services that fall under civil services. The purpose of this was to make you aware of the actual nature of the services because I have seen that the youth, especially those who come from far off towns and cities are not aware of the services. That's why they face problems when listing down their preference and sometimes they do not give preference at all. They may have to regret this later on. I'm not claiming that my telling you this will solve your problem 100 percent, but you will at least be aware of the facts. I would suggest you collect information about various services while preparing for IAS. It will help you set your preferences right.

Friends, you may think in the beginning that how does it matter whichever job you get, at least it's a job, but you will repent this. Do not take the preference of the services lightly. You may get any service but every service comes attached with its own policies, culture, prestige and comforts, and in a sense this becomes our lifestyle. So you should give your preference after giving this a serious thought.

Promotion in civil services

If we consider the top Indian services and Group A services (except Group B services), then we can say that the chances of promotion in all services which are bagged through civil services exam are very good. We can also say, without a doubt, that among all these services, the chances of promotion are best in IAS. Anybody can see the reasons behind it. If the promotion is being hampered at any level, the officer can get it fixed because they are the ones who have administrative control. In other services, there may be hurdles but since these appointments are through Indian civil service, the odds of promotion are higher than in other jobs.

In general, promotion in civil services takes place like this -

(1) The first two years of service you are on probation. The officers are called probationers and this is their training period. They are assigned a particular department and given practical training. They are also given a designation which lasts till they finish their training. The probation period is quite sensitive. An officer is not permanent yet and if his character is found lacking he can be removed from the service. If the same problem is spotted later on when an officer is permanent, the government has to follow a strict set of rules and it is not an easy process. So this probation period should be taken seriously.

(2) After joining the service, an officer will work at a position of the same level for the next four years- he may be assigned various departments and have different designations though. You must keep in mind that an officer's level and his designation are separate. There can be many designations at the same level depending on the department and its work culture. For example, in the initial four years, an IAS officer will be an SDM and an ADM, but his level will be same.

(3) The first promotion in all services is known as 'time-scale'. This means that when an officer completes four years in the service he is promoted. Generally, a

promotion is given when there is a vacancy. After the 'time-scale', all promotions are given whenever there is a vacancy. But 'time-scale' promotions have nothing to do with the availability of vacancies. It is concerned with the time only. Once you complete four years, you will get your first promotion. Sometimes a promotion can be given even before four years have been completed, in case there is a vacancy. It's true for many services.

(4) After nine years of service, another promotion can be expected, an officer can be promoted to the rank of deputy secretary. This is also to be remembered that this job is at the centre-level, and not state. Usually, state secretary is appointed at the centre at a lower level of joint secretary.

(5) On completing 14 years of service, 'selection grade' is received and an officer is appointed as a 'director'.

(6) The promotion which is received after 18-19 years of service is known as senior administrative grade. The officers at this level are known as joint secretary at the centre. At state-level, they are known as secretary or commissioner.

After this, promotions are based on how many higher posts are in the service and how many are vacant. Who gets the promotion and when depends on-

(a) The officer's age when he entered the service.

(b) His rank in his batch.

(c) The age of officers in the senior batch, who must all be his superiors.

(d) The number of higher-ranking jobs.

Generally, young people who give a lot of importance to their careers, keep two things in mind during their preparation. First, they try to join the service at an early age. If they join early, they will get more years of service, and if they work for longer they have better chances of getting higher-ranking jobs.

Another thing is about rank. These students try that their rank in their batch is very good. Generally, the rank in all civil services is decided by the marks scored in the UPSC exam. A higher score will ensure a higher rank. If a student scores 1054 marks, he is ranked higher than the student who scored 1053. Let's imagine that 20 candidates were selected in the IPS. Obviously their ranks will not be in continuous order. So if the first student to enter IPS has 48th rank, it's not necessary that students ranking 49, 50, 51, 52 will also join IPS. Since everyone has its own preference so rank is not chronological. It is possible that in these 20 IPS officers, the topper is ranked 48th and the 20th student may rank 100th. Anything can happen here, except two students having the same rank. If two students have the same number of marks, then UPSC will decide the rank based on the marks obtained in general knowledge.

There is a principle followed for promotions according to which a subordinate will only be promoted after his superior.

It can be evident right after 'time-scale' promotions. The first promotion is given to the entire batch. But the future promotions depend on how many posts are lying vacant. When there is a vacancy, due procedure is followed and the senior-most officer is promoted.

Later on, the officers of the same batch get promoted at different times depending on their rank in the UPSC exam. So, prudent students are cautious about this from the beginning. If you dream of becoming cabinet secretary or state chief secretary, it would only be possible if you fulfil two conditions- you should become an IAS officer at a young age and top your batch.

There is one more thing. Except for the time-scale, none of the promotions are in your hands. It is not that you complete a particular number of years in service and get a promotion. A process is followed and a committee is appointed which discusses an individual's confidential report (CR) for the past few years. If something negative were to come up at this point, the committee can recommend that the individual should not be promoted. In case this happens, a subordinate might get the promotion and this situation will last throughout an officer's career. Thus, civil service expects its officers not to engage in any questionable activities.

(7) As far as becoming a secretary/chief secretary in the state government and secretary in the central government is concerned, these posts are mostly held by IAS officers. This is not mandatory though and some posts are filled up by officers from other services as well, but this is rare. These posts are the top jobs in administrative services and all policies are formulated and implemented by them. IAS officers are given preference for these posts because the government believes that though the IAS officers are known as generalists, they are specialists when it comes to administration.

To sum it up you, as a civil servant, can be rest assured that even in the worst situation, at the time of retirement, your rank would be that of a joint secretary at the centre or state secretary. At least this much can be guaranteed. How long an officer would want to work as a joint secretary would, however, depend on the possibilities of further promotions seen by him.

Although it is not a good idea to start worrying about this right now, it is not foolish to do so. I have noticed that IAS aspirants have a great desire to know about all this. This is why I decided to discuss about this here. While this discussion is not related to the exam preparation, it is related to mental preparation. I think the information in this chapter will motivate students to study harder so they can not only get a job they want but also a good rank. This will help them reach the pinnacle of their career.

Chapter 8

Choosing the Optional Subject

You can't underestimate the choice of optional paper in the process of becoming an IAS. Before 2013, choosing an optional paper was twice as much challenging because students had to pick two subjects. But now only one paper has to be chosen, so I believe that this challenge has been reduced by half. In my experience, students seem more troubled when asked to choose 'another' optional subject; one is quite okay for them. For example, engineering students would choose a subject relevant to their stream which is simple and easy for them. The problem would arise when they had to opt for a second subject. Similarly, for post graduates, the subject of their post graduation is an obvious choice for an optional paper. But they would also face difficulty when choosing another subject. So now that candidates are not required to choose two optional papers, their difficulties must have eased.

But is that what has really happened? I regret writing this but the answer is no. Although, the challenge has somewhat diminished compared to before, it hasn't been wiped out. Even now students ask me, 'Sir, what subject do I choose?' I feel sad because I have to disappoint them. But I also feel hurt that this student does not have the ability to even choose a subject for himself. At this initial stage only I detect this as a weakness in their personality and this is hardly ever wrong. You tell me, who else other than you can decide which subject you should take? After all, how much does the other person know you that he can tell which subject you should choose?

There is another danger in asking others. You will get different replies from different people about this. If there is someone who didn't get selected because he scored less in public administration, he may not advise you on which subject you should choose, but he would definitely suggest, 'Do whatever, but do not choose public administration'. But it is quite possible that the same day you meet someone who scored very high in public administration. Obviously, before you can even finish questioning him, he will tell you to choosc public administration. If you ask coaching centres they would tell you to opt for subjects which they are teaching. Remember, none of these people are wrong; they just view the truth differently. Even coaching centres teach subjects they think are important. This is their truth. The fact is you have your own truth and someone else's truth is not going to work for you.

On the basis of my years of experience of guiding civil services aspirants and my successful juniors, I say this with conviction that there is no subject in UPSC's list that no one has ever opted for or no one has passed. If there were a subject like that, UPSC would have removed it from its list.

I think this problem needs to be addressed in a more logical way, because students unnecessarily worry about this. Ponder over these questions-

(1) What is the reason that a subject in which one student succeeds becomes the reason for another's failure in the same year?

(2) Why is it that a subject that seems simple and interesting to one student appears difficult and boring to another?

(3) Why has UPSC introduced scaling of marks? Don't you think the aim of this move is to ensure equality in the marks scored in all optional subjects?

If you think about these questions seriously you will begin to see more clearly. This will save you from choosing the wrong subject. When I say 'wrong subject' here, let me clarify that no subject is wrong in itself, it may just be wrong for us.

What influences your decision the most while choosing a subject for yourself? It is 'rumours'. In the community of IAS aspirants, various subjects keep coming in the limelight. Some candidates think that because high numbers of people are being selected from a particular subject, their chances of selection will also increase if they opt for it. Both the facts are wrong here. People don't get selected because they choose a particular subject, more number of successful candidates from a subject means more students are opting for that subject. If you look at it from the point of view of percentage, you won't find much difference. If you just look at the numbers, they will appear higher, and this is what is happening here.

The other fact you are not considering here is that you can wear someone else's hat, but would it fit you? You need your own hat. You know how many students who opted for a subject got selected; do you know the number of people who didn't? I do not mean to say that you should shy away from choosing popular subjects. I'm not saying that at all. If you feel comfortable with the subject, there is no need to doubt whether you should take it.

There is one more thing. It has been observed that every year the paper of one subject or the other is very tough. This results in a bad score and the subject gets a bad reputation. This happens regularly. Sometimes this could happen with one subject continuously for two three years. But it will happen to one subject or the other that is for sure. In this situation, you should not think that since last year the paper was easy (or tough), it will be easy (or tough) this year too. UPSC creates high and low tides in these papers to strike a balance. So I think you should be very careful when deciding to opt for a subject based on its popularity.

So what should you do?

I'm giving you a torch that will shed light on which subject you should choose. You can have faith in this torch of mine. Although I have called this my torch, the battery in it belongs to UPSC. In discussing the syllabus of the mains exam, UPSC has already clearly mentioned that "The main examination is intended to access the overall intellectual traits and depth of understanding of candidates rather than merely the range of their information and memory."

It is then clear that the subject is not important; your knowledge of the subject is what matters. When you start being analytical about a subject, you gain a deep knowledge of it and start developing your thoughts accordingly. This renders even a simple subject important. On the other hand, even the most important subject can be turned simple.

So use this torch when you are deciding upon a subject for yourself. Do not be in haste when it comes to choosing your subject. Think about it calmly. You can take advice from other people, listen to what they have to say, but do not get so influenced that their suggestion becomes your decision. Think about it logically, analyse your facts and then take a decision.

Once you have made your decision, stick to it, do not change it easily. Alter your decision only if you cannot fall in love with the subject, or cannot get a complete hold of it despite trying everything. Or you should change your decision if you feel that you love your subject, you have a good hold of it, but the exam results are too bad for you. I'm not talking of exam results being bad, I'm talking of the results being really bad. If your results are too bad, do not blame UPSC or the paper; do not blame the books you have studied or the examiner who corrected your answer sheet. Instead of finding faults in all the other things, find out where you were lacking. By blaming things, you will get a false sense of self-satisfaction, but not success. It's up to you now, whether you remain happy with a false self-satisfaction or should you opt for real success. If you want success, work on your own shortcomings because you do not have control over UPSC or your examiners.

I'm mentioning this because I have seen students change their subject. They do not change themselves, they keep changing their subjects and consequently their results do not change. As I mentioned above, students get selected from every subject and if we are not getting selected the problem lies with us.

However, there is one more truth. If you are not getting the hang of a subject initially, you should not take too long to change it. Even if you have wasted a year on that subject, it is better not to waste five more years over it. This will not just save your years but also your future.

The 'mantra' of choosing your subject

The mantra here is nothing magical. I have used it in the sense that it should be the first and most important basis for your selection. The optional subject in itself is very important. Compared to other five papers in civil services exam, it is this subject that you can master. As far as the four papers for essays and general knowledge are concerned, the syllabus is not limited. The preparation is also subjective, every student prepares in a manner he sees fit. However, your optional paper is one that you have chosen. Its syllabus is clearly defined and it is taught in a systematic way in colleges. You have been studying it since long. But general knowledge has not been taught to you like this. This is why you can see a huge difference between scores in general knowledge while there is not much discrepancy (leaving aside any exception) in optional papers' scores. This is why you should do the best preparation you can for your optional paper. You should try that your score is in the higher range. This would be quite difficult if you do not choose your paper wisely.

I will now tell you the most important scientific principle behind how to choose your optional subject. This method is time-consuming but you will reap benefits. So let us talk about the most important aspect of choosing your subject.

After talking to various people -and after giving it a deep thought- if you have decided on one particular subject, let me congratulate you. However, if you could not settle down on one subject, or you are confused among two/three subjects then you can use the following method-

First stage

Buy a few books for the subjects you have shortlisted. But take them at the medium level, not advanced. These books should be of graduation level (first or second year) and they should cover the basics and core knowledge about the subject. Also, these books should not be too analytical in nature. They should be written by ordinary authors in a simple manner.

Now read the book of a subject. Take at least three-four days to read it thoroughly. You can jot down important points, such as 'whether you liked studying the subject or were you bored? Did you find the subject easy or difficult? Was it easy to understand?' Now try recalling the topics that you read and see how much of it do you remember. Write all this down somewhere.

Second stage

Now take a look at the UPSC syllabus. Read properly the syllabus for the subject whose book you have studied. Once you read a book for a subject, you get a fair outline of it. You also form an impression of that subject. When you see the UPSC syllabus, you will find that your brain is interacting with it. You will find it surprising that after reading the book, when you read the syllabus, you will form an impression about the syllabus too. Now write down whatever impression you have formed of the syllabus.

Third stage

In this stage, take a look at the previous years' unsolved papers of the subject. Read the questions asked in the papers carefully. Don't just read them, read them carefully. You will start noticing different shades of the questions. You will notice the hidden angles in the questions. UPSC rarely asks questions that can be answered straight-forwardly. This stage will help you figure out whether you are able to detect the hidden angles or not. If you are able to detect them, it means the subject may be right for you.

Fourth stage

This is the last stage and you have to work hard here. Select a chapter in the book and see what kind of questions have been asked from that chapter in the previous years. Write down the questions somewhere. Now read the chapter again, numerous times if required, but read it in such a fashion that you have a strong hold on the chapter. When you are satisfied that you have studied the chapter the best you could, take the questions asked from that chapter in previous years' papers and write down the answers for them.

This will be the deciding moment for you. If you are able to write the answers, you have found your subject. Let me tell you that at this point your answers will not be of the level that UPSC requires. You will achieve that level when you have studied the subject thoroughly and have a hold on it. As of this stage, the level of the answer is not very important. The important thing is whether you are able to answer the questions, even if your answers do not match up to UPSC standards.

Now after completing all the stages, you find that you cannot see different shades of a question or you are not able to write decent answers, this means that this subject is not suitable for you. Now, repeat the stages with all the other subjects you have shortlisted. Even if it takes you a month to complete all these activities, it is not a big deal. After all, you are going to become an IAS, and becoming an IAS is no joke.

You may face a third situation as well. You go through all the stages and the results are the same for all the subjects. Then you will be faced with the problem of what to choose. It is not very difficult to solve this. See which of the subjects can also help you prepare for your general knowledge paper. This subject will kill two birds with one stone. For example, history, geography, sociology, political science, economics and public administration are subjects that play an important role in your general knowledge preparation. Even if these are not your optional subjects, you will have to study them. Of course, you would not have to study them in depth as you would have otherwise.

So, this was if you were in a dilemma regarding the choice of the subject. Now I will tell you some ways that will prevent you from getting confused in the first place. If you rise above the rumours and stop being influenced by others, these ways will show you a clear path. Let us discuss them in detail:

(1) If you are a post graduate, I would advise you to think very carefully about why you do not want to take the subject of your post graduation as your optional paper. After all you have invested two years on the subject. Unless you

spent two years on the subject just for a degree, this subject will prove to be your best companion. In any case, if you do not choose this subject, you will choose some other subject and it will be a subject that you know nothing of. If you think about this logically, it is better to take up a subject about which you know something.

Also, when you go for the interview, it is likely that you will be asked questions about your postgraduate subject even if you have not chosen it for the mains. This means you will anyway have to brush up on your knowledge of the subject when you go for the interview. This is why I take it as a fact that the subject of your post graduation is the ideal choice for an optional paper.

However, there are exceptions to this rule. It could be that you didn't give your subject a serious thought during post graduation. Maybe you did not get the subject you wanted and had to settle for another. Perhaps you did get the subject of your choice but you did not enjoy it or could not master it and scored less as a result. In this scenario, it is better to avoid the temptation of choosing this subject.

Normally, there are three subjects that students do not want to take up in IAS, and this even includes students who have done their post graduation in these subjects. Students believe these subjects have a vast syllabus or they say that the subjects are very tough. Also, since these subjects are dynamic, it is difficult to keep up with the constant changes. This makes these subjects less scoring. These three subjects are- Math, physics and economics. This does not mean that no one opts for these subjects. It also does not mean that anyone who chooses one of these subjects will not succeed. Students get selected from these subjects too. These are students who have an interest in these subjects and are able to answer according to UPSC standards. Now you decide what your situation is.

(2) It is possible that you are a graduate, and not a postgraduate. Then what should you do? Every student studies at least three subjects during graduation. You should choose one of these three. Choose the one you like best. B.E. students can take either civil engineering or electrical engineering. MBBS students can choose a subject like biology if they are not opting for medical science. In fact they could even go for anthropology or psychology.

The logic behind choosing the subject when you are a graduate is similar to the logic I gave you when I told you about how to choose when you are a postgraduate. You do know something about the subjects you studied in your graduation, so you should make use of this knowledge.

(3) Although the number of students pursuing this degree is gradually decreasing, some still choose to do B.Sc. It has been observed that B.Sc students do not like to choose any of the subjects they have studied in graduation as their optional paper. For a science student to opt for an Arts subject would not be wrong. Choosing a science subject as an optional paper is beneficial only if you have done your post graduation in it.

Science students should keep two things in their mind. They should figure out which subject is somewhat familiar or adjustable to what they have studied as science students. For instance someone who studied geology could choose geography; a math student could opt for statistics and a biology student could go for anthropology.

Another advice is to take a subject that also helps you prepare for the general knowledge paper. This is not a necessary thing but if possible you should follow this advice.

There is one other important thing which I want to tell you- do not ignore your interests. Our brain is wired to gain in-depth knowledge of only those subjects that it enjoys. It is difficult to have a long and fruitful companionship with a subject which is of little interest to you. To figure out which subjects you enjoy apply the mantra I told you above.

4. You cannot figure out which subject to choose depending on whether it is difficult or easy. There are two reasons for this. Firstly, whether a subject is tough or easy is subjective and varies from person to person. It's possible that a subject considered tough by you is found very easy by somebody else, and vice versa. Secondly, if some subject is actually easy, then it is easy not just for you, but for everybody else too. And you must be aware that in a competitive exam, you are not concerned with just scoring passing marks. You are required to score sufficient marks to make it to the final list.

5. How vast is the syllabus of the subject should only determine in part whether you should choose it. So do not base your decision solely on the length of your syllabus. You should make sure whether there are enough books for you to study to cover the syllabus and whether you can handle them.

6. If you are choosing a subject completely new to you, keep two things in consideration. Firstly, figure out whether you will be able to gather study material for the subject.

Secondly, if you would require help from someone to understand the subject, find out if that help is available to you. If you cannot fulfil the above two conditions, then the subject will not be able to fulfil your expectations.

7. Lastly, remember that no subject can make you an IAS. It is you who can become an IAS with any subject. So do not give the credit for your success or failure to your subject, give it to yourself.

I have told you some things about how you can choose an optional subject. But I cannot guarantee that I have told you all important points that you need to consider while choosing your optional subject. If you get some help from my advice, it would be my pleasure. However, if my advice could not help you, do not worry about choosing your paper based on something else you see fit. Do not think that your decision will be wrong. The subject is not important here, your treatment of the subject is what matters.

Chapter 9

How to Study For IAS

Let us start this chapter with a question- 'What is the reason that toppers are unable to crack the exam while a second division holder qualifies?' The books are almost the same, so are the notes available in the market. In coaching classes, students listen to similar lectures. The question paper is the same and there is not much difference in the examiners either. However, the result is different for everyone.

I have another question- water pours down on sugarcane as well as bitter gourd. It becomes bitter when absorbed by bitter gourd and sweet when exposed to sugarcane. The water is the same then why does it change its taste?

Friends, I'm not going to dwell on scientific reasons as this is not important for us. I will give you an answer that belongs to life. Life is an art, and art is all about interpretation. How you interpret a thing depends solely on your mettle; it depends on the mechanism of the person how he imbibes something, how much of it does he imbibe and what he makes of it after.

This also applies to students preparing for IAS. When I tell students to learn how to study, they look at me with disbelief and are slightly offended. I can understand what their eyes are saying, 'Are you saying we don't know how to study?' I'm unable to answer with a straight 'yes' but I do not hesitate to say, 'yes, it is something like that'.

Then I ask differently. When in class, I say, "raise your hands... those of you who do not sing." Not a single hand is raised because everyone sings, even if they are bathroom singers. Then I say, "raise your hands... those of you who are singers." Silence falls over the class of 100 students and I only see a few raised hands. Then I tell them that one who sings is a singer and since all of them accepted they do sing they should have raised their hands. There is no answer from them and this is what I expect.

This is where the secret of success (in life as well as in IAS) lies. I let them know that they are not making a mistake but rather they are unable to understand how things are. Each & everything has a certain 'way of being' which I call grammar. Everything on this Earth- even the way we speak, walk and talk- has its own grammar. Problem is that we do all these things but do not understand the grammar. One who understands the grammar becomes a true scholar.

We all sing but do not understand the grammar of singing. The grammar of singing includes knowledge of rhythm, pitch etc. Those who know the grammar are singers and those who do not know also sing but they are not singers. Does this same thing not apply to IAS aspirants who study for years, but do not know the grammar of studying?

In this chapter I will address this. But if you want to study this in great detail, I suggest a reading of my book, 'The Art of Study'. This book is also available in Hindi and Gujarati.

I would advise you to read the book not because you are preparing for IAS but also because you have to study something all your life. After sometime, you will teach others too, maybe not professionally. So let us now learn the grammar of study.

Learning and the mind

Only the thing that stays with us is ours. We can study anything and as much as we want but we would be able to use (especially at the time of writing an exam) only that part of it which gets stuck in our mind. Needless to say, our brain is the bowl in which we store everything we study.

There are two challenges posed by learning. First you have to store information in your brain. If you study and nothing is getting absorbed by your brain, then there is no point in studying. It is better you do something else.

The next challenge is that information must be readily available. If you cannot remember anything while writing the exam, then it does not matter whether you have the information. These two challenges must be kept in mind while preparing for IAS.

Importance of visuals

Anything that we hear, study or see is absorbed by our brain as images, not sound or letters. When you hear or read the word 'horse', then the image of a horse is formed in your mind without any effort. You cannot understand the meaning of a sound or a letter if your brain is not capable of imaging it. This is the principle followed when it comes to studying. If you follow this then you should study in a manner that your mind forms images. Your study will be better if the images are clear and deep. Now keeping this fact in mind I will tell you how to study so that you can do justice to images formed in your mind.

(1) You should study only one chapter or topic from a subject on a given day. Why? If the same subject has two different chapters, there will be some similarities. Due to these similarities, images from different chapters start merging. For example, if you watch three back to back romantic movies today you will find that after few days the stories have merged. But if one movie is a thriller, one is a love story and the other is an action flick then you would remember each story for a longer time.

(2) I'm saying here that you should study only one topic or chapter from a particular subject. I'm not saying that you should only study one topic a day. You can read a topic each from various subjects. But not more than one topic per subject.

(3) You stare at your reflection in still water. Now move it and stare again. What difference did you notice? You could see your reflection better when the water was still, right? Similarly a calm mind develops clearer images. This is why I am not in favour of forced studying, studying while trying to stay up with the help of tea/coffee, studying continuously for 15 hours or studying when you are sad and depressed. I consider it to be 'pseudo study' which is done only to keep occupied. It produces nothing.

It's a universal truth that the best time to study is in the morning as the mind and body is fresh, calm and not tired. The ambience is also not distracting. Therefore, the images on the mind are etched deeper. The three-hour morning study is equivalent to studying five hours in the afternoon or late at night.

(4) Here comes a question: how many hours should you study? The answer is: Can you draw infinite number of images on a canvas? I mean to say our mind has a limit. If your body can get tired, how do you expect your mind to work ceaselessly? Science agrees that our body can work energetically for 8 to 10 hours. Our mind is also energetic in this time period. However, when it comes to rigorous studying, this limit is only 6-7 hours. The ability of the mind to focus diminishes when you study continuously. Your mind would not be as energetic at the end of six hours as it was in the beginning. But if you want to continue studying even after this time, you can do a bit of light studying such as reading the newspaper or revising. You can also read some other books on the subject that are easy to understand and the ones you don't need to memorise.

The right speed to study

Your train is at the station. You can watch all the scenes around you clearly. When the train starts moving the scenes are shaky. Once the train passes the station, the scenes fade away but you can still identify which tree this is or which office. After the train gains speed, you cannot see the scenes clearly. You can figure out that it is a tree but you cannot identify which one it is. Why is it so? After reading this metaphor do you believe that speed contributes to forming images in our mind?

Many young students claim with enthusiasm, 'I can study

for 15 hours a day and that too at a great speed'. I don't disbelieve this because I know they can do so. But I pity them because this won't help. They can study but would their brain register all of this? Their brain would absorb some information but not enough to make an IAS out of someone.

How our mind absorbs what we study is related to our speed of studying. If you study very fast, you will finish the pages but not your study. The images that are formed are not deeply etched in the brain. So those who study very fast soon forget whatever they have studied. The images they form in the brain quickly fade away or get merged. That's why I'm advising you to study 5 to 6 hours every day in all seriousness.

Continuity

You must have heard the story about the tortoise and the hare. The tortoise wins against the hare, an animal that runs very fast. Why did this happen? The moral of the story is that the hare stopped midway but the tortoise kept walking. Continuity holds a great potential. It has as much power as compound interest. And compound growth has been regarded as one of the greatest powers in the world by scientists such as Einstein!

There are many students who, out of their ungrounded enthusiasm, do not hesitate in claiming that they will crack IAS in just a year, even though their background is not suited to this. By claiming this, they lay down the foundation for their claims to be falsified later and also waste an entire year. Such students don't really know what IAS is and how to study for it. This knowledge you will gain only after studying unsolved papers of the mains.

So let me tell you the 'law of nature' when it comes to IAS preparation. Suppose it rains, on a given day, 5 cm in an hour. On another day, it rains 5 cm in 5 hours. Now tell me which water will be absorbed better by the Earth? I know that you too know the answer: 5 cm in 5 hours. This is the law of nature, and since our brains too are a part of the nature, it also governs them. When we expose our brain to bits of information it is absorbed better. This is only possible if you follow the principle of continuity. Instead of reading up a lot in a few days you should read a little bit every day. If you finish your monthly dose of vitamins in just five days, they will not have any effect on your body.

Revision

This is also related to images. You remember only those incidents from your life that you keep recalling- either you are telling someone or simply thinking of them silently. People tend to forget stuff. But this is a blessing in disguise. If we could remember each and everything, sooner or later we would lose our minds. Problem arises when we forget something that was needed to be remembered or when we find ourselves unable to recall a thing when it is needed the most. There could be another side of this problem: we are unable to forget what we don't want to remember at all.

So it's clear now that the chances of not forgetting a thing have a direct relation with whether we have revised it enough. Even the brightest, boldest colours will fade after a while and they will gather dust. Now the only option we have is to dye it again and wipe off the dust. The same applies to studying.

Let me now explain what is meant by 'studying hard' for IAS. This 'studying hard' does not mean you study for 12 to 15 hours, read several newspapers and magazines every day or read many books on the same topic. This 'studying hard' is actually related to two things- studying for 5 to 6 hours a day and revising it daily. When we do so, we re-colour the images on our minds. This will help us write better answers.

Friends, I would like to tell you a scientific truth about revision that was put forth by Aving Has. He researched the human habit of forgetting and found out that we forget 47 percent of a topic within 20 minutes, 53 percent after 1 hour, 66 percent after a day, 75 percent after a week, 79 percent after a month and about 95 percent after a year. And the five percent that we do remember is just a faded memory.

So, in order to not forget what we have studied, it is important to convert information to knowledge (by reading, analyzing and remembering things carefully) and then to keep revising it. Another scientist called Epping has come up with a method to revise -

(a) Read a topic at least four times in one day.

(b) Read it again after 24 hours. Now repeat it as if you are reading this for the first time.

(c) Read it again after a week, though you can increase the reading speed.

(d) Revise the topic again after a month.

Epping believes that if a subject is read like this, it becomes a part of your mind. He also said that as the revision frequency increases, so does the reading speed. This will then take very little time.

I would like to add something in it that stems from my own experiences. Underline all the important points while reading a book. You can even write on the margins. The underlined text and the notes will help you revise. You will be amazed to see that after just reading the underlined text you will recall what you studied on the entire page. This will only happen if you follow the scientific principle of studying.

You can call this principle the 'science of studying', it won't be wrong. But when you express what you have studied, it becomes an art. Science deals with how to do something but it turns into art when we start doing it. Any work is a mix of the two- ratio to each other may be varying, though. It is more science when you are reading and more art when you write down the answer. If you believe this, and if you follow my advice on the principle of image-forming in the mind, it will benefit you a lot.

Now let me tell you what your attitude towards books should be.

How to behave with your books

There are variety of books and various types of readers. There are many ways to study and many aims behind it. The same book can be read with different goals and this is what decides the method of studying. You can read a novel for pleasure but if it is included in the literature syllabus, a student will read it differently because the purpose is write the exam, not entertainment. A common man watches a movie for entertainment. But a film critic watches less of the movie and focuses more on its creativity.

You have to study in a way that you can crack IAS. The purpose of such study should be -

(a) Understanding the facts.

(b) Storing them in your mind.

(c) Acquiring the ability to put them to paper.

Keeping these in mind, I will now discuss with you how to study a book. You can include this method in general knowledge books and books for optional papers as well. IAS students are advised to read a few other books as well. These books are not directly related to your syllabus. But they help to provide you with a clear and in-depth viewpoint which is linked to your syllabus. The method of studying books I am going to mention here need not be applied to these books. These are supporting books that don't have to be taken very seriously.

Now let me explain how to study a book.

1. About the author

There are very few students who read up about the author before reading a book, even though they sometimes buy the book because the author is famous.

You must be wondering why I'm asking you to read about the author before reading the book. Firstly, if you know the author's background, you would understand the origins of his thoughts. If the author's academic background and achievements are strong, you feel a certain respect towards him. This increases your mind's receptivity for the words written by the author. It will take less than five minutes to read up on the author but it holds great value.

2. Introduction

Most students skip the introduction because it is not a part of the syllabus. But if you read the introduction, you will understand two things at once. First, you will understand why the book was written. This will make the purpose of the author clear. You can also gather information about how much the book will benefit you. It usually does not take more than 10 minutes to read the introduction of a book. Is sparing just 10 minutes too much to ask for students like you who spend years preparing for IAS?

3. Read the index

If you are a true consumer of books, then you must read the index before buying the book. This is a very good habit. But there are many students who buy books just based on the author. They only check the index when they are searching for particular chapters. But this is not what I'm talking about. You need to read the index after reading up on the author and the introduction to the book. This is somewhat similar to reading the map of a place before actually going there. How many minutes do you think this will take?

These are the things you should do before reading a book. Just like a farmer ploughs the land before sowing seeds, similarly you should prepare your mind as a 'ready-to-paint' canvas on which bold colours of your study can emerge.

4. Do not jump to chapters or topics of your choice

After reading the index, you may want to read particular topics. Please don't do this. You should avoid doing this, even if you are very tempted to do so. This will damage the continuity of the book. The images that should have formed in a chronological order will go haywire. Would you watch a film from the middle? If you do so, you would find that this is not much fun. The same rule applies to books too.

5. When and how to read

I will now tell you how to get the most out of any book, when to read it and how many times.

You should read every book for the first time like you read a novel, story or an autobiography. Do not worry about how much of the book you can actually understand. You do not need to memorise it at this stage, you just have to read it. You must have read in the newspapers that when a state is ravaged by floods, ministers do an aerial survey. This gives them an idea about the flood situation. You also have to do an aerial survey of the book.

Study according to your regular speed. Do not read too fast in order to finish the book sooner or read so slow that you get bored. Read in a fashion that you get an introduction to the book.

During your second read of the book, you have to be more serious and read it in parts. You do not have to read it like a novel. Read it like you read a short story collection. You read one story a day; similarly you have to read only one chapter of the book every day.

Now you don't have to just read but also try to understand the book. This will slow you down. There are some things you should keep in mind-

"Keep marking and underlining important points you come across while reading. This way all the important points will get etched in your mind. This will also help you revise.

"You can also write your comments on the margin of the book. If after reading a paragraph you feel that it can be better remembered with a certain word, jot it down. These will function as 'keywords'.

"If you can recall other information about the topic you can jot that too on the margin of the book. If in another book, there is some updated information on this topic which is not mentioned in the book you are reading, you can write about that too. This will help you expand your knowledge on the topic. Now that you are reading the book again, do not be lazy or careless. If you read the book scientifically at this stage you will save yourself a lot of trouble and unnecessary struggle. Also, do not be in a hurry to finish the book.

If you do not understand something, keep trying. Do not skip it or learn by rote. If you cannot understand it yourself, take help. If you do not understand it here, you might have troubling understanding things ahead. A book or a subject is like a chain that has 100 joints. If even one joint is weak, then this chain with 99 strong joints will still be considered weak. A single joint will render the whole chain weak. Similarly, when you do not understand a topic, you will also have trouble understanding other things.

While reading you will come across many words that you do not understand. Some students think how does it matter and proceed. But this matters a great deal. If you cannot understand a word, how will you understand the meaning of the sentence? If you do not understand sentences, how will you understand the subject?

Knowing the meaning of words is important not just to understand the text but also to express your thoughts and emotions clearly. This will also help you score better. After all, exams are all about expressing your thoughts in an impressive language. So understand the meaning of words and then use them in your conversation.

I know this must have disappointed you a bit. You must want to read many topics of a subject in a single day to finish studying it fast. But I cannot give you wrong advice on disciplined learning. However, you can always read three topics a day, but they should be from three different subjects, not one.

After reading a single topic from a book, revise it multiple times a day. You don't have to sit at a table, you can revise it while walking, or on a bus or just in your mind. It will give you a strong hold on the topic.

Do not just repeat the topic in your head, also try to analyse it. Think about what new idea you can come up. If you cannot think of anything, do not get upset, it is a difficult task. If you keep trying, you will be able to do this because your brain will be trained to do this. This is why you have to keep trying even if you fail in the beginning, you will get success later.

Now you have to read the book for a third time. This will be somewhat like your first reading of the book. Now, once again, you have to read the book continuously like you read a novel. You will find that though you are reading like you did for the first time but this experience is different. You are enjoying now because you can understand things. During the first read, you may have got bored and even frustrated. Now you are enjoying and your confidence is building up. When this starts happening you can believe you have won the subject and you are climbing the Everest.

I asked you to read the book for the third time because it helps us develop an overall opinion of the subject. This is somewhat similar to you opening a sack and then understanding every single thread. After doing this we gathered all the threads and tied them up again in a bundle, so they don't disappear.

Don't you find this method more scientific, more reliable and more enjoyable? This may not be the case initially, but be patient, it will happen soon enough.

After reading like this three times, the subject will be very well understood by your brain. The roots of the subject are now deeply in your mind. They will not leave easily. But no matter how deep the roots are they still need moisture, meaning you will need to keep revising. When you revise, you will not be studying like you were studying before. Now if you even give the book a cursory glance, you will remember everything you studied. Keep doing it.

I feel that if you read any book following this methodology you will be able to do justice to it. You will also be able to do justice to the time you are spending on reading this book as well as your purpose of reading it.

This is how you should spend time with your book, so it

can prove to be a trustworthy companion. I want to clarify once again that it is my logic which I have come to after my experience and experiments. You can learn from your own experiences and I have no hesitation in saying that your experiences may be better than mine. So you don't have to take what I say as the ultimate truth. You can adopt the suggestions that you think would be useful to you, and make them applicable your way. You are also free to completely reject my way of reading.

So far you have learned how to read a book. Now I want to tell you how to treat the subject matter in the book. It means I will tell you what kind of relationship you should have with the material and the knowledge in the book. You can call this section 'how to study'. Let us talk about this in detail.

How to study

Before I explain to you how a book should be studied, I want to remind you that you have to study in the context of IAS preparation. There are three levels of studying. When we read a book and want to absorb its subject-matter we see that there are three levels.

(a) Information
(b) Knowledge
(c) Wisdom

(a) Information

The first level of studying is information and it is mostly superficial. This is the beginner's level. Most of us see books as mere sources of information we want to gain and store in our brains. This is the level at which we study from first grade to college. This is a weakness that renders us unable to crack the IAS exam because merely gathering information does not get you success here.

What is information? It is the bits and pieces we collect from books. It is important to store them in our brain, but many students cannot differentiate between knowledge and information. I have often seen students engaged in debates when leaving their study rooms and coaching classes. They try to outdo each other by bombarding each other with bits of information. The listener also gets impressed with their 'knowledge'. But do you really think you will be able to crack IAS based on a strong information database in your mind?

(b) Knowledge

It is true that knowledge does not come from thin air. It is gained through information. But it is also true that only storing information is not knowledge- and you should be very clear about this. If you really want to succeed in IAS, information should only serve as raw material. You have to cook this information in the kitchen of your brain to turn it into knowledge. Information left on its own will be like a conked out skeleton. Whether you have to answer intelligent questions in the preliminary exam or the analytical questions in the mains exam, it will only be made possible when you understand the subject at the level of knowledge. You can achieve the level of knowledge only when you have understood a subject, and not merely memorised it. Thus, information is memorised but knowledge is understood. Knowledge is gained at a deeper level than information.

(c) Wisdom

When a scientist achieves this level, he becomes an inventor and a writer becomes a philosopher. Einstein was a great scientist but it is not that he never read Newton. Karl Marx was a great thinker but he also read the writings of Hegel etc. Information transforms to knowledge and ultimately wisdom.

However, you do not have to worry too much to achieve this level. This is the last stage of our analysis, thinking and study. This level is not very important for IAS success but if you are able to achieve it, it would do you good. But right now I would advise you not to worry too much about it. So we don't need to go into details here.

I will now tell you some facts related to your treatment of the subject-matter in a book that will help turn the information in your mind to knowledge. I want to make it clear that I have not been a science student. My understanding of science is limited to a basic level. So I'm not sure how applicable my wisdom is to science subjects. But I know that if you follow my methods and apply them to arts subjects, you will definitely benefit. Let us now discuss how to absorb the subject-matter in a book.

(1) Importance of the first chapter

Arts students have a tendency to take the first chapter of a book lightly. However, I believe that the first chapter is very important as it lays the foundation of the entire subject. It is possible that a question from the first chapter has never been asked in the exam, but this does not mean you should not study it. You need to not just read this chapter, but also understand it. If you understand it properly, you are on to a great beginning to study that subject. This is a master key that will help you unlock the doors to future chapters.

(2) Understand the concept

Students seem very surprised when I tell them that even arts subjects are scientific. Is this not true? If it is not true then why has the prefix science been attached to politics and you must have heard of sociology. This proves that art has its own science, even though it may not be conventional science.

If you accept this truth, you will realise that your viewpoint towards studying arts subjects has changed. Now you will not read the subject but try to grasp the concept behind it. Every subject and every new chapter of a subject has a strong, solid concept behind it like every human being has a spine. It is the spinal cord which holds the body together.

Take geography, for instance. I consider it the master of all sciences. The concept of this subject lies in the globe or the map. If you understand the science of and the relationship among longitude, latitude, sea, air, Earth etc., geography will become a child's play for you. Then you don't have to memorise the social, economic, political and cultural situation in any country.

The same logic applies to political science, economics, history and all other subjects related to humanities. This book does not allow me to go into detail on this.

(3) Understand the relationships

'No humanities subject is an isolated island cut off from everything else. Every subject is not only related to the chapters preceding and succeeding it but also to different subjects. When you study history, don't you read about the political, economical, social and cultural situation during that time? Is sociology so different from anthropology, and does it have no association with science or geography? I don't have to explain the link between psychology and life sciences to you. It is not easy to understand a nation's present political scenario without knowledge of its past. All the subjects in the field of humanities are like the oceans illustrated in a map. The oceans have different names and are located at different places in the map but they have the same water. Water flows from one ocean to the other. This is called interconnectivity and when it comes to studying subjects, it is known as interdisciplinary approach i.e., studying different subjects in relation to each other. When you study in this manner, you develop an unimaginably strong habit of converting information to knowledge. IAS is seeking young men of this ability only.

(4) Prepare models

This is similar to studying after forming images in the mind. The difference between the two is that image is formed of a topic or a chapter. But model covers a larger area which can span across many chapters and even the entire subject. For instance, let's imagine you are reading sociology. Your own family, your village or town, the local culture, behaviour and attitudes of the people and traditions serve as the model here.

If you are reading public administration then the office of the collector, Panchayati Raj system, Rajya Sabha and Lok Sabha elections can serve as the model here. If you have any experience living in a rural area, the lifestyle of villages where local zamindars have a lot of power - even though law has made the zamindari system illegal - can help you understand history better.

For now, I would advise you to try to find real-life situations associated with the subject that you are studying. If you do come across a real-life situation like that, then every time you study, you should relate it to the facts in your text book. You will feel as if a miracle has happened and you can now understand things clearly. Now you will have no problem understanding the topics, and since you have no difficulty in understanding them, there should be no difficulty in analysing them either.

To study after forming models is an amazing thing to do. I have done the same thing, although I don't know how I came across this. Maybe this happened because I had a tendency, since beginning of my school days, to develop a thorough understanding of every subject. So I kept discovering and learning new ways of studying a subject. When I started guiding IAS students lately, this model forming technique proved to be the basic idea. Students found these models very interesting and it changed their way of studying and understanding the subject. They found it hard to believe that someone can study this way too.

I will now narrate an incident that happened in October 2013. I was teaching a hall packed with students at a coaching institute in Mukherjee Nagar, Delhi about how they should prepare for IAS. In two hours of my presentation, I told them quite a few things, including the model of how to study geography. It took me hardly 20 minutes to explain it. You may not believe that after understanding these models, the students were able to answer difficult questions related to geography in the preliminary exam 2013 with ease. Even after answering them, they could not believe that their answers were correct. It was only after I told them their answers were correct that they believed it.

A week later, I got a call from a man who was not preparing for IAS exam but was present to video record my presentation. What he said on the phone made me think. He said, "Sir, that day whatever you told about the model was amazing. All the students were talking about it after the lecture. Why don't you write books about these models? It will make it very easy for students."

At the time I gave him a reluctant answer, 'let's see'. Later when I thought about it, I realised that it would be a good thing if I could write down the models. I toyed with the idea for a few days, it is easy to explain a model in 20 minutes but to write a book on it is no easy task. There are many who will say a thing, but how many would actually jot them down?

But I'm thinking of writing down the models in a book. I can write books containing models on geography, political science, economics, sociology, history and public administration because I study and teach these subjects. I don't know when I will be able to do it. I wish to finish writing the books as soon as possible.

Anyway, I want to bring the 'how to study' section to an end after telling you once again that if you study in this fashion, then you will remember things for a long time. You will not forget important information. In fact, your brain will process information quickly when you are writing down your answers. Don't forget, the art of writing is connected to the art of reading. If you want to write down good answers, then you need to adopt a good method of studying.

Importance of support books

UPSC has decided upon a syllabus- even for subjects like general knowledge. Most students restrict their studies to this syllabus. The books, notes and study material available in the market are written keeping this syllabus in mind. It is very convenient for students to study these books and material which are based on the syllabus. This method of studying is also correct because you have to study the syllabus, ultimately questions will be asked from it.

But is there any other method that can improve upon the knowledge acquired through syllabus-based books? When I say improve upon your knowledge I mean 'what is new or innovative about you?' Every student studies, memorises and understands the same books and writes answers based on them. If you do this, you also become like them. This is why I believe that studying books outside your syllabus can benefit you. I have many reasons to say this -

The support books are written by renowned specialists in the subjects and they dwell upon the subjects in detail.

Books based on the syllabus are very mechanical and

mostly store facts and information. In support books, the author goes into the depth of a topic and describes it in a way that makes the reader curious and interested. This can help make things clearer in the mind of a reader.

In these books, the author also writes about his personal experience. These experiences are in the form of stories, examples and case studies. This makes the subject interesting as well as easier to understand.

Support books explain a particular subject in detail. It is true that studying these books will take time, but can you get a job like IAS in seconds? You should be willing to give it time.

The syllabus books can be dull and bland but it is important to study them. Support books can help you get over the boredom.

You can memorise the facts in syllabus books but not support books. The same book will be studied by many students who will take their own material from and understand it in their own way. This own way of studying is what sets you apart from the rest of the candidates and this is what UPSC is seeking. So keep reading support books after regular intervals.

I will now mention some books that you can read -

(1) India Unbound - Gurucharan Das
(2) The Argumentative Indian: Writings on Indian Culture, History and Identity - Amartya Sen
(3) Bharatnama - Sunil Khilnani
(4) India after Gandhi - Ramchandra Guha
(5) My experiments with truth - Mahatma Gandhi
(6) Discovery of India - Jawaharlal Nehru
(7) Swaraj - Arvind Kejriwal

(8) Emerging India - Nandan Nilekani

(9) This matter of culture - J. Krishnamurti

(10) Whose century? Whose millennium?- Aizaz Ahmed

How to deal with statistics

Statistics are often scary and overwhelming. However, they are needed to complement your answers. The problem with figures and statistics is that it is not easy to remember them. Even if you do remember them, you might mix them up. The numbers will help us score well, but they have to be correct. Instead of giving wrong figures, it is better to not give them at all. So you should not try to guess these because you are likely to go wrong.

I will now tell you how to make statistics your strength. There are three ways to remember the figures. Firstly, do not cram too many numbers. Only remember the most important ones. For example, there are so many statistics available for the Indian population - the number of houses, cars, the number of people belonging to a certain caste, population in the cities, literate population, national per capita income etc. Now which ones should you try to remember? If you try to memorise many of these, you will end up forgetting everything.

So we need to know how to say 'no'. Saying 'yes' means you are ready to learn everything that is in front of you. Saying 'no' means you refuse to cram most of the figures. Make space in your mind only for the most important figures which would be useful to you, and useful in many ways. For instance, if we talk about population, we should know the population figures for India. We should know the total population as well as the numbers of rural and urban population. We should know the literacy rate and we should know the number of literate men and women. We should know the average age and income of an Indian. We should remember the population density with the percentages of men and women. It is enough to know these basic numbers. You can use them anywhere to support your answer.

Another thing about figures is that you should interlink them. If you try to study and memorise a particular figure alone, you will not be able to store it in your brain for long-term. But if you link it with other figures, it'll become easy for you. This is exactly the same mechanism that I mentioned earlier when talking about interlinking subjects and studying them.

Lastly, it would be better if you try to remember statistics as prose and not numbers. So instead of learning that India is 2,933 km long and 3,214 km wide, we can learn it as - India is almost three thousand km long and about 3,200 km wide. We can also remember it by understanding that the width of India is 300 km more than its length. If you remember the numbers like this, you will not mix them up.

If you want to remember statistics for a long time, you have to keep using them - while talking, reading or studying. We are better able to remember the statistics that we use frequently.

Chapter 10

How to deal with newspapers

Let us start with asking what is a newspaper and what does it mean to you? Is a newspaper just a collection of events that happened during last 24 hours? Is a newspaper just a bundle of pages bought for three rupees which is of no use after a day and sold as garbage a little later? Are newspapers just one of the means to pass time while you wait at the salon for your turn? Or is it just a news medium to know what is going on in your country and the world?

Actually, the newspaper is every one of the things mentioned above but what the newspaper should mean to you is beyond all this. What a newspaper is depends on who is reading it and for what purpose. If I have to answer an IAS student on "What is a newspaper?", then my answer would be, "Tell me what it is not."

Pick the general knowledge question paper from the preliminary exams. Also see all the four question papers on general knowledge from the mains exams. Read the questions asked from those who reached the interview stage. You will find that you can use the newspaper to prepare three-fourth of all the questions asked in the various levels of the IAS exam.

If you are planning to write an essay on a contemporary issue do not do it if you have not read the newspapers regularly.

Now you can understand how important newspapers are for you. If you are averse to reading newspapers, I would assume that you are also averse to being an IAS officer and you should drop the idea. It is the newspapers which turn IAS into a wonderful, prestigious, difficult and challenging exam. Books are books; anyone can cram them and become something on that basis. But newspapers are completely different and this is what sets IAS apart from other exams.

I'm aware of the questions that IAS candidates have when it comes to newspapers. Their main questions are -

- How many newspapers should I read?
- Which newspapers should I read?
- What to read in the newspapers?
- How much time to spend on newspapers?

Most students understand the importance of newspapers but they do not understand what the important issues in the newspaper are. As a result, they read a number of newspapers. I'm not surprised when someone tells me that they spend 2-3 hours every day reading more than five newspapers. If you spend this much time on the newspaper how will you have time for anything else! But this is not what the candidate is concerned about. The concern is that he spent so many hours reading so many newspapers, but what did he actually study? The truth is, he read everything but studied nothing, because he did not understand anything.

These are the kind of students who are very scared. They believe they will be asked anything in the name of general knowledge. They want to study everything, so nothing is left untouched. But they overlook the science of our brain functioning. If you fill the brain with so many facts, none of those will remain of any use then. The meaning of general knowledge is not 'knowledge about anything'. General knowledge means knowledge that can be expected from an educated citizen. It is only after you understand these facts that you will be able to read the newspapers correctly. Otherwise, this is a web in which you will get very deeply entangled.

It is definitely a challenging task to read newspapers in a disciplined and scientific manner from the perspective of IAS exam. But preparing for IAS without understanding this challenge would be foolish. This is why I decided to devote an entire chapter to this.

Which newspapers should you read ?

Should you read the maximum number of newspapers? Should you read all the important newspapers as students who are very academic do? I'm against this technique. I have a task for you. Get all the newspapers you consider important for a given date. Take an entire day to scan them. Note which important points are missing in which newspaper. I'm not talking about small news items but the really important ones. You will notice that all the newspapers will have the important news of the day. The news angles and description may differ but all newspapers will cover the important events.

Then what will be different among the newspapers? The editorial page. The articles on the page could be on different topics and even if the topic is the same, the write-ups are by different people. The quality of the articles will thus differ. The editorial comments will be different in different newspapers. If they choose the same topic to comment on, the quality will be different.

So should you read many newspapers just to pore over the editorial page? I do not think it is necessary. In any good newspaper, only the important topics will be commented upon and given space in the editorial page. The newspaper would have already covered or would cover at a future date topics on which articles and editorials are now being written in other newspapers - if the topics and events are really important. Even if this does not happen, you do not have to get upset; you cannot possibly know everything about the world. Someone who tries to hold onto everything will be left with nothing. This is the law of nature, do not forget it. Even if your friends warn you about this, do not be worried.

Therefore, the very first point in your approach towards newspapers is that instead of selecting many newspapers for yourself, you should choose only one national-level newspaper and stay consistent with it. Don't change the preference so often- unless you have a big reason for it. It does not really matter which newspaper you are reading as long as it is good quality. What matters is how you are reading the newspaper.

As much as possible, you should read the newspaper in the same language that you are choosing as your medium in the exam. Don't be worried about it. If you are a Hindi medium student do not think that you can't become an IAS officer without reading 'The Times of India' or 'The Hindu'. But yes, if you have a good English vocabulary, you can give some time to these newspapers, especially to the editorial page. You do not need to do more than this.

What should you read in a newspaper?

Just the size of the newspaper and the number of news items in it are enough to create confusion in the mind of the students. The students behave with the newspapers just like a hungry person gulps down food, even if he gets a tummy ache later. The students fail to understand that newspaper is a forum that has separate choices for every reader. From a rickshaw puller to an administrator, the newspaper has something for everyone. But every piece of news is not for everyone. Every individual has to choose and read items according to his needs and wants. You too have to choose which news you should bc reading.

Now you are not reading the newspaper just to keep abreast of the current affairs or to pass time or for entertainment purposes, so you need to know what you are reading it for. If you are reading it to prepare for IAS then you have to immediately decide on two things.

Decide that all the things in a newspaper cannot be equally important to you. So what is important for you? I will explain this to you but if you are new to this, it will take a while to understand. If you follow my advice, you will become an expert within three months. Another step you have to take is to rid your mind of the fear - God knows what they will ask! If you are scared, you will lose your power to choose the most important news. You will not be focused and this mistake may cost you. Now let me tell you what you should read in the newspaper -

(1) Main page

The main page of every newspaper -regardless of the quality of the newspaper-contains the most important news items. All important events that happened a day ago in any region or any sphere of life are published here - even if they are given less space. Whether you want or not, you cannot skip this page. You have to go through it in detail. A map of the previous day's events should form in your mind after reading this page. You will also get an idea which are the events that will unfold gradually over the next few days and which ones can be written upon.

The last page of the newspaper is also important. If after the main page, there are some other important news items left they are usually placed on the last page, although this is not a rule.

(2) Editorial page

This is the most important page of the newspaper, especially for you. Although very few people like to spend time on this page, you cannot take this liberty; you have to read the page. Why is it so? In a way, the editorial page is not just a page but the essence of the newspaper. It contains views, not news. And as I have been telling you again and again, for the mains exam you need more views and less news. Your views should not just be informative but also analytical. If you skip this page, it is as if you never read the newspaper. If you skip the main page, you can still make up for it by listening to the news on radio or television but nothing can make up for missing out on the editorial page.

Do not be in this illusion that you can make up for the lack of this by reading monthly magazines related to competitive exams. These magazines are useful to you but they are not a replacement for newspapers. Articles in the magazines lack the lucid thoughts found in a newspaper article. This is because newspaper articles are written by specialists keeping a particular angle in mind. This is not the case with magazines. In fact, articles in most magazines seem like they are a mix of articles from many newspapers. While such an article gives you good knowledge of facts, it loses the critical ability to analyse an issue. This does not mean that you should throw away the magazines. Just remember they are substitutes. There are two kinds of material in the editorial page -

(1) Editorial articles

(2) Editorial comments

Editorial articles mean one or two long articles on the page that are written by the specialists. The uniqueness of these articles is that they are related in some way to the current events. This is why they become so important for you.

Read these articles carefully. You will find how the writer took one small incident and created a solid structure of thoughts and information around it. The event may have happened a day before or recently, but when you read it you will understand the following things -

☑ The background of the event

☑ The history of the event - if any

- ☑ The political, social, cultural and economic impact of the event
- ☑ The writer's attitude to the event

When you read about an event, on the news pages of the newspaper, you get to know only the facts that this and this has happened at this and this place. It lacks in-depth understanding of the issue. So you simply read it and forget it. But when you read an article (full of insights) on the editorial page of the newspaper, it is absorbed by your brain and it gives more space to it. Needless to say, you have a better chance of finding a larger thing in your cupboard than a smaller one.

The other important part of the editorial page is the editorial comment. You will find one or two in every newspaper. It is possible that a day's newspaper has an article on a topic and the editorial comment on the same topic. However, they both are different. While an article reflects the thoughts of a person, editorial comment represents the public view. Another major difference is that an article talks about a topic in detail while an editorial comment is brief. When you get time, compare the two. You will find the key to success for IAS exam. You will be amazed to see that where an article takes about 1,000 words to put forth a single point, an editorial comment can convey even multiple points (and even more important ones) in mere 300-350 words. If you want to score well in IAS, you have to be as good as the editorial comments.

Editorial comments not only give you important facts, but also make you think. When I tell my students how to improve upon their analytical skills, I give them the example of editorial comments. An incident occurs and an editorial commentary is prepared after viewing the incident from various angles. The most important thing for analysis is being aware of these 'angles'. We should be aware of all the angles the event could be viewed with. This is the key to critically analyse any topic. My advice is that don't read editorial commentary just to gather facts and thoughts, also read it to understand how a fact can be analysed. You will also develop the habit then.

There is one more thing. There are sentences used in the editorial commentary that are understood only when you know the context. Many students leave it and miss the opportunity to understand the context of the sentence. You cannot understand the meaning of a sentence without knowing its context. For example, a sentence reads, 'the country needs Chanakya today'. If you do not know who Chanakya is, how will you understand what is being said. Editorial commentary is, thus, not simply a means to boost your knowledge but also to help you revise a subject.

I have used the word 'study' in context of editorial article and commentary till now but if you allow I would like to use the word 'analyse'. So at least these two things you should try to analyse just like you analyse a serious book.

(3) Other news

All newspapers devote an entire page to sports news. Sports are an important part of national and international news. However, just because newspapers are giving huge space to sports does not mean that you should consider them very important. Just glance once at those sports those are important at a national and international level. In any case, news about sports of this level makes front page news. If you are interested in sports, it is a different matter; otherwise you don't have to give sports news that much importance. But if there is an editorial article or commentary about any sport then it is as important to you as any other editorial article. Also, if the government announces a policy related to sports or if there is a new report or the courts give a verdict related to sports, you should pay attention to the news items.

The same rule applies to awards. You don't have to focus on small awards. Do not fall into the trap of trying to learn about all important personalities. If you do this, you will just be crowding your mind with facts which is not required.

Science and environment are very important subjects. Usually they do not make front page news. You will have to look for news items related to these in the inner pages. If you find some, read carefully.

National newspapers give some space to news from various states as well. These are, of course, important news. You should focus on news related to your state; it will help you during your interview. As far as news from other states is concerned, you can give it a quick glance. In any case, if there is some important incident in any state, it gets published in the front page.

The last thing I want to tell you regarding newspapers is that you should quickly go through the entire paper once. At least check out the headlines. This will help you get an idea of what is happening around the world - even in your own neighbourhood.

How should you read the newspaper?

I have come across strange experiences of newspaper readers. In one instance, a reader reads something and says something else. In another instance, they have not read the newspaper but claim about something that they read it in the newspaper. Sometimes, the reader will read something in the newspaper but claim "I did not read anything like that". Those who are reading more than one newspapers wrongly attribute news items to the newspapers. There are few who are not sure of the plain facts in big and bold letters either. This is a problem because readers do not take this seriously. This might not be harmful for other readers, but this cannot be the case with you. As long as you are preparing for the IAS exam, at least during that time, take newspapers very seriously.

This is the first step in how to read the newspaper. You have to change your psychology. Our brain has the special ability to prepare itself according to the signals you send it. If newspapers are just an obligatory task for you then that is how your brain will react to it. But if you take the newspaper reading seriously, your brain will act like an obedient slave and absorb information seriously. I have already told you how to read the editorial commentary. The art of reading editorial commentary is the core of the art of reading newspapers. You can even spend 50 minutes on the editorial commentary which usually takes only five minutes to read - but only if you spend time thinking about what is being said and try to understand the contexts. Editorial commentary requires you to analyse and think about what you have read rather than just reading it with concentration. More you do it; more will be revealed to you.

Now I will give you some pointers that will help improve your newspaper reading:

(a) I have already told you which pages of a newspaper to focus upon and which news items to read. Also, that you have to give a quick glance to the rest of the news, except editorial article and commentary. However, this does not apply to a business newspaper. All news items in a business newspaper are important in their own way and you have to treat them equally.

(b) You don't have to just read the newspaper, you have to analyse it. So when you read the newspaper, you should be holding a pen so that you can underline the important parts. When you underline them on paper they also get underlined in our brains, meaning the images formed in our minds are darkened. It also helps while revising.

Why am I putting so much emphasis on it? You read a book multiple times and they last you for years but newspapers are a daily affair and everyday there is something new. This way the newspapers pose a challenge - how to store all this information in our mind? You can solve this problem by underlining things. I have experimented with this which is why I'm telling you to do this. However, underline only keywords from important news that you need to remember.

(c) Also, you should keep clippings of important editorial articles and editorial commentaries. But you do not need to keep a thick file of newspaper clippings; you should only choose the most important ones. Do not forget to underline the important bits and keep going through them once in a while. You will find that after a few months, articles which you once thought were important now appear to be old and unimportant. If you do not discard them time to time they will increase the garbage on your desk as well as burden on your mind.

(d) Keep a separate diary for newspapers. When you come across an important fact, jot it down. I'm not asking you to write down the news, only facts. When I say facts, I mean a statement by an important personality, important new statistics, important names, reports etc. Do not include too much here either, else it won't be of any use.

(e) If there is such a context in a news item which you do not know about, do not be lazy. Try to know the context first and then read the news. I already have told you much about it.

(f) Any important event occurs at a certain geographical place, so every time something important happens, you should look up the region in a map. If you keep doing this for three months, you will obtain miraculous knowledge of geographical locations.

(g) After you finish reading the newspaper, think for 15 minutes about what you read. Do not be under the illusion that everything was easy and you remember everything. This is correct if you are talking only about today, but not if you are talking about a month. These 15 minutes will help solidify the 90 minutes you spent reading the newspaper. Try to save these 15 minutes and you will lose those 90 minutes as well.

(h) I mentioned earlier about noting down important facts.

It was related to statistics and statements. Now I will talk about some other stuff. Many students ask me if they should make notes. I don't know what they mean by making notes. If by this they mean jotting down important points from newspapers, my answer would be yes. The biggest benefit of this would be that you would have a collection of important facts. You will not have to go through magazines again and again. This will save you time and prevent a messed-up situation in your mind. Your viewpoint towards the subject will also become very clear. I want to assure you once again that to score well in general knowledge, you don't need to know too many facts. The most important thing here is how you use the facts that you do know. If you keep noting down and revising important news from newspapers for a year, you will find the general knowledge question papers in the mains exam quite easy. But you have to continuously revise and keep practicing how to use the facts you have learned in your answers. I don't think it is too much to ask for a prestigious exam like IAS.

I will now give you some details that will help you understand precisely what you need from newspapers. I would also suggest you keep reading unsolved question papers from the mains exam as well as preliminary exam. It will guide you in what to study else you may lose focus.

Here are some of the things you should focus on -

☑ New schemes and policies announced by the government, especially those related to rural development, poverty, health, education and those associated with social development.

- ☑ Latest information related to the economy such as changing economical scenario, budget and things related to industry and agriculture.
- ☑ Important facts related to the constitution.
- ☑ Reports presented by the government and other agencies which directly impact policy making.
- ☑ Events related to administration- specially those showing its efficiency.
- ☑ New scientific discoveries, especially advances in the field of information sector, space, biotechnology and medicine.
- ☑ Things that have to do with natural disaster management.
- ☑ Environmental problems and their solutions.

I want to warn you again that do not fall into the trap of trying to note down too many things. You have to only focus on important things even if you miss out on few other important things.

I believe that after everything I have told you about newspapers, it must have broken your illusion about newspaper reading. This is just the beginning. We have only talked about it theoretically. When you actually implement everything I said you will find that things have become clearer.

Chapter 11

Preliminary Exam : Preparation of General Studies (Paper-1)

Do you know that preliminary exam is actually a very deceitful exam? Lakhs of students sit for the IAS exam every year. Most of them go on to see the nature of preliminary exam (objective type questions), find it easily negotiable and assume that they can crack the IAS. They think that this is everything. They prepare for it and many even stand successful. It is only after they find themselves in this situation that they start preparing for the mains exam. However, it is too late and then they are unable to crack the exam. To keep you away from this deception, I will talk about what exactly the preliminary exam is.

What is preliminary exam ?

It is just an entrance test. I won't go into detail here, because a lot has already been said about this. You also know this but you are unable to believe it. Believe me, this exam is nothing more than an entrance test. It is an admission card for the mains exam. It is just an elimination process so that less people sit for the mains exam.

So when you are preparing for IAS exam, you cannot

prepare only for this. Firstly, it does not have some special form of preparation. Secondly, even if you crack this exam you will achieve nothing because the mains paper is the most important. So you should accept this truth that whatever preparation you have to do for IAS is actually preparing for the mains, the preliminary exam will be covered by this; you just have to adopt a slightly different technique for it.

(1) **Difficult or easy ?**

There are two contradictory views on this. Most people find the exam easy but some find it difficult. Those who find it easy think that answers are already given and if we have read the subject then it is easy to choose from the option. You don't have to write anything on your own. It is also easy because if you get a 60 percent score, you get selected. It is not very difficult to score this much. Those who find the exam easy are mainly candidates who haven't taken the exam yet.

However, when they sit for the exam, they do not find the exam easy. Interestingly, the reasons they gave for the exam being easy are now the exact reasons they find it difficult. Now they think that all the options are so similar that it is difficult to spot the right one. The options you have to choose from are like a maze, your mind gets lost in there. A major problem is that of negative marking. If you answer based on your guesses you are taking a risk. When you read the question, you will feel that you know the answer but you lose confidence when you read the options. We feel we read something similar but we are not sure if it was the same. It is not easy to answer it then. This is why getting a score of 60 percent can become very difficult.

Then which one is true? Friends, the exam being easy or difficult is very subjective actually. When we have prepared well and we have a good hold over the subject, then the exam is easy for us - no matter how difficult it is. But if we are not prepared even an easy subject becomes difficult.

Another thing that matters is the process of studying. If you try to prepare for preliminary exam keeping in mind the objective nature of the questions asked in the paper, you will definitely find it difficult to score even 60 percent marks. This is not the way you prepare for the IAS exam. You can apply this technique of studying for state civil services, but you need basic understanding for preliminary exam and this you can get from preparing for the mains paper. You should accept this fact and then prepare accordingly.

(2) Clarity

If the options are easy, then obviously the questions asked are not too difficult. The entire problem is that of the options. The only way you can overcome the difficulty of options is through the clarity of your thoughts. If you are not clear about the questions being asked, your mind is not strong enough and the chances of you giving wrong answers is high. But this clarity of thoughts will only come when your hold on the subject is very strong. This hold is not just knowledge of facts but also a deep understanding of facts. All this requires 'updated knowledge'. Even if you pick up unsolved question papers, you will find many questions that appear connected to some subject but they are linked to current affairs. You will find this especially true for economics, political science and geography. Current affairs are anyway an important part of general knowledge.

(3) Speed of your mind

If you take a lot of time to understand the questions, reading the options and answering, preliminary exam can become very difficult for you. You need to be very fast here. You need to understand the question immediately. Read the options very carefully so that you can navigate the maze to narrow down on the right one. A lazy mind will not do, you need a fast one.

How do you gain good mental speed? You need a good understanding of the subject and then you need practice. We will talk about this later. For now, it is enough for you to know that preliminary exam requires your mind to be fast.

(4) Patience

It is also required to have patience in your heart. When we come across something complicated, we are troubled; we lose our patience and then panic. When we panic, we are prone to making mistakes. If you panic and decide not to face the trouble, you will miss out on questions. If you panic and hurry, you will choose the wrong answers. Negative marking has made making mistakes pricier than missing out on questions. So it is important for you to develop a strong mind and heart.

I have told you certain things about the preliminary exam so that you don't take it lightly. However, do not consider this everything. You should accept that only after preparing for the mains paper can you prepare for the preliminary exam. This is the only way you can face the challenges posed by the preliminary exam.

What to study ?

Students are so scared of general studies, they generally panic. However, there is nothing to be worried about. UPSC has decided the syllabus of general studies for the preliminary exams. Yes, there is a lack of detailing but I think no syllabus is given in too much detail. Only the important things are mentioned and they should suffice. Isn't it true?

Therefore, the panic that general studies create is mainly due to current local and international events. This preparation is done using newspapers and newspapers are awe-inspiring in themselves. But this is not true and I have already talked about this. Other than this, the syllabus is quite lucid. I don't think that you have to worry too much about it. However, since students worry, I have decided to write about this. If there is a problem, it cannot be solved merely by my saying there is no problem. There has to be a solution and that is what I will present you.

The seven most important points of the syllabus of the preliminary exam are -

(1) Important events at national and international scale. These are related to newspaper and magazines.

(2) Another subject is Indian history and struggle for Indian Independence.

(3) Third subject is geography which requires you to know the geography of India and the world.

(4) The fourth subject can be called political science or constitution.

(5) The fifth subject is economics and this is related to behavioural economics.

(6) Environment is another important topic. Climate change and biodiversity falls under this category.

(7) The last subject is that of general science. Biology, chemistry, physics, zoology and medicine fall under this.

I want to make it clear that all the subjects in the syllabus fall under general studies not specialist studies.

Now I have a question. If we remove the first point about important national and international events, then is there any subject that you have not studied till tenth grade? You must have studied all of this. So you are expected to know these basics before you specialise in a particular field. Whether you become a doctor or an engineer, you need basic knowledge of these subjects. There is nothing new in this.

If you find them to be new, this is your own problem. This is not a problem of the education system or UPSC. Your problem is that you read all this 7 to 8 years ago and have now forgotten. You faintly remember some of it. You have forgotten it because you did not study it to understand but only to qualify exams. Once the exam was over, you forgot about it. If you were to miraculously remember everything you read until tenth grade, you will start considering yourself qualified to be an IAS. Won't you?

You forgot what you studied, it is okay. This is the case with most people. Now let us see what can be done. I will tell you what to study for general studies paper for the preliminary exam:

(1) NCERT books

If you think that preparation for general studies is easy then you are wrong. The books will be average, the knowledge you gain from them will be average too but your effort should not be average. So what we refer to as general studies would be better defined as foundation of learning. This is information that every educated person should know - whether he is taking the IAS exam or not.

There are many text books and guide books to help you prepare for general studies. You can choose either one of these or both. It is not just me but even other successful candidates suggest NCERT books. There is a strong reason behind this.

NCERT is an organisation of the Indian government. Books prepared by NCERT are studied in CBSE schools across the country. We can call these books national books for 1-10th grade level.

Then there are state boards. These boards have their own syllabus and the books are prepared according to it. The state boards have different syllabi; the subject matter in the books also differs and so does the level of the exam.

So logically, it makes sense that UPSC should make NCERT books its medium. And generally, if not all the time, it stands true. So if you study NCERT books from grade sixth to grade tenth and understand the important points and memorise the necessary facts then you would have developed a very strong foundation for general studies.

There is another added benefit to this. If you have been a student of the CBSE board, then you must have already read these books. Now you are just revising them. You will not find these books unfamiliar. Students whose first language is Hindi will also benefit. The books are also available in Hindi although they have been translated from English. I agree that the translation is quite difficult and not easy to understand. But there is no way around this. You should see the Hindi in the question papers of the mains and preliminary exam. You will only understand half of it. This is an unfortunate situation and we don't know when Hindi will get its place. For now, you will have to struggle to read and understand NCERT books, but it will help you understand the kind of difficult Hindi that is asked in the civil services paper. This will give you practice.

But if you are not able to understand Hindi in NCERT books at all, do not fret over it. It would be better if you read books written by other authors on the subject. Do not think that you are making a mistake or missing out on an important part of learning. You will get information from other books too. This will also help you build the foundation of your studies. Understanding something is better than understanding nothing.

(2) General knowledge guide

I'm not talking about some thick guide. I'm talking about an average-sized guide. Do not feel terrorised or attracted to thick books. Such books claim that 90 percent questions have been asked from them. But is it possible for any student to read, understand and remember the entire book? The claim of the books is correct but it not very feasible. You do not need these heavy books.

So keep a medium-level guide with you and keep going through it once in a while. Guide books store information which is scattered in books in one place. Guides give you the material in a focused form. However, do not try to memorise everything.

Read the previous years' unsolved papers to decide what you should read from the guide.

(3) Newspaper

I have talked about this in detail. Newspapers are as important for you as blood circulation is to the body. There should not be even a single day when you do not read the newspaper. Wherever you are, you will find a newspaper. It is not important that you should only read your favourite newspaper. If you are outside and cannot find your favourite newspaper, this does not mean that you should not read the newspaper at all. You should read any newspaper you can get your hands on so that there is a continuity of news in your mind. This continuity is extremely important. It is possible that you miss a day's newspaper and something very important happens on that particular day. If you miss this, then you will lose out on the stability of your studies.

You should read the newspaper daily. I have another purpose behind giving you this advice. I know that if you are given the liberty of not reading the newspaper 2 to 4 days in a year, you will start taking this liberty for 2 to 4 days every month. This will be very harmful to you.

To save yourself this information, when you see that you are missing out on your favourite newspaper, you should ask someone to collect them. Later, you can go through the old issues. You don't have to devote too much time to these, but just a glance would be enough. I used to do this and I still do, not because I have to prepare for IAS but because I write columns for newspapers. I don't want to miss anything. You should do the same thing.

Why is reading the newspaper so important? I want to add something to what I have already told you. You will listen to news on radio and TV, but those are mere pieces of information. These will not tell you the entire background of the story or how to analyse them. The newspaper will fill this gap. Another benefit is that you get to revise the news. I have already told you the benefit of revising. So do not even try to think of an alternative to newspapers, you have to read them.

(4) Magazines

Magazines can be thought of as chosen thoughts of the newspapers. While newspaper brings you news every day, magazines discuss events that happened over a week, 15 days or a month. They also mention opinions and thoughts related to these events. The news items that get space in a magazine are the most important ones of that time. So, magazines help you cultivate a vision that allows you to identify important news items. Also, they help you to revise the important events you read about in the newspaper.

The magazines I'm talking about here can be divided into two categories. The first category is that of magazines related to competitive exams. You should choose one magazine and read it according to your need.

The other category is that of magazines based on particular subjects. The important ones in this category are 'Yojna', a magazine about developmental policies of the Indian government and 'Kurukshetra' based on agriculture.

Students often get confused about what to read and what

to leave in these magazines. Please note here that the entire magazine is not for you to study. These magazines have not been created keeping your IAS goals in mind - even those that are meant for competitive exams. So you need to know which material is important for you. Guides and unsolved papers can help you determine this. After a few days, you will develop the vision to see which articles you should be studying. I don't think that in any magazine, there are more than 3 to 4 articles that would be of use to you. Sometimes you won't find up to that much.

(5) Everyday news

Not many people advocate this, but I do. I strongly recommend it. I think that all students who want to clear the IAS exam have a moral duty to listen to the news every day. As far as I'm concerned, if I did not listen to the radio, I would not have become a civil servant. News on TV was not available that time. But why am I advocating listening to the news so much?

Everyday news keeps us alert and informed. The presentation of news on TV and radio is such that it instils in us the ability to choose important knowledge. Radio first broadcasts the main headlines and then elaborates upon them later. After that many other news items are broadcasted. At the end of the bulletin the headlines are repeated. So two things happen automatically -

(1) You get to know which are the most important happenings of the day.

(2) We are reminded of important happenings of the day thrice. Do you consider this any less important?

When I say everyday news, I mean the news at night on radio and the news at night on Doordarshan. You are going to be a civil servant, a part of the government. Truth be told, you will be the government. It is important then that you should be well aware of governmental policies and the government's viewpoint. If you compare the news on Doordarshan with the news on other private news channels, you will observe a difference. Private channels focus on news which can generate a high TRP for them- burglary, murder, rape, politics, corruption, suicide, celebrity, cricket etc. They talk little about governmental policies on rural development, heath, education etc. News on developmental issues is also not given much space. International relations have been completely ignored by private channels, unless there is some conflict.

News on Doordarshan is different. The channel has its own discipline and they broadcast the 'real news'. Do not ignore Doordarshan because you are watching news on other channels. Even if you sometimes miss the news on Doordarshan, never miss the news on radio.

There are many news items on radio that are not in the news otherwise. This suggests they were not very important but still listening to them adds on to your knowledge. You will not believe that listening to the radio news only takes fifteen minutes but they save you many more. You can do your own experiment. You listen to the news at night and read the newspaper in the morning. You will find the news familiar. You will be able to read the newspaper fast and understand quickly.

As far as learning is concerned, it is said we better remember things that we hear than those that we read and things we say than those we see. In general knowledge, you cannot do anything special but you can hear the news.

Many students face this problem of how to learn the names of premiers of various countries. It is difficult to learn which union minister has which portfolio. Should you cram this? No, you just hear the news on radio and watch it on Doordarshan. These names will often come up and you will remember them without effort.

(6) Watch discussions and take part

Television and radio both broadcast discussions on various important topics. Specialists take part in this and the best part is that they are from different fields. This helps you understand the same topic from different viewpoints. Definitely, this understanding is beneficial for the general knowledge section in the mains exam.

You need to take time out for this and do this seriously. By being serious, I mean you should sit with a pen and paper. You should jot down important points else you will forget them in sometime. If you get time you should take part in discussions yourself. I have already talked about this.

I believe that this should suffice for the general knowledge preparation for both preliminary exam as well as the mains paper.

Which subjects should you study ?

There are two things in front of you - the syllabus given by UPSC and the unsolved question papers by UPSC. This is true that anything can be asked in the general knowledge section but this does not really happen. UPSC asks only those things that it expects to be known by you. Only those things are asked that must have reached you through some medium. It is a different matter whether you had access to that medium and whether you paid enough attention to this item. Generally, very random questions are not asked.

You should see the syllabus of the preliminary exam and unsolved question papers from previous years. Based on this, we can conclude that there are four main subjects that account for two-thirds of the questions asked in the general knowledge section. And what is even more important is that these are the four main subjects based on which three papers have been prepared in the general studies section in the mains exam. These four subjects are - geography, economics, political science and history. After this comes general science.

The first paper of general studies in the mains paper is primarily based on history and geography. The second general studies paper is related to the Indian constitution and Indian political system. International relations also fall in this section. After all they are also a part of politics. The third paper of the General Studies is on Economic Development, Technology, Biodiversity, Disaster Management, Environment, and Security.

Therefore, if you prepare these four subjects very well then you have prepared nicely for three general studies paper in the mains exam as well. The only difference is that in the preliminary exam, you only have to choose the right answer, in the mains exam you have to write the correct and precise answer on your own.

There is no arguing that the syllabus given for the general

studies paper in preliminary exam is not very detailed. It is mostly indicative. Many students are unable to understand the indications and get lost trying to decide what to study and what to leave. They also cannot decide which chapters are important and which ones are not. Due to this, their preparation is not very disciplined, solid or scientific. To avoid this, I'm giving you details on which subjects you should master for preliminary and mains exam and which topics you should focus on.

(1) Geography

I consider it the most important part of general studies. It is the master of all sciences and if you understand the science behind this subject then you don't need to cram anything. Always use a map while studying geography. A science student requires a lab and a geography student needs maps.

There are three main parts of geography - physical geography, world geography and Indian geography.

Questions are asked from all three in the preliminary exam but most questions are asked from physical geography and Indian geography. Physical geography means - scientific knowledge of geography. If you understand this well you will find the subject very easy and will quickly understand the world and Indian geography.

(a) Physical geography: The main topics you should focus on are :

- ☑ Make-up of the earth - through longitude, latitude etc.
- ☑ Geographical division of Earth on the basis of various zones.

- ☑ Rotation of the Earth that causes night and day and seasonal changes. This also includes lunar eclipse, solar eclipse, and high tide, low-tide etc.
- ☑ Internal make-up of the Earth which includes types of rocks and their special characteristics.
- ☑ Earth's landscape which includes mountains, hills, plains, snow-capped mountains and valleys etc.
- ☑ There are many changes on Earth. Elements that bring about changes are rain, air, earthquake, volcano, climate, temperature, pressure, moisture, seasons etc. You should understand the science behind this.
- ☑ Oceans, streams and rivers make up the water-bodies on the Earth. You should be aware of important tributaries in the world as well as important rivers.
- ☑ You should also study the atmosphere. You should have a deep understanding of the science of the natural phenomenon such as layers of atmosphere, presence of the Sun, rainfall, snowfall, fog etc
- ☑ Many students keep maps but do not understand how to read them. Learn it.
- ☑ Geography has its own terminology. Many words have their own definitions such as continental climate or frigid zones. These need to be studied.

(b) World geography: If you have understood the basic principles of geography, then understanding the geography of the world would not be too difficult for you. When studying the geography of the world you just have to keep applying principles of geography to it. For instance, if you are reading that the densest forests are found in equatorial regions then apply principles of geography to it to understand why this is the case. You will find that the region experiences heavy rainfall. Due to heavy everyday rainfall, the densest forests are found there. If you are able to do this, world geography will never be a pain.

And remember, you don't have to study geography; you have to study the general knowledge behind it. General knowledge means practical knowledge. So keep your studies confined only to information that has practical applications. Keep this in mind and pay special attention to the following points when studying world geography-

- ☑ Mining of minerals in various parts of the world.
- ☑ Cultivation of important crops in different areas of the world.
- ☑ Forests in the world and other natural resources.
- ☑ Establishment of important industries in important regions of the world.

When studying world geography, your focus should be on the economical aspect of geography and not environmental and political geography. Although from the perspective of the mains paper, you should also pay attention to the environmental geography of certain countries such as China, Japan, America, Germany, England, South East Asia and India's neighbouring countries (Bangladesh, Nepal, Maldives, Sri Lanka, Afghanistan, Myanmar etc).

(c) Indian geography: Given that you are a citizen of India, you should have a deep knowledge of your country's geography. Geography is not just a subject but a foundation on which a nation's economical, social, cultural and even political structure is standing. As an administrator you cannot fulfil your duties until you know the geography of the place. So your level of knowledge of Indian geography should be higher than the level of general studies. You should pay attention to the following points when studying Indian geography -

- ☑ Geographical conditions of India such as its location, boundaries and size (especially Himalayas, important mountains, Ganges, Deccan Plateau, Vindhyas, Satpura and Aravalli ranges, island and coastal regions).
- ☑ Tropic of cancer and tropic of Capricorn.
- ☑ Water flow which includes sources of main rivers, their paths and their endpoints.
- ☑ Important lakes and waterfalls. Also, methods of irrigation.
- ☑ Climate and weather - especially in the context of monsoon.
- ☑ Vegetation especially in the context of forests.
- ☑ Soil - especially in the context of crop cultivation.
- ☑ Agriculture - types of crops and their distribution across different states. You should focus on which state has highest production of which crops.
- ☑ Projects with multiple aims - in the context of dams of national importance and sources of energy.
- ☑ Minerals- especially in the context of availability in different parts of the country.
- ☑ Industry - you should know the 'when, where and how' regarding the development of main industries in India.

- ☑ Castes and tribes of India
- ☑ 2011 Census and its details- especially in the context of literacy, population density, male-female ratio etc.
- ☑ Important cities and important tourist spots.

You may think there is too much to study in geography but this has been done in order to make the syllabus clearer to you. You should not look at the above points and think that the syllabus is vast. If you give only one month to this subject, you can prepare it well. If you understand a subject well, the knowledge will stay with you throughout life and you can use it in any competitive exam. This is very fortunate.

(2) Economics

The importance of economics has now increased in the IAS exam. After economic liberalisation, the world is now an open market. Today, international relations are determined not by political forces but by economic conditions. In this scenario, the importance of economics is bound to increase.

Most students find economics difficult, and it is difficult - if you see the theory part. But it is also an easy subject if you understand its behavioural aspects. There is no man who can say that he has nothing to do with economics. I can say I learnt economics when I ran a shop and went to the market. If you keep your eyes open and understand the workings of the market, you will be covering up at least half of your economics syllabus.

You must have a bank account. You must visit the bank. If you pay attention to their work process, you will understand banking. The same thing applies to industries. You should visit an industrial centre one day and talk to the officers there; you will understand how industries work. If you stay in a village you would be aware of the economical situation there - if you are a responsible citizen. Do you think it is very difficult to understand rural economics? Do you think it should be hard for you to answer why prices of vegetables are higher in the summer?

There are two parts of preparing for economics. The one I mentioned above is the first part. This is the behavioural, practical aspect of it. You keep your eyes open and you will understand everyday economics. When you visit a place, you can see which crops are sown there or which industries exist. This knowledge helps you prepare for geography. But when you bring the market into this, it will improve your knowledge of economics. I believe that IAS preparation should not be limited to books but should also be done at a practical level which includes everyday society. You don't have to take any special steps for this; you only have to stay alert. If you go to the market and observe which vegetables are available in which season and what their prices are, some of your questions will be automatically prepared. Your knowledge of geography will be boosted as you will be able to identify Rabi crops from kharif crops. This question was asked in the IAS exam. You also get to know the law of demand and supply. According to the law, "when the supply of a commodity is higher than its demand, the price of the commodity will fall." This question was asked in the preliminary exam.

Now comes the theory part. I will advise you to go through NCERT books. If you want you can pick up some other books, but not the notes. Notes will not be of much help. Pay attention to the following points in these books -

☑ Important laws of economics such as that of

demand and supply.

- ☑ National income-how it is estimated, how it is counted, gross domestic product and its distribution etc.
- ☑ Various five-year-plans and their main goals.
- ☑ Population: structure, growth, problems etc.
- ☑ Indian economy - especially in the context of the developing countries.
- ☑ Employment status - various sectors of employment, unemployment etc.
- ☑ Poverty and inequality.
- ☑ Natural and human resources.
- ☑ Agriculture production, irrigation and development of dry and infertile land.
- ☑ Crops - oilseeds, food and cash crops.
- ☑ Agriculture marketing: market, transport, agencies, storage, price determination, loan policy etc.
- ☑ Fertilizers- methods of consumption, subsidies on it.
- ☑ Agriculture modernisation: Technical know-how, new crop species and seeds, crop insurance etc.
- ☑ Rural development: related policies of the government.
- ☑ Land development - zamindari abolition, forest land acquisition etc.
- ☑ Industrial development - especially in the context of public sector, private sector, big scale, small scale and cottage industries.
- ☑ Currency and its value- especially in the context of monetary policy.
- ☑ Monetary and fiscal development

- ☑ Banking system - Reserve bank of India, public sector banks, other important banks and financial institutions.
- ☑ Public finance - sources of revenue, gross financial loss, financial organisations, public debt etc.
- ☑ Fundamental infra-structure: energy, railway-road-air transport, telecommunications and postal services.
- ☑ Tax system
- ☑ Green revolution, white revolution, blue revolution
- ☑ Agriculture price-policy
- ☑ Public distribution system
- ☑ Industrial policies, industrial sickness and financial institutions
- ☑ Foreign direct investment
- ☑ Stock exchange: a general get-to-know of the share market, SEBI.
- ☑ Foreign trade - new trends, stock, balance of payments, export policies, India and World Trade Organisation.
- ☑ Economic liberalisation
- ☑ Current economical scenario
- ☑ Pre-budget economic surveys
- ☑ General budget for every year
- ☑ Important terms related to economics.

Once you understand the topics above then you will be able to analyse current economic policies and problems. Current political events grab headlines, so do economic happenings. While political events are easy to understand but if you do not have a solid background in economics, it will be difficult to completely understand the economic events. They become a mere piece of information. That's why you should have a good knowledge of economics in general.

(3) Political science

Knowledge of political science is required in the civil services at every stage - mains, preliminary and interview. If you think about it, you will find that a citizen's life is closely linked to his country's political structure. Therefore, it is expected from an educated citizen to be aware of the political structure in his country. Perhaps, it is this thought which has rendered this subject so important in IAS.

As we have seen, in economics, two types of questions are asked- introductory questions to economics and contemporary events related to economics. Same is the case with political science. The subject also has two parts. The first one is the constitution. These are direct questions which you can answer if you have studied the constitution. The second part is related to recent events. You will be asked questions about important political events in the past year. Questions related to articles of the constitution can even be asked on the recent events. In this scenario, you have to do the following:

- ☑ Understand the constitution in general
- ☑ In-depth knowledge about some important parts of the constitution
- ☑ Sharp knowledge of recent political events

But you need not worry too much about this. You don't have to become a specialist on the constitution. You only have to pay heed to important articles of the constitution. Keep a close eye specially on those points of these articles that have been in news for some reason or are related to some way to the events occurred during last one or one and a half year.

In the subject of political science you are required to know the following:

- ☑ Preamble of the constitution
- ☑ Characteristics of the constitution
- ☑ Federal form of government: formation and work of Lok Sabha and Rajya Sabha
- ☑ Election, work, responsibilities and powers of the Prime Minister, President and Vice-President.
- ☑ Fundamental rights
- ☑ Directive principles of state policy
- ☑ Fundamental duties
- ☑ Citizenship
- ☑ Legislatives
- ☑ Executives
- ☑ Judiciary (specially High court and Supreme court)
- ☑ Election Commission of India: formation, work, powers and constitutional protection to it
- ☑ Parliamentary committees
- ☑ Constitutional article related to Jammu and Kashmir
- ☑ State's Legislatives, Executives and Judiciary
- ☑ Governor and Chief Minister
- ☑ Distribution of power across states and centre
- ☑ NITI Aayog
- ☑ Financial commission
- ☑ Information commission
- ☑ National commission for minorities

- ☑ National commission for women
- ☑ Relations between the union and the states-specially in the context of Sarkariya commission
- ☑ Important amendments to the articles in the constitution
- ☑ Self-governmental organisations - focusing on Panchayati Raj
- ☑ All Indian services
- ☑ Union Public Service Commission and State Public Service commissions

Now I'm presenting some facts that will help improve upon your preparation of the Indian constitution -

- ☑ Fundamental rights and directive principles of state policy
- ☑ Emergency powers of the President
- ☑ Passing of Money Bills
- ☑ Appellate jurisdiction of the Supreme Court
- ☑ 42nd, 44th, 93rd and 94th constitutional amendment
- ☑ Constitutional provisions ensuring social justice
- ☑ Impeachment of the President, Vice-President, Supreme Court Judge and Chief Election Commissioner
- ☑ The process of constitutional amendments
- ☑ Constitutional protection given to the Election commission and C.A.G.
- ☑ Constitutional provisions ensuring judicial autonomy
- ☑ Resolution of issues between centre and state
- ☑ History of Panchayati Raj system and its

development

- ☑ 91st constitutional amendment to prevent elected MLAs and MPs from changing parties.
- ☑ Civil Societies etc.

(4) History

History is a vast and detailed subject. The challenge is where to start from and where to finish. However, the syllabus given by UPSC addresses this issue. This can be seen in both preliminary exam as well as the mains exam. For the preliminary exam the syllabus mentions - Indian history and India's struggle for Independence. In the mains exam, three important points are mentioned. Firstly, the syllabus mentions Indian culture, art, literature and sculpture from ancient time to modern period. The second part includes important events from 1850 to present. The third point is related to India's struggle for independence. You should prepare for history keeping all this in mind.

History has been my subject. You are lucky that now you don't have to choose an optional subject in the preliminary exam. I had to do so and I chose history. What did I do! Every single line in that subject could have been asked as a question in the preliminary exam. Since I have never been good at learning things by rote, it was going to be very difficult for me. Anyway, it all went right in the end.

My sole purpose behind saying all this is to advise you do not try to prepare everything (about history) from the beginning till the independence of India. However, if you have studied history before you can revise all of this else the time spent on studying all this would not be worth it. So what should you do then? Let me discuss the strategy you should follow when it comes to history -

- ☑ Indian culture has been included in the mains exam. So you should focus well on this subject.
- ☑ Independence struggle is a part of both mains exam and the preliminary exam. At least 30 to 40 percent of the questions asked in the preliminary exam on history are from this section. Around 10 to 15 percent of questions are asked on art, literature and culture.

When you see questions on Jainism, Buddhism and Bhakti movement, they seem to be a part of history but they actually belong to culture. Culture is actually an important part of the history of any country. So you should prepare well for this part.

Now if you combine the questions asked on Independence struggle and culture, you will find that 50 to 60 percent of questions asked are based on this.

Now the question remains about the remaining questions. Let's suppose there are 10 questions asked on history. This means, the challenge in front of you is only 4–5 questions. It does not make sense for you to struggle with the entire history syllabus just for these 4-5 questions. So what should you do?

I'm not saying you should not study history at all. You have studied the subject till grade 10th. You can pick up NCERT books again. It will give you a general idea. Besides you can pay attention to important sections where questions are usually asked from. These are -

- ☑ Indus valley civilisation
- ☑ Jainism and Buddhism
- ☑ Art and culture of Maurya and Gupta's period
- ☑ Art and culture of Mughals

- ☑ Read up a little on Shivaji and Ranjit Singh
- ☑ British entered India in the 1600s. They, from then on, went on to fight three important wars - Battle of Panipat, Battle of Plassey and Battle of Bastar. Study them.

Modern Indian history begins from 1765. You have to study history after this in detail because it's a part of the mains exam as well.

So how will you prepare the above mentioned points? Well, I have already suggested studying NCERT books for this.

Now I am going to give you a special advice. You can call it a task. You will only be spending as much time doing it as you would spend watching 13 films- I consider the duration of a film to be 4 hours, including commuting time. Shyam Benegal made a TV show called 'India: a discovery' that was aired on Doordarshan. It is available on DVD now and it sketches the entire Indian history beautifully. It will take you 50 hours to watch this. If you do this, you will understand Indian history and India's struggle for independence in detail. I have conducted experiments on this and achieved good results.

(5) General Sciences

The importance of this is increasing in the IAS exam, but the degree of uncertainty is very high with it. One year only 3 questions out of 100 are asked on general science and the very next year 15 questions may be asked. Initially very basic questions were asked but now some of them are specialist questions. However, they are not so specialist that you would require graduation level studies. You just need to regain the knowledge you acquired till 10th grade.

Questions asked in general sciences section can be divided mainly into five groups -

(a) Physics (b) Chemistry

(c) Zoology (d) Botany

(e) Environment

Most questions are asked on Physics and Zoology. After that comes Botany and last is Chemistry.

Now I will list details that will help students, especially those not from a science background, to prepare for the paper.

Usually students from arts and commerce stream are scared of science but thankfully this fear is not as great as the fear of maths. I don't know how to assure you that there is no need to be scared. When you see science questions in unsolved papers you get very disturbed. You feel you will not be able to solve them. Why? Is this paper really tough? Not at all. You are the reason for this problem, not the subject of science. When you have not prepared for a subject at all how can you determine whether it is difficult or easy?

If you study the points I'm telling you with patience you will be able to get rid of all your problems. If you have decided to become an IAS, then also decide to study science.

I suggested that you read NCERT books to study science. But you might find the Hindi in the books difficult. In this case you can prepare with a good guide. Also, there are some books available keeping especially civil services in mind. The important part here is preparation, not preparing using NCERT books.

The basis for preparation for questions in Science, both in Pre and Mains examination, has changed completely. This change is to be seen mainly in two forms :

The first is that there is far more emphasis on current knowledge than on book learning now. As a result, preparation for this is better done reading newspapers and watching the news than reading up on books.

The second is that basic sciences are not being studied the same way as before. As an example—Archimedes principles, and correction of vision defects—such basics are no longer being asked. These appear childlike questions to ask in the face of the sweeping influence of science in our daily lives. Instead, advanced science questions are being given prominence now. Some of the areas from which questions come up now are:

- Electronics
- Meteorology
- Atomic physics
- Robotics
- Nano technology
- Bio technology
- Fourth generation industrial revolution and associated technologies like:
  - Artificial Intelligence
  - Quantum Computing
  - The Internet of Things
  - 3 D Printing
  - Block-chain
  - Big Data
  - Machine Learning

Apart from these topics, there could be others that are in current discussion in the news. Therefore, you will have to be on the alert in this regard. Don't just go by past information.

You will have to prepare for these from two angles. First, understand the basic principles underlying each of these. Second, get a general knowledge about these sciences from a topical point of view.

(6) Environment

This subject has become extremely important for both preliminary and Main examination. It has to be prepared while keeping following points in mind-

1. Problem of environment
2. Solutions to this problem (including international treaties) and
3. International institutions associated with this issue

And ofcourse you should pay special attention to the events related to this subject arising in current scenario (current affairs).

(7) Contemporary events

This is the most important part of general studies. Generally, this includes events that happened up to a year or a year and a half ago. This is not a fixed rule though. Although the syllabus mentions 'national and international events', it has been observed that the focus is on national news. The ratio is 8:2. So you should largely focus on national news in your studies.

(a) Main national events: Do not worry that 'anything will be asked'. If you do not do this then you will not be able to do justice to the facts that you should know.

The question here is how you will identify important national events. One of the parameters is that any important event related to what you have studied under geography, politics, economy and science can be considered an important national event. Politics and economy should obviously be given the most importance here.

Other criteria to judge important recent events are:

- ☑ Events that impact the society
- ☑ Cultural facts
- ☑ Awareness of challenges faced by the country
- ☑ Development-related programmes
- ☑ Important people and places in the news
- ☑ Important awards and honours
- ☑ Sports-related news
- ☑ Important scientific facts and discoveries

There could be other contemporary events which cannot be predicted. But you don't have to worry about these. If you read the newspaper and listen to the news regularly, this will be easy for you.

(b) International events: I have mentioned this in the chapter on newspapers. International news is a field that is vast but you will notice that newspapers give little space to it. This is because only news related to our country is related to us as it would affect us directly. Therefore we are not presented with irrelevant news.

How will you determine the important news among the news that has been served to you? You have to determine how the event will affect our country. The more an event impacts our country, the more important it is. For example, most of the events that happen in leading countries such as US, or in Pakistan, Afghanistan, Nepal and other neighbouring countries have a direct political and economical impact on our country.

You should consider the following points when preparing for international events -

- ☑ India's relations with important countries
- ☑ Challenges being faced by the world
- ☑ International organisations, such as United Nations, World Bank, World Trade Organisation, International Monetary Fund etc.
- ☑ Important organisations such as Non-aligned countries, BRICS, QUAD, G-21, SCO, ASEAN etc.
- ☑ Important events in different countries that affect India directly or indirectly, such as economic policies of China and America, decisions taken by the European Union and changing political and economic landscapes of Latin American countries & African countries.
- ☑ International meetings and events in the perspective of economic liberalisation.

While I have listed some important points for you, it does not mean that anything outside this cannot be meaningful to you. But it is true that most of the important events which may be meaningful to you will fall under the topics I have mentioned.

I have tried to produce a detailed syllabus of subjects under the general knowledge section of preliminary exam. This will help you study the subjects in a logical manner. If you prepare well according to the above mentioned points, I can't claim that your preparation will be 100 percent but it will be sufficient for you to succeed. Will it not be enough for you to succeed?

Studying strategy

It is as important to know 'how to study' as much as it is to know 'what to study'. I have talked a lot about this in previous chapters. So I don't want to repeat myself. I'm telling you things here that will help you in the preliminary exam-

- ☑ I will repeat myself that do not try to study for preliminary exams separately. When you study for the mains exam, it will also cover the preliminary exam.
- ☑ When you study the unsolved papers, you will see that the questions which have been asked are very easy but the options that you have to choose from are not. It is possible that two out of four options are easy but the very thin line between the other two options will make it difficult for you to succeed.
- ☑ There is an increasing trend of offering cluster options in UPSC. Cluster options mean - four options are given and then another four options are presented with different choices. This creates a lot of confusion and these questions demand time. You will only be able to solve these questions when you understand the subject very well. This is why I'm emphasising that you should prepare for preliminary exam on the basis of the mains exam.
- ☑ Scrutinise what you have studied and ponder over it. For e.g., if you are reading a definition you should be familiar with the terms. The following question was asked in the preliminary exam -

Question - Who among the following rulers in ancient India had assumed the titles 'Mattavilasa', 'Vichitrachitta' and 'Gunabharata'?

(a) Mahendravarman I

(b) Simhavishnu

(c) Narasimhavarman I

(d) Simhavarman

This history question, which appears simple at first glance, is slightly different from the usual ones. You will not be able to solve it easily. So I would advise you to read slowly and think over it.

- ☑ There are plenty of books with model questions to help you prepare for the preliminary exam. You should practice with them as well; not only will it clarify some 'still unclear' facts in your mind, but will help train your brain as well.
- ☑ Preliminary exam also requires you to master time management besides having knowledge about the subject. Your thinking speed needs to be fast. This will only come with practice. So keep solving model test papers on a regular basis. But your sole purpose of doing it should not be just to check your score; you should aim at getting more out of it. Going through this process, you can evaluate yourself in a reverse order. To do so, give attention to the following points:
- ☑ Mark the questions you are unable to answer without any confusion. Now figure out why you were not able to solve these. Rectify this weakness.
- ☑ There will be questions you were able to solve with confidence but they turned out to be wrong. Think about why this happened. This is a dangerous situation which is responsible for the failure of many students. If you don't understand where the mistake

was made, how will you work upon it? There are many students who claim they will score 60 percent after they take the exam but they are unable to even qualify. I worry that the same thing will happen to them the following year too, and often it does.

☑ Mark the questions you are unable to solve. Now think about it: Could you not solve them because you didn't study the topic? If you did study the topic, did you not understand it? If you understood it, why couldn't you solve the questions? Did you get confused because of the options? If you got confused with the options it means you studied the subject but could not catch the nitty-gritty's.

These questions are now very important for you. You need to read the related chapters again so you can answer the questions next time.

☑ You need approx 45-50 percent marks to qualify the preliminary exam. Do not get complacent if you score 60 percent in the practice papers. Leave that 60 percent aside and focus on the 40 percent you could not score. Think why you could not solve these 40 percent questions. You have to study for that 40 percent. This I call 'reverse evaluation'.

Remember, the purpose of practice questions is not just to evaluate you or increase your calculation speed, but its purpose is also extension of knowledge. Every time you practice, you should gain some knowledge.

Sometimes you come across unknown facts when you are solving practice papers. It is also possible that your books say nothing about these new facts. Don't bother. It is quite obvious as no book can claim that there is no knowledge beyond what it contains. This is good for you though, you learned some new facts which you should jot down.

Friends, I have churned out everything I knew, thought and experienced about the preparation of preliminary exam in this chapter. Now it is up to you, how you use this knowledge to ensure your success. My best wishes are with you.

Chapter 12

Preliminary Exam : Preparation of CSAT (Paper-2)

After being implemented, the CSAT examination became a subject of controversy. There were doubts that this exam is mainly in favour of engineering, management and English-medium students. The doubts turned out to be true. This examination came as a boon for students from these backgrounds, and their number among those who qualified for the mains examination increased unbelievably.

This caused discontent among students from other backgrounds and thus led to protests and outrage, with students demanding that the exam is scrapped. In fact, this issue was even raised in the parliament with great emphasis. As a result, the government removed English language questions, which carried 15 marks, from this paper in the 2014 preliminary examination. The paper was thus, reduced to 185 marks. The government then next year did not remove the CSAT, but made it merely a qualifying examination.

So from 2015, the CSAT is just a qualifying exam. This means that the marks scored in this exam are not going to matter when a student's merit is being determined. A student's merit will be decided based only on the marks scored in the first paper of General Studies. The student just has to pass the Paper-II (CSAT). The qualifying score for this examination is 33 percent. If you can score 67 marks out of 200, your purpose would be solved.

Students appearing for this paper have been divided in two different groups. One group includes the engineering and management students. For these students, this paper is very easy, since there background has been the same. The other group is of the arts and commerce students and the students from the other fields. It's completely new for them. It's not only new for them, but difficult too. Especially, mathematics and mental ability's questions seem to be too difficult to them. They have to prepare them from the beginning. However, the first group's students don't have to do any extra preparation for this. As far as comprehension is concerned, it is the same for everyone. People who don't find this paper challenging, don't need the information about its preparation. But, there are many students who really need it. This chapter has been written only to guide such students.

Friends, the first thing I would like to say is that you should be free from mental inertia. Whether it's the question of general mental ability, logical skills or analytical skills, or mathematical and statistics, they seem to be very scary and confusing, but, this is till the point you are scared. If you muster courage and decide to fight with them, then they will become your friends.

Anyway, I would like to tell you whether it's the number game or analytical skills or mental ability's puzzles, these are actually exercises for the mind. By practicing these, our mind's ability increases- even our ability to think, ability to decide and our memory too. That's why this will give you double advantage. You can think of this too and try to befriend them.

I know that you haven't been in touch with them for a long time. Since when? Since the day you reached class ninth. But doesn't matter. You just have to believe that the seeds of knowledge are still there in you. Now you don't have to sow the seeds, but just provide them water and warmth. They will sprout. Keeping these things in mind, I am going to give detailed information about the facts, on the basis of which, you should prepare for this paper. A little struggle is required in the beginning. Once, only once. After this you will become an expert in this and will start enjoying it too. That's why I would like to suggest that it would be better for you if you don't look at the unsolved question papers till the time you prepare well for it. Otherwise, it is possible that you may be so scared by it that you may leave it before even giving it a try. So, let's talk about it in detail.

There are six main topics in 'CSAT' syllabus. In this the comprehension is like unseen passage. We will discuss separately about the preparation of general mental ability, logical skills, and basic numeracy. I would like to make it clear here that I'm not preparing you for the paper here, but, I am telling you how to prepare for it.

Logical Skills

This includes neither the numbers nor mathematics' formulas. In this, those questions are asked which help in checking your reasoning ability. To understand how easily you can solve a complex subject. For example-

Panna is older than Yamuna. Sita is older than Chanchal. Rita is not as old as Sita, but she is older than Chanchal. Chanchal is not as old as Yamuna. Who is the youngest? (a) Rita (b) Chanchal (c) Yamuna (D) Sita

Literally, to solve such questions concentration is needed. These questions are easy, but using the words, they are made complex in order to confuse you. This confusion can be removed only by concentrating. Look at the above question. In this, girls' names and their age difference have been given in a complex manner. Now the problem is that how would you solve it?

To solve such questions, you should first understand what has actually been asked in the question. In the above question, 'who is the youngest of all' has been asked. You have been given four names for the same. You should start looking for the answer from the options you have. Here, the first option is Rita. Now, you have to find out if Rita, actually, is the youngest. You should read all the sentences related to her. It is clearly mentioned in the question that Rita is not as old as Sita, but she is older than Yamuna. Hence, it's evident that Rita is not the youngest since she is older than Yamuna. The second option we have is Chanchal. Now you should determine her situation in the question. There are two sentences related to her. First sentence is- Sita is older than Chanchal. This means that Chanchal is younger than Sita. Second sentence is that Chanchal is not as old as Yamuna. So, it's clear here that Chanchal is younger than Yamuna too. Your mind should speculate here that there is a possibility of Chanchal being the youngest. If you are even a little careful, you can give the answer to this question without considering the next two options. You have already cancelled Rita. When you were determining Chanchal's situation, you noticed that:

(i) Sita is older than Chanchal, and

(ii) Yamuna is older than Chanchal.

If you look at the options, Sita's and Yamuna's names have been given in the third and the fourth options. You are already certain that Yamuna and Sita are older than Chanchal. This means that Chanchal is younger than Sita and Yamuna.

You can have a doubt here that who is younger, Rita or Chanchal? It is possible that Chanchal is younger than the (c) and (d) options but older than (a) option. Hence, you can determine this also from within the question. Now you have to find out who is older between Rita and Chanchal. You should look for those sentences in which both these names came together. However, you will not find such a sentence in this question. You will have to determine it in an indiscernible manner. Look for the sentences that are related to Rita. The sentence related to it is: Rita is not as old as Sita, but is older than Yamuna. Hence, Rita is much older than Yamuna. And you have previously proved that Yamuna is older than Chanchal. It would be clear to you that if Rita is older than Yamuna, then, naturally she is older than Chanchal too.

Such questions are of course tough, but they are enjoyable too. You can become capable of solving such questions after some practice. It's important to understand and then do these questions. There are different types of such questions:

(i) Blood relations : Some blood relations are given in such a way that it confuses the reader. Although, the answers are quite simple, but, the way they are given, makes them difficult. For example :

☑ "A lady introduces a person as her mother's brother's son. What is the relationship between this lady and this person?"

It is very simple but it has been said in a complex manner. Mother's brother means uncle. And his son means cousin.

There are two ways of preparing these questions:

☑ Few relationships should be memorized, like, the only daughter of grandmother and grandfather is mother. Mother's daughter means sister, etc.

☑ Second way is to understand the complex relationships in the question patiently, rather than getting nervous. It would be better to do some rough work as the interpersonal relationships will be clear to you. This will help you in finding the answers easily.

(ii) Puzzle : This is also the way of saying a simple thing in a difficult and complex manner. These confuse the person. We have to find a way out from this confusion only. For example :

(a) There are six friends, whose names are: P, Q, R, S, T and U. They are the members of a club. They play football, cricket, tennis, basketball, badminton and volleyball.

(b) T, who is taller than P and S, plays tennis.

(c) The tallest member plays basketball.

(d) The shortest member plays volleyball.

(e) Q and S neither play basketball nor volleyball.

(f) R plays volleyball.

(g) Q, who plays football, is in between T and P, according to his height.

So, who plays basketball?

1. Q
2. R
3. S
4. U

How will you solve this? You will have to do some rough work for this. Make a chart with three columns- club members' names, sports' names and players' height. It will be made like this:

Members	Sports' Names	Height
P		Shorter than T
Q	Football	Shorter than T
R	Volleyball	The shortest
S		Shorter than T
T	Tennis	Shorter than U
U	Basketball	the tallest

On looking at the chart, it is clear that U plays basketball. In the beginning, it will take time, but, with practice, your speed will increase.

(iii) Directions knowledge: The questions which are generally asked are such in which a person walks in a certain direction and after covering some distance, he turned in some other direction, so, where would he be now? For example :

"After walking for 8 kms in the East, a person turned towards North and walked for 6 kilometers. Then, after taking left, he turned towards South-West and walked for 10 kilometers, so how far is he from his current position?

(a) 2 kilometers

(b) 3 kilometers

(c) 0 kilometer

(d) 1 kilometer

It is advisable to solve such questions using line diagrams. You should make a diagram using lines with an estimated length. Like in the above question you draw a line from left to right, which is considered to be 8 kilometers. Its direction is from west to east according to the map. After this, draw a line of 6 kilometers towards North, that is, towards the top. Its length will be little less than the previous line since this one is 2 kilometers less than the previous one. Now draw another line which turns towards the left and then it continues towards the South-West direction. If you now connect these two lines, you will realize that the person has reached the same point from where he started. The line of 10 kilometers will look a little longer than the 8 kilometers one.

General Mental Ability

Logical skills, which has already been discussed previously is somehow related to General mental Ability. I have kept the number related questions under this topic. In this, numbers are given, on the basis of which mental ability is tested.

The main quality of such questions is that they appear to be scattered and pattern less on the face value, however, there is a rule of a fixed pattern that has to be followed. These patterns can be of numerous types. You just have to find the right pattern and then get the answer through that. To be very honest, there is neither a fixed rule nor a formula to solve these types of questions. This can be done only with practice so that you can finish the questions in time.

I am presenting few samples of the numbers which are asked in the Civil service examination:

(i) Numbers' series: In this, a series of numbers is given, from which any one number is missing. You have to find out the missing number. For example :

15, 55, 59, 99, 103, 305, 507,?

(a) 710

(b) 790

(c) 709

(d) 754

Look at its pattern. If you inverse 15, it becomes 51 and if you add 4 to it, then it becomes 55. If you add 4 to 55, then it becomes 59. The same pattern will continue till the end. If you apply the same pattern to 507, then, on inversing it, it will become 705. Now if 4 is added to 705, then the answer will be 709.

However, I would like to tell you that it is not an easy job to detect this pattern. You will have to remain relaxed for this, which can happen only through practice. Mind will understand different kinds of patterns that exist with practice. Then it will start thinking in the similar way.

(ii) Letters series: We read about numbers' series before this. In that a number is missing, whereas, a letter is missing in the letters' series. You have to find that. For example:

Z, U, Q, ? L

(a) I

(b) K

(c) M

(d) N

The easiest way to solve this is to find out the number of letters missing between the two letters. In this, you will observe that there are 4 missing letters between Z and U, and 3 between U and Q. That means the number of missing letters is decreasing. Now you have to find a letter which comes on missing 2 letters and that is N. The next letter in the series is L and you will notice that only one letter is missing in between L and N.

This was a general example. More difficult questions are asked, but, the way of solving them is the same. The letters' pattern has to be found out in such questions too.

(iii) Knowledge of Status: The status or the sequence of people, things or places is given in the questions which are asked under this category. From this, only you have to find the relative status of either one of those. For example :

"Rajesh is at 15th position from the beginning and 13th position from the end in his class. How many students are there in the class?"

(a) 27

(b) 26

(c) 25

(d) 24

These questions are comparatively easier than the numbers' series questions. If your logical skills are strong, you can verbally solve these questions too else, you can use the general mathematical formulas. Like, Rajesh's position is 15th from the beginning. So, there are definitely 15 boys in the class. Now, his position is 13th from the last. That means if we count from the end, there are 12 boys standing in front of Rajesh since he is at 13th position. So, the total number of students in the class would be 15+12=27.

Basic Numeracy

Although the meaning of numeracy is with numbers, but, here we are talking about mathematics. These can be understood as questions related to mathematics. This is not higher level mathematics, but just of the level of eighth class. If you understand the basic principles of mathematics, then, you can easily solve these questions. You, anyway, don't have any other option. You have to do it.

I am going to discuss that part of mathematics here, which will make your preparation easy and focused. This includes those formulas related to which there is a higher possibility of asking the questions. You just need to practice it to be relieved from its tension.

(i) **Simple fractions:** Simple fractions means there is a number at the top and the other one right below it. That means on dividing the number at the top by the number below, the number we get is the right answer. Like, ½ means 1 has been divided into two parts, so, the answer is ½. So, ½ means half, that is, 50 percent.

There is a question: 405 sweets were divided among children in such a way that the sweets obtained by every child were 20% of the total number of the children. So, how many sweets did every child get ?

(a) 15

(b) 45

(c) 9

(d) 18

This question can be answered using only simple fractions. I will not go in detail. You should duly understand this. I am now going to tell you only that fraction, with the help of which the answer to this question can be obtained. The fraction would be: 45*20/100. The problem, here, would be to understand from where we have got 45 and 100. It would be better to understand this through mathematics as only it can give you the ability to solve such questions.

(ii) Simplification: It simply means simplifying the given numbers by using addition, multiplication, subtraction, division etc. By using this, even the most difficult questions can be solved very easily. There is a question :

"A person spends 1/3 of his income on food, 2/5 on his house rent and 1/5 on his clothes. If still he has Rs.400 left, then, how much is his total income?"

In this, "the assumption formulas" of mathematics are used. That means you have to assume that his total income is Rs. x. Then, you have to use the given fractions and go on simplifying them. Finally, you get the answer. It is difficult to get the answer without doing this. By doing mental calculations, you can get the answer, but, it takes time which you don't have.

(iii) Highest common factor and the least common multiple: This is the most important formula of mathematics because it is used to simplify the given numbers and to do their basic calculation. When we apply this formula, it becomes very easy to solve those difficult questions which appear simple but they are actually very confusing. There is one such question:

"There are 4 bells that ring at the following intervals respectively: 10, 12, 15 and 18 seconds. If they are ringing together right away, then after how many seconds will they ring again together? "

(a) 270

(b) 90

(c) 180

(d) 360

In this, you have to find the least common multiple of 10-12-15-18, which is very easy. You can do this and find the answer on your own.

(iv) Average : This is one of the easiest parts of mathematics and it is very useful for practical life too. Its simple meaning is if 2 or more than 2 numbers are added, then, what will be the common factor. There's a simple formula:

Average = sum of numbers ÷ sum of things

For example :

"The average age of 5 members in a family is 21 years.

If the youngest person's age is 5 years, then, at the time of the youngest person's birth, what was the average age of the family? "

(a) 24
(b) 25
(c) 20
(d) 28

It is relatively a complex question for average, but, it's not difficult at all. If you multiply 21 with 5, then, the total current age of the family will become 105 years. Its value would have been 80 years 5 years ago. This number has been obtained by multiplying 5 members and their age of 5 years. Now, you can use your common sense. The members' average age was 80 years 5 years ago. However, keep in mind that there were only 4 members at that time. The 5th member took birth later on. Now you can divide 80 years among 4 members, you will get the answer.

(v) Age related questions: Mental ability generally includes the age related questions. For example:

"The difference in Pankaj and Mudit's age is 16 years. After 6 years, Pankaj's age is thrice Mudit's age, so, how much is their current age?"

(a) 30 and 14 years
(b) 18 and 2 years
(c) 20 and 4 years
(d) 14 and 30 years

Its correct answer can be found using the mathematical formula which you will have to learn. To solve such questions, you should generally, focus on the following three points :

(1) What's their current age

(2) Their age few years ago

(3) Their age after few years

(vi) Percentage: It means on every 100. If we say 40%, then it means 40 out of 100. This is one of the most important parts of mathematics. So much so that even the practical life cannot go on without this. Hence, you should already be aware about this. Questions related to this are generally asked. It is used even in the other types of questions. For example:

"If there is a 20% increase in the price of wheat, then how much consumption should be reduced in a family, that it doesn't affect their total expenditure on wheat?"

(a) 16.33%

(b) 16.37%

(c) 16.89%

(d) 18%

You can solve this using the formula of percentage; else, it will be very difficult to solve it.

(vii) Profit and Loss: In the basic calculation, questions related to profit and loss are also asked in the CSAT exam. This is the most practical topic. If we buy something in our day to day life, then we sell something as well. In this, calculating the profit and loss is our ability. Its basic premise is the same, but the given situations are not that easy. Because of this questions become complex. However, they are still relatively easier. For example:

"On selling an item for Rs.500, there is a profit of 25%. How much should it be sold for to get a loss of 10%?"

(a) Rs.400
(b) Rs.430
(c) Rs.360
(d) Rs.370

There are actually two things to be considered while calculating profit and loss. First, if a thing was bought for more than maximum retail price, then, there will definitely be loss. Second, if it is bought for less than maximum retail price, then, there will be profit. After finding out these two main things, you need to use fractions, percentage etc. The answer can be found using it.

(viii) Ratio and proportion: Its meaning is derived from comparatives. Two or more than two numbers are given and the figure telling about the relation between them is ratio and proportion. For example: the ratio of 10 and 5 is 2:1. There is a similar question:

"The ratio of students of three classes is 2:3:5. If the number of students increases by 20 in these classes, then, the ratio becomes 4:5:7. So, how many students are there in these classes? "

(a) 10
(b) 90
(c) 100
(d) None of the above.

Generally 1 or 2 questions of this kind are given in the paper. You need to practice the formula needed to solve these questions. If you, anyway, get to know the basic mathematics, then, solving such questions is not difficult.

(ix) Work, distance and time: Every year, at least one question is given from this. Under this category, normally, five types of questions are made: (a) work and time (b) distance and time (c) train related (d) boat and stream (e) tap and tank. For example:

"Ram does twice the work than Shyam. Both of them, together, finish a work in 14 days. So, how many days will Ram take to finish the work alone?"

(a) 28 days
(b) 24 days
(c) 21 days
(d) 14 days

Actually, whcther they are questions related to ratio; work, distance and time; or interest and partnership related- these questions can be solved only by "assuming the price". It is very difficult to get an answer without this. That's why you should focus on practicing such questions.

There is an example related to distance and time:

"A person completes half of his journey at the speed of 30 kms/hr and the rest half of the journey at the speed of 20km/ hr, so what is his average speed?"

(a) 25 kilometers
(b) 24 kilometers
(c) 23 kilometers
(d) 22 kilometers

It appears to be a question of average, but, it isn't. You

have to be careful about this. You have to believe that such questions which look simple on the face value are actually not that simple.

(x) Train related questions: This is the popular question of CSAT. One such question is given as an example :

"A train crosses a pole in 15 seconds and a 100 meter long platform in 25 seconds, then, what is the length of the train?"

(a) 125 meter

(b) 200 meter

(c) 220 meter

(d) 290 meter

(xi) Boat and stream: Although such questions are rarely asked, but, it is better to be aware of them. This category's questions are anyhow solved using similar formulas. For example:

"A sailor travelling at the speed of 18 kms/hr reaches in 4 hrs in the direction of the stream. He takes 12 hours to return in the opposite direction of the stream. What is the speed of the stream? "

(a) 6.5 kilometers

(b) 4.25 kilometers

(c) 2 kilometers

(d) 1.5 kilometers

In the similar way, the questions related to tap and pipe are asked. For example:

"Two pipes can fill the tank in 10 and 12 minutes respectively. The third pipe can empty it in 20 hours. So, how much time will the three pipes take to fill it together? "

(a) 9.30 hours
(b) 9 hours
(c) 8 hours
(d) 7.30 hours

(xii) Simple and compound interest: A question is usually asked about this. If you have a bank account, then, you would have some knowledge of it. Simple and compound interest have their own formulas, after knowing which, you get the courage to solve even the most difficult questions.

An example for simple interest :

"If Rs.848 has to be returned in 4 years, then, how much money should be paid every year, if the simple interest rate is 4%?"

(a) Rs.232
(b) Rs.218
(c) Rs.200
(d) Rs.195

Compound interest means an addition of the interest amount into the total amount of money after a certain time period. Hence, the compound interest rate increases a lot. Generally, simple interest questions are asked, but, since it is also a part of interest, it is better to have some knowledge about it. There is a question:

"An amount of money doubles in 4 years because of compound interest. In how many years, will it be 8 times?"

(a) 8 years (b) 12 years (c) 16 years (d) 24 years

(xiii) Mixture and partnership: When two or more than two things are mixed in a decided ratio, then it is called a mixture. We do get questions from this. An example is given below:

"A milk seller claims to be selling the milk at the value he bought it. Even then, he earns a profit of 20%, so, in every 3 liters mixture of water and milk, how much water does he mix?"

(a) 400 ml
(b) 500ml
(c) 600ml
(d) 800 ml

After knowing the formula, you can very easily solve it as it is very simple.

When few people work together, then, it is called partnership. It is generally used in the context of business. Questions are asked from this as well. An example is given:

"Kamal, Yogesh and Sachin started their own business by contributing Rs. 10000, 14000, and 12000 respectively. After a year, they earned a profit of Rs.5400. If the profit has to be divided among them according to the ratio of their invested amounts, then how much money will Yogesh get?"

(a) Rs.1500
(b) Rs.1800
(c) Rs.2100
(d) Rs.150

This is also not a difficult question. Difficult questions are generally not asked in civil services exam. You just need to practice, that's it.

(xiv) Trick questions: To check your mental and logical ability, sometimes such questions are given which cannot be solved using mathematical formulas. Actually, there exist some tricks which you need to remember. On doing this, the questions which seem to be difficult and complex, can be easily solved. These questions mainly include calendar's date and clock's time. For example:

"What was the day on 28th March, 1900?"

This question cannot be solved without a trick. There is another similar question:

"Tell a time between 4 and 5 o'clock, when both the hands of the clock are 4 minutes away?"

As far as the questions related to time are concerned, some help can be taken from mathematics. But, it is not true for the calendar related questions. If you practice a little more, you can become expert in the calendar related questions, so much so, that the other person will be shocked.

Geometrical Figures

In CSAT's paper, questions related to geometrical figures are also asked under the heading of basic mathematics. Geometrical figures mean quadrilateral, triangle, line, circle, angles etc. In the unsolved papers, you will find line related figures. To solve such questions, there is the need to do definitive study. It is majorly a question related to geometry and most of the students are scared of it. If you can be patient for a while, you will realize it is not that difficult. However, it is so important that you should take somebody's help. If you try doing this on your own, then, you will definitely get tensed and will leave it thinking it is tough. If you want to be an IAS, then you have to face it.

You have to study mainly four geometrical figures in this:

triangle, quadrilateral, angles and circle.

You are given pictures related to these and are asked to either the number of figures, the type of angles or such type of questions. You have definitive formulas for these too, just like mathematics. You just need to understand these. Then you can easily solve these questions.

Interpretation of data

It has been noticed that in CSAT's paper, few questions related to interpretation of data are asked every year. This was, anyway, a part of the second question paper of General knowledge in the mains test before 2011. In a way the same has been used in CSAT. In these questions, data is generally presented either as tables, bars, circle diagrams, or line diagrams. After that some questions are asked on the basis of that diagram or the table. The answers of these questions are based on the analysis of the data presented as the table or the diagram. Generally, 3-4 questions are asked from one table. That means if you read and understand a table properly, you can very easily answer 3-4 questions at once. I would like to clarify this using the following table.

The consumption of goods (in tonnes) in different cities of India in a year is as follows:

Grains

City	Wheat	Rice	Maize	Millet	Jowar
Mumbai	750	700	550	340	480
Kolkata	650	750	480	260	240
Delhi	700	820	640	120	150
Jaipur	350	720	650	300	270
Chennai	250	850	300	210	150
Bangalore	430	850	280	160	120

Q1. What's the ratio of the consumption of millet and wheat by the people of Kolkata?

(a) 1:4
(b) 2:3
(c) 3:5
(d) 2:5

Q2. Which grain's consumption is the least in all the cities?

(a) Millet
(b) Ricc
(c) Jowar
(d) Maize

Q3. What's the average consumption of maize in all the cities (in tonnes)?

(a) 390
(b) 483
(c) 495
(d) 500

Q4. In which city is the lowest consumption of rice?

(a) Jaipur
(b) Kolkata

(c) Mumbai

(d) Delhi

The way the data has been mentioned here as a table, in the same way, it is mentioned in different ways. Hence, you should practice the other ways too. The different types are (1) circle diagram (2) line diagram (3) bar.

To analyze such numbers and figures, practice is required.

I have given a detailed syllabus of questions related to mental ability and mathematics which are related to the preparation of CSAT. I have also stated how to prepare for this. I believe that it will really help in your preparation and your mind will also be cleared.

I would, now, like to tell you about the other two important parts of the CSAT paper. These two parts are: comprehension and decision.

Comprehension

What does this mean? This just means how intelligently you can understand and assimilate the given passage. Here, we have called it 'comprehension'; it is also called as 'unseen passage'. That means it is a piece of composition in prose which has a possibility of not having been read before by you. This is deliberately done because if you have read it before, then, you would be able to answer the questions very easily.

If you generally say to someone that 3 questions are asked based on a passage of 300 words, then, the other person would reply: 'what's the big deal in it? This is very simple'. Maybe, before looking at the unsolved papers, you used to say the same. But, not anymore.

Actually, if it was that easy, then there would be no purpose of giving it in the paper. Other questions could be asked instead of this one. You would be surprised to know that around one-third of the questions asked in CSAT paper are of comprehension. Just imagine 30% of the questions from single topic. I think this should be enough for you to get an idea of the seriousness and the difficulty level of this.

(A) Challenges in comprehension

This topic which seems to be easy is definitely not easy at all. This creates a lot of challenges at the psychological level for the candidate. It would be better to know the challenges here:

(i) The first challenge is related to language- if you are from a Hindi medium background. It is not a problem for those from English background. It is a problem for Hindi students because the given passage is not a Hindi one rather it is translated from English. Hence, the language becomes difficult unnecessarily. You come across words you may be reading for the first time. This is definitely an unfortunate situation. But, till the time this situation is not changed, you have to face this challenge.

(ii) The second challenge is to keep your mind calm. The passages which are given are generally related to general knowledge. You read and understand the passage. When the time comes to answer the questions, it is then, that you face difficulty. The challenge is to protect your mind from being intruded by general knowledge facts. The questions are easy and that's why on reading them, answers start flashing in your mind- automatically, even before you look for them in the passage. Here, you have to be careful since the answers being flashed in your mind are the general knowledge's answers, but, not the passage's answers. And you will get the marks for passage's answers only.

The options that are given to confuse you include the one which is similar to the general knowledge's answer. Hence, if you are not careful at this time, you can be deceived.

(iii) The third challenge is to remain focused. While reading the passage, you should not only be focused on reading it, but, also on the facts in it. Even if it is for a short period, you should keep the facts in your mind. You should keep this in mind that if facts are misunderstood, then, the answers will be wrong too.

You should stop thinking about other things while reading the passage. You should be tensed neither about the time nor about the length of the passage and the type of questions which have been asked. You should concentrate on reading the passage and remembering the facts.

(iv) The next challenge is related to how fast your mind works. The challenge is how fast can you read and understand the passage and then answer the questions that have been asked. This is definitely not an easy task. If you are given enough time, you can very easily answer all the questions. However, to complete the questions in the given time, you have to think and understand faster, and this can happen only with practice.

(B) The art of reading a passage

After mentioning the problems above, I am going to talk about the method of reading a passage which will help you in overcoming them. According to me, all these problems are related to the way you read the passage. I have tested this on myself and also on my students. I am mentioning below the results of these tests:

- ☑ I have tested both the methods of reading the passage. In the first method, you read the passage and then you read the questions. The second is the one, where, you first read the questions and then the passage. The results of the second method have turned out to be much better.

The benefit of reading the questions first is that while reading the passage, you closely observe the points related to the information which is asked in the question. You read those parts with much more concentration which helps you in getting accurate answers. Hence, you should read the questions first. Moreover, it is important to note here that you read only the questions and not the options. I am saying this with only the time constraint in mind. If you don't have time problem in the paper or if your reading speed is fast, then, you can read the options too.

- ☑ You should read the given passage twice. You should neither read it once nor thrice because by reading it only once, you will not get answers, and by reading it thrice, you will spend more time on it. Hence, reading twice is the appropriate number.

- ☑ While reading it the second time, you should underline the words or the points which are related to the answers. It would be better if you do it while reading it for the first time itself. By this you will get to know where your answer is and you will get an accurate answer by focusing on that point only.
- ☑ The intent of the whole passage is also asked sometimes. You should, hence, read it in such a way that you understand the gist of the passage. That means you understand what the passage is related to.

I would like to state a fact here that it is not the complete paragraph or prose, but, it is just a passage from it. That means a whole article was written, only a part of which is given to you. It is quite possible that the subject matter of the article was completely different and when you try to fit this passage in the actual article, then, it may not even fit. However, you shouldn't be bothered by it. You should only bother about the text that has been given to you. You should focus only on this and not the main article. For instance, an article can be about pollution, but, the passage can be about noise pollution. So, now, you will choose the word 'noise pollution' for the given passage and not 'pollution'.

You need to practice this and many books are available to practice unseen passages. You should read them in a scientific way, the way I have told you. You may find an answer in an unorganized way as well, but then your mind will not be able to develop a systematic approach towards it which is needed in the exam when you feel the pressure of time shortage. Hence, it's in your own interest if you keep your mind organized, so that, in the examination hall, it works scientifically, and can help you in scoring more. It is easy to score highest in the comprehension questions.

Decision making and problem solving

The most important role, in our lives, is played by the decisions we take. We are here today because of the decisions we had taken in the past, and 'where will we be tomorrow' would be decided by the decisions we take now. We are actually the product of our decisions. Every deed of ours -no matter how insignificant it is- comes into existence only after we have decided to make it happen. That means every action of ours follows the decisions we take. Our life will be based completely on our decisions.

Why are you reading this book? If you say that this is a good book, then, don't you think everybody should read a good book? Actually, your answer is not accurate. You are reading this book, not because, it is a good book, but, because you have decided to become an IAS. Others are not reading it because they have not taken this decision. This doesn't mean that other people aren't reading anything. They are reading those books about which they have taken a decision.

I feel that now you would have understood the reason for including decision making and problem solving as a part of the CSAT exam. Maybe, you are thinking that both of these are different, but, they are not, they are the same. You have to take a decision to solve any problem. No action can be taken without decision making and without taking an action, a problem can't be solved. It is only with your decision that a problem can either be solved, or increased, reduced or it will remain the same. As an administrator, you will face a lot of problems and to solve them, you will have to take a decision.

The scale to measure an administrator's success is only by looking at the kind of problems he had solved and the decisions he had taken. The decision becomes a policy here. Decision sometimes becomes a rule in itself too. Are the decisions taken by the Supreme and the High court not called laws? That is why decision related questions have been included in the CSAT paper, which is the right thing to do.

If you look at decision related questions given in the unsolved papers, you will face some difficulties. These difficulties would be like: the problem which has been given is complex. It is not easy; however, it is not that difficult that you cannot even understand it. As soon as you read the problem, you will be capable of thinking of at least one solution. It means your brain has taken a decision regarding it. This decision can be made on any basis- your habits, religion, policy, compassion, humanity, or traditional thinking.

When you read the options, you will be confused. There will be two types of confusion. One, that after looking at the other options, you will doubt your own decision. And second will be related to choice. You will be in great dilemma that if you choose one answer, then, this will be the loss. Or if you choose another one, then there will be a different kind of loss, hence, what should be done in such a situation? I am going to tell you a solid solution in brief, and after reading it, you should decide as to what extent it will help you.

The formulas for decision

The way a passage is given in the comprehension question, a problem is given in the decision related question. Whenever you read a problem, you should derive two facts:

- ☑ First is that you should understand the way you have been asked to solve the problem. You should find your status. Since a problem can be solved in different ways, it all depends on the person's identity. A robbery's solution will be given in a different way by the police and in a different way by the public. An old man will come up with a different solution, whereas, a judge will talk about a strict law. Hence, it is very important to find out your own identity regarding that particular problem.
- ☑ Then, you should find out the kind of solution which is expected for the problem. There can be many solutions for one problem. However, it is only the problem that will decide the best solution. For example, the solutions can be as follows:

  I. Constitutional provisions
  II. Administrative rules
  III. Sense of responsibility
  IV. Foresight
  V. Courage
  VI. Humanity etc.

If the problem is related to political system, then constitutional provisions will be used to solve it. If it is linked to government related work, then administrative rules will be used. If it is related to the society, then, you will have to see by which decision most people will benefit even if few people have to bear the loss. If it is related to the person's honesty and integrity, then, no compromise should be done.

Using these two facts, you can solve such questions very easily. Bring this into practice and you will know the truth behind my words.

Friends, I have told you about the preparation of CSAT in detail. I don't think, in the context of this book, anything more can be added in it. Although I believe that it is not hard to score 33% marks in any MCQ paper. What do you say?

Chapter 13

Preliminary Exam : How to solve the question paper

There are two papers in the preliminary examination of civil services. First is general knowledge and second is CSAT. Both the papers are for 200 marks each. Hence, the target for you is of 400 points, for which you continuously practice hard. For this you not only need to practice hard, but, you also need to have a scientific method of reading and answering. You should keep in mind that for success in competitive examinations, only hard work and courage are not required but a scientific way of working hard and tricks are also needed.

This is a scientific fact that water boils at 100 degrees Celsius. If I ask you if the water can boil at 99.9 degrees Celsius, then, of course, your answer will be "no". That means we need an extra 0.1 degrees for water to boil. That means, even if the temperature is a little less than the required one, water will not boil.

My dear friend, the scientific principle of getting success in competitive exams is same as the scientific principle of boiling water. The difference between the students who prepare well and the students who prepare hard without knowing how to prepare well is only of 100 and 99.9 degrees. Or you can say that the difference between success and failure in this exam is only of 100 and 99.9 degrees. But this small difference becomes a big one in life.

I am going to tell you the method of solving the preliminary exam question paper, to help you eliminate the difference between 100 and 99.9 degrees. I would like you to believe that this method is almost the same one with which I got success. And then, after speaking to other participants who got success, I have come up with the best way. I would like to state here that if you follow this method the way, you can very easily remove the difference of the temperature without extra hard work. So, I would like to start now.

As soon as you get the question paper and think of marking the right options of the questions, your mental status would be either of the following:

i. You are aware of the right answer. In such a situation, you will straightaway tick the right answer.

ii. Maybe, you had read about it before, but, after looking at the options, you are confused between, either two options or 3-4 options.

iii. Maybe, you don't know anything about the question.

I am going to tell you a technique keeping the above scenarios in mind. The students who have used this have been benefited. This technique does not ask for more hard work or efficiency from you, if you use the already existing hard work and efficiency in a more organized way, then, you will definitely see an increase in your score.

In the preliminary exam, you are given about 2 hours for each paper i.e. 120 minutes each to answer 100 and 80 questions respectively.

Basically, about 1 minute is given to answer a question, which means 100 questions have to be answered in 120 minutes. The technique being told here is based on the knowledge which you already have, and in spite of this, you can increase your score by at least 5-7 percent very easily by just following these instructions:

- ☑ There are some students who want to read the entire paper at once as soon as they get it. Whereas, there are some, who don't read the entire question paper, but, they read few questions in between to have an idea of the kind of question paper it is. Basically, both these ways are wrong. What do you get by doing this? Nothing, except that you get to know if the paper is easy or difficult. If the paper would be easy, then, you may tick wrong answers in excitement. If not, then you may answer incorrectly because of the tension. In both the situations you will have to bear a loss since your mental status will change. Moreover, you will also waste few minutes of your valuable time. Hence, you should remember that reading the entire question paper as soon as you get it is a psychological problem and not a necessity to get success.
- ☑ Rather than doing what has been mentioned above, you should immediately start answering the questions. You shouldn't answer all the questions at once; you should do that in four phases.

a. **First phase :** As soon as you get the question paper, you should start answering the questions. In the first phase, you answer only those questions after reading which you immediately get the answer or after reading its options you know which one to select, without any doubt. If you can answer immediately upon reading the question, then, that means that you have complete knowledge about that topic. It is difficult to find an answer sometimes, but, you can choose the right answer as soon as you read the given options. This is a psychological problem. You must have experienced that sometimes you forget the other person's name, but, as soon as he tells his name you remember it. Meaning that you don't have further doubts that this may not be his name. Hence, you should only attempt those questions in the first phase whose answers you are sure of.

It is natural that since you are sure of the answers to these questions, you will take hardly 50 minutes to read all the 100 questions. You can try this. Now suppose, you have the following figures:

Total questions	:	100
Solved questions	:	40
Questions left	:	60
Total time	:	120 minutes
Time taken	:	50 minutes
Time left	:	70 minutes

You have solved 40 questions, which we are considering will be correct as you have attempted only those questions which you are completely sure of.

(b) **Second phase :** While doing the first phase's questions, you should make a small dot in front of the questions which you have already answered. This is to save time while attempting the second phase's questions as you will not have to read all the questions once again. You should note here that the dot should be very small and light and should be made in front of the order of the question and not the options. This will help you in identifying which questions still have to be answered.

You should start reading rest of the questions from the beginning in this phase. Now, you need to answer only those questions in which you were confused between only two options. Suppose in the question of availability of more black soil, you are confused between Maharashtra and Madhya Pradesh, but you are sure that it is not found in Karnataka and Tamil Nadu. You are confused here because you must have read or heard from somewhere that cotton is cultivated in Maharashtra. At the same time you must have heard or read that in Madhya Pradesh's black soil, there is very good gram cultivation. That is why it has become difficult for you to choose the right answer. You have to solve such questions in the second phase in which you are confused between two options.

In such questions, you should think patiently and shouldn't get nervous. You will notice that you will be able to find the correct answer of most of the questions, but, not all. You have to keep in mind that you mustn't answer those questions in which you are confused in three options.

Now the calculations will be like this.

Now suppose, that out of 60 questions, around 25

questions were such in which you were confused in two options. Since the confusion was between only 2 choices, hence, according to the "probability theory", about 50% of the questions should be correct. However, this will not be the same case here, as here you have thought and answered and not just guessed. Since you have tried to answer these questions after a deep thought, hence, you should consider at least 15 questions correct out of the total 25 questions. Now the calculations will be :

Total right answers: 40 (first phase) + 15 (second phase) = 55

Questions to be answered: 45

Total time taken: 50 (first phase) + 30 (second phase) = 80 minutes

Time left: 40 minutes

(c) **Third phase :** The questions which you answer in the second phase should also be marked so that you don't read the same questions again. The benefit of this would be that you will get extra time to think on the other questions. You took 50 minutes to answer 100 questions in the first phase, whereas, in the second one, you took about 40 minutes to read 60 questions. Now you have only 30 minutes to read 45 questions.

In the third phase, you have to answer those questions in which you are confused between 3 options. There would hardly be any question in which you will be confused in all the 4 options. If there is any such question, then, you should cut it as per the elimination system. Elimination system is the one in which you don't find the right answer, but, you find which cannot be the right answer. For example, if you think about Tamil Nadu, then, black soil cannot be found there as it is near to the sea. The coastal regions have different climate and soil. This way you can at least cut off one option as per the elimination system. In the third phase, you have to find the option which cannot be the right answer.

The number of options will reduce with this method. You should try to think about these options, which will finally lead you to the right answer. First effort should be made to reduce the number of options from 4 to 2. When you are left with only 2 options, then, you should think about them. If you are sure of the right answer, then, you should tick it. If you can't reduce three options to two, then, you should leave that for the fourth phase.

This way, you can at least answer 10 questions. Hence, the calculations will be :

Total correct questions : 40 (first phase) +15 (second phase) +10 (third phase) =65

Total time taken : 50 (first phase) + 30 (second phase) +30 (third phase) = 110 minutes

Time left: 10 minutes

Questions left : 35

(d) **Fourth phase :** This phase is totally dependent on luck. In this phase, only those questions are left which are either completely new for you or for which you have 3-4 options in your mind. Now you should see how much time you are left with. If you have enough time, then, you shouldn't leave hope. You should think of utilizing every second. You should try to find the possible solution to all the 35 questions. If you don't have enough time, it is better to leave them unanswered than making wild guesses.

Union Public Service Commission has made the evaluation of the preliminary exams negative in 2007. According to this rule, if an answer is incorrect, then 33% of the total marks would be deducted for that question. For example, general knowledge's question is of 200 marks, but, only 100 questions are asked. That means every question is of 2 marks. If you answer a question incorrectly, then, 1/3rd marks would be deducted from the total marks. The same way if you answer 3 questions incorrectly, then two marks would be deducted from the total score.

Looking at this situation, it is advisable to leave such a question in which you are confused in all the four options. You can still take a risk and answer those questions in which you are confused in three options. For example, if you answer 4 questions in which you were confused in three options, then, the chances of having a correct answer would be 1/3rd according to 'probability theory'. That means 1 question can be correct out of 3. Suppose you answered 4 such questions, and only 1 is correct out of that. So, you get 2 marks on getting the correct answer and 2 will be deducted for the wrong answers. This way, the account is the same. That means, at least you didn't suffer a loss.

In another situation, it is possible that 2 are right and 2 are incorrect. In this way, you can score more than one and a half marks. That is why I said that you can answer till the 3 options' questions, and not more than that.

It is obvious that you should solve the 2 options' questions as there the chances of scoring more are 50%, whereas, the chances of losing marks is only 33%.

I would like to say one more thing at the end. Before trying the method that I have told you in the examination hall, it would be better, if you try it beforehand. If this helps you it is only then that you should use it in the examination hall, else, we can find another method for you.

Chapter 14

The Biggest Preparation : The Mains Exam

After reading the previous chapters, if I have succeeded in making you believe that the mains exam is the true exam of IAS, then, I would consider that my hard work has paid off. This is the exam which actually helps you to become an IAS. The major part of the marks, 1750 out of total 2025, depends on this paper, making this paper very important.

What is mains exam?

Before I tell you about this exam, let's first see what UPSC wants from you. The Commission's purpose of this exam is not to check how much the student knows or how strong his memory is. The actual purpose is to evaluate his complete scholarship and the depth of his understanding.

Therefore, we should prepare for the mains exam only keeping this in mind. Even the subjects which UPSC has shortlisted for the mains exam, their syllabus, the papers which are made on the basis of the syllabus, and the evaluation procedure, everything has been made keeping in mind the evaluation of the candidate's complete scholarship and the depth of understanding. Hence, it is clear that neither the abundance of knowledge nor the magic of photographic memory will be useful.

Having taken all these things into account we are now able to draw an outline for the basic nature of mains exam at present. Let us have a look:

(i) Explanatory

The preliminary exam is about objective system, whereas, the mains exam is about subjective system. In this the answers are not provided to you. Questions are given here and you are expected to answer them, which means you will write either what you have studied or what you have thought about. So, your ability of expression will also be checked here that how clearly and convincingly you can put forward your thoughts.

(ii) Practical

You should look at the unsolved papers of general knowledge and of the optional subjects too- if your practice was limited to only the books and notes, then, you would feel that 'nothing has been asked from it'. You will declare that it is 'out of syllabus'. What does this announcement mean?

The clear meaning of this is that 60-70% of the questions are related to the practical side of the subject. These questions are not lifted directly from the books; rather, these are the questions that are based on the subject matter in the book and address the issues of today's time and society. Hence, it is checked if you can convert the theories given in the book into practical knowledge.

So, it is clear that the exam cannot be qualified only by studying books, memorizing the facts and writing them as it is in the exam. This was okay for universities' exams, but success in IAS's mains exam can only be achieved by studying, understanding, thinking and then applying the acquired wisdom in the real life.

(iii) Original ideas

You only read the writer's views in the book based on any topic. The same way the incidents and the views in the newspapers and magazines are that of the journalists. The challenge is how you form your own opinion from this. Your original ideas will help you score better than other candidates in the mains exam. That is why you will see instructions like, 'what do you understand of this?', 'interpret it', etc. with the questions. These instructions indicate that there is an opportunity to include your own opinion in the answers. If you neglect these instructions then you are also neglecting your success.

(iv) Relatively small answers

There is a word limit of 150-250 words in questions related to general knowledge. In the optional papers, a few questions have approximately the same word limit and some do not have a specified word limit. However, the questions which do not impose word limit, it is expected that you should not write more than 800 - 900 words. What is the purpose of this?

There are two purposes. First is to prevent you from over-writing (or I should say, from writing irrelevant things). It is just not allowed here. The second is to see how well you can write important things using minimum words.

I think these are the necessities (four points given above) of the mains exam and these should be kept in mind while preparing.

Parts of mains exam

I will be discussing about the preparation of mandatory Hindi, mandatory English and the essay papers in the forhcoming chapters. That is why these will not be discussed in this chapter. In this chapter, only the remaining papers of the mains exam will be discussed, which include: 4 question papers of general knowledge and 2 papers of optional subject. I have divided these 6 papers in 3 parts. These three parts are: (i) 3 papers of general knowledge (ii) a single paper of ethics, integrity and aptitude, and (iii) 2 papers of optional subject.

Now, I am going to discuss these three parts in a way which will give you a focused and planned idea to prepare for this. So, first we are going to talk about general studies and the papers related to it.

(i) General studies

Once again I am insisting you first read the unsolved papers. They will give you the following instructions:

- ☑ All the questions of general studies are mandatory. There is no choice, not even, between two questions.
- ☑ This is a good thing. You should not be tensed as it is not just for you. This is for all the people who are your competitors. If there is a question that cannot be answered by you, in the same way, there will be a question which the others may not be

able to answer. Hence, there is no reason to be scared.

- ☑ However, it is important that you do not leave any topic of the syllabus completely while preparing. You have to read everything. Yes, you are free to choose which topics you want to give special attention and which to study in a general way.
- ☑ All the questions have a word limit of 150-250 words. That means you are not asked to write much. Then what are you asked to do? UPSC has very clearly mentioned that "Contents of the answer are more important than its length". Then how should it be prepared?
- ☑ Your strategy should be to read more topics rather than reading only one topic in detail. Read only the important points in each topic.
- ☑ Most questions under this heading are related to contemporary issues and trends. Studying the books is like a beacon which shows the path ahead. The light cannot make you walk, but, can only show you the way. So, how can this be dealt with?

It is not difficult to deal with them. Newspapers, magazines and news on radio & Doordarshan can be of great help. I have written a separate chapter 'how to deal with newspapers', keeping this in mind. You can fulfill the commission's needs by adopting this.

(ii) Ethics, integrity and Aptitude

This is a new addition to the civil services examination

and it is very challenging, important and enjoyable. You should look at the unsolved papers. In the unsolved papers, you will clearly see two sets of questions. One set is related to the theoretical part and the second is related to practical part (case studies). The ratio of marks is 130:120. But this is not a problem provided you know how to use any knowledge practically.

All the questions are important in this section too. Once again, you have no choice but to read everything. Theoretical part is also important. A good number of questions are asked from it which has to be answered in about 150 words. An effort, by UPSC, to cover most of the syllabus can clearly be seen here.

Now the question is which strategy should be undertaken to prepare for these two sets? Your strategy should be to first understand the theoretical set. If you don't understand the theoretical set then you cannot provide in-depth answers to the questions in the practical set.

I would like to clarify here that by practical set I am not talking of pure practical knowledge. You have to keep the section of practical knowledge with the theoretical knowledge. The solutions you suggest must be supported by the principles. Only then your answer will be convincing. Hence, you should not take these questions as pure 'common sense' questions. Your common sense should be complemented by knowledge about that topic.

Section B of the paper requires preparation based on case studies. To prepare for section B, you should read as much case studies as possible; because the more case studies you read the better you will be at finding new solutions. You also need to understand and analyze the recent incidents. Case studies should not be limited to bookish knowledge only. If you identify a problem in your society, try to solve it practically. You will realize that there are many problems which you will face and also that many people will give their own arguments. This will be a 'vibrant practice'.

(iii) Optional subject

The optional subjects that I am referring to here are related to Humanities. I am not too sure if it can be applied to other subjects like science or not. You should understand this if you are Science or Commerce students.

I would like to re-emphasize the importance of going through unsolved papers. The Commission has changed the way of asking questions now. Now they don't ask questions that can be answered straight from the book. Since Arts subjects are focused on the society, these subjects are naturally contemporary and necessary. This is the only part that makes the subject of Humanities in civil services exam a little challenging. But, this is a good part because only with this, correct evaluation can be done. Otherwise anyone can qualify this paper.

I am going to mention a few important things here that are not very different from the ones above. It is very important for you to not to solely concentrate on book's knowledge, but focus on the contemporary issues as well. Whenever, any important incident happens, you should analyze it according to your subject and then you should have a stand on the same. This can also be called your subject's lab. You should be very observant while preparing for the optional paper. You cannot afford to ignore things around you. You should think and even have a group discussion on the topic you have read. You will have a deep understanding of the topic with this. It is only then that you will be capable of using the topic practically.

Some important tips for the mains exam

I get a lot of questions mainly about the mains exam through phone or email. Keeping in mind all those things, I am going to give you a few instructions. These instructions are also based on my experience and on other students' as well as examiners' experience. These are few facts, with the help of which, students can get more success. They are mentioned below:

(i) After clearing the preliminary exam, students become very sensitive to the mains exam. That is why they think that they should have more and more content and should read more and more books for the same.

This thought is actually incorrect. Students should not focus on having more content. If they have a good book by a good author on the topic, then, they should not be worried about reading more authors. You should know that the important information given in various books is not different. However, there is definitely a difference in the way of presentation and explanation. If you try to read more books, more notes, you will end up having a scattered mind. You will find yourself lacking the required clarity and solidness of thoughts. You will not be able to focus on the main points about the topic.

Hence, you need to have a book by a good author and

prepare on the basis of that only. You can read the books by other authors too, but don't let them confuse you. If you come across some new information while reading them jot it down in your main book.

(ii) It has also been seen that students try to acquire expertise on every topic. Actually, this is not right. First, your syllabus is vast and it is impossible to acquire expertise on every topic, and even if you succeed in doing that, then, there is no need. The only thing expected from you is sufficient knowledge about the topics. However, when you try to become an expert, then, it creates a problem as you don't understand what to write and what to leave. Moreover, if a word limit is given, then, it will be a bigger problem for you.

Hence, you shouldn't try to become an expert; rather you should have sufficient knowledge of the same. The opinions of different scholars should be known. You should also have critical knowledge for the same. It is not evaluated in the mains exam that how much knowledge you have, but, if you are capable of explaining it well or not.

(iii) If you like to read books other than your syllabus, then, you should not stop doing that. This knowledge can be useful, not only in the elementary exam, but, also in the mains. However, it should not become the only basis of your exam. You shouldn't think that reading more books can help you in scoring more marks.

(iv) You should read every subject's syllabus carefully and according to it, you should get books and the other content. If you get to know that for a particular point, a particular book is good then you should get a photocopy for the same. It is quite possible that a particular topic is well explained in a book, but that doesn't mean the other topics are well explained too.

After you have gathered enough study material, you should start studying from them in accordance with the syllabus. The preparation for any subject should be started from the beginning and not from the middle. This way you will acquire a systematic knowledge of the subject. This way it will be easier for you to understand the subject thoroughly and you will not get confused midway.

(v) There are some subjects which need regular updating. Economics, public administration and political science are a few of them. You should have the latest knowledge related to these subjects all the time. As soon as something important happens related to these subjects, you should write it down (in an analytical manner) in your notebook. This creates a very positive effect on the examiner.

Listen to audio lectures on www.afeias.com

I have started a new website since March 2014, keeping in mind the current challenges of the civil services exam. The website is www.afeias.com and features 20-minutes daily lectures by me. It also includes a lecture on life management. These lectures became quite popular quickly and not just in the country but also among Indian students living in nations such as England and US who are preparing for the exam. You can include these lectures in your preparation. Mobile app by the name of AFE IAS is also available for IOS and Android version.

The audio guidance will provide you with -

- ☑ Daily 5-6 minutes of motivation. This will help you keep your energy levels high as well as live your life happily. This part is very important for your personality development (interview), essay-writing and analytical ability.
- ☑ There is a 12–13 minute lecture based on current affairs.
- ☑ It features daily articles and editorials (properly underlined) from 10 main newspapers in the country which a civil service aspirant must read. This will help you understand two things -
  - (a) Which topics to read
  - (b) What points to focus on in a particular topic
- ☑ A review of the above articles is also provided.
- ☑ Important articles from Yojna and Kurukshetra (English and Hindi) magazines are provided.
- ☑ You can hear radio news bulletins that go on air at 8.45 and 9 pm in the night. An analysis of news items that are important for civil services preparation is also available.
- ☑ The website is interactive and answers queries of students and addresses their problems via email.
- ☑ You can also learn the technique of preparing for the exam and writing good answers. All important information and instructions are issued as and when required.

I believe this daily audio guidance will be very helpful to

candidates preparing for competitive exams and even to students in general.

Make notes

There are many books and readymade notes available in the market these days. However, it is advisable to make your own notes. Yes, you can take help from those readymade things but you shouldn't be dependent solely on them. This is because a different answer is always appreciated, as most students generally write the answers based on the same books and notes due to which their answers are similar. If the examiner gets to read a different answer amidst the same answers, he definitely gets impressed. This will happen only when you make your own notes.

Your notes should be of two types :

☑ Detailed notes

☑ Point wise notes

In the detailed notes, all the information should be mentioned in the notes to fully understand the topic. This will include the critical review as well. These are the notes which you will read from time to time. You should even keep them updated. You should leave a page after every topic to add extra information when you get it.

Point wise notes are related to the points of a topic. Suppose you are making detailed notes on economic liberalization. This will include the following details:

☑ In which situation did it start?

☑ What are its main qualities?

☑ What is its profit?

- ☑ Its disadvantages
- ☑ What progress has been made in it, and
- ☑ How has it affected the Indian economic system?

But you should write these details as precisely as possible while making point wise notes. If your detailed notes are for 3 pages, then, these should only fill one-fourth of a page.

You should also make sure that important facts should be mentioned in the point wise notes. For example, important latest figures, a prominent economist's views, a major report information etc. Exceptions should also be included in these.

Point wise notes are most important at the time of exams. At this time, the whole course can be revised in few hours only using the point wise notes. Every student makes detailed notes. If it took you 5 hours to make detailed notes, it will hardly take 15 minutes to make the point wise notes. But, these 15 minutes will ensure your success.

It is expected from you that the notes be made 1 year prior to the examination. You should remember that:

- ☑ You should not wait for the preliminary exam's result; you should start preparing for the mains.
- ☑ You should keep reviewing the prepared notes even during the preliminary exam.
- ☑ The general knowledge's notes should be kept updated. Keep including the latest happenings till you clear the exam.

Should you make notes for the whole syllabus ?

This is one such question for which most of the students are excited. Following are the results based on the experience:

- ☑ 75% of the course should be well prepared. Hence, the notes will be made.
- ☑ The rest 25% of the course can be casually prepared, even without the notes. It can be read directly from the book.

Now the question is that what part of the syllabus should be prepared with notes and what part should be done without them?

For this, you should take help of the questions which have been asked before. You should try to know the following from the unsolved papers:

- ☑ Questions have been asked from which topic every year?
- ☑ Topics from which questions have been asked occasionally?
- ☑ Topics from which no questions have ever been asked?

After sorting out the topics this way, you should make notes on the topics chosen by you. You should keep in mind the following points while choosing the topics:

- ☑ None of the important topics should be left.
- ☑ You should give special attention to those topics, which are somehow related to the contemporary situations.
- ☑ You can leave those topics in which either you are not interested or you don't have the content.
- ☑ While choosing the topics, you should also keep in mind the different parts of the syllabus. Suppose there are two parts of a question paper. So, you

should first find out from which part 2 questions have been asked and from which 3 have been asked. You should also keep in mind that the questions, by solving which you can score more, should be practiced more. It is obvious, hence, that the preparation of notes will be done accordingly.

One more category of making notes should be determined. This category would be of possible questions. You can guess the topics from which most number of questions would be asked by looking at the previous years' question papers. At least 20 topics should be selected from the whole syllabus. After selecting the topics, proper notes should be made. None of the points should be left. It is not necessary that all the questions will come from the topics you have chosen. However, if 8-10 questions are asked from the 25 questions that you have chosen then it is possible to take your score from 50% to 55%. Do you consider this increment of 5 percent unworthy?

Practice writing

There is one more technique of being successful and that is by writing the answers for the questions which you think are important. After writing, you should check that no fact has been left. This will help you in not only mastering these answers, but, will also help in increasing your writing speed. You will get benefitted by this in the exam.

Revise

Most students (leave aside the exceptions) do not have

the memory to remember information that they read only once. The things that are registered in mind start blurring after a time interval. That is why it is important to revise the topics. This process of repetition can be done using books, or by using the detailed or point wise notes. Although this practice should not be neglected, most students are prone to it. They keep reminding themselves that they remember the topic very well. However, not all information from a topic is retained unless you revise the topic regularly.

Time-table

It is also advisable to prepare for the mains exam using a time table. You should decide the time in which you will finish a subject. You should decide how much time you will spend daily on a particular subject. You should also write down when and how many times will you revise a subject. You should keep one subject as main and the rest should be given lesser time. But don't commit the mistake of leaving a subject aside for long. Talking about the general studies, you have to devote little time to it daily.

How many hours should you study?

Students are also excited to know the number of hours they should study every day to prepare for the mains exam. It is difficult to answer this question. This totally depends on the subjects you choose- if they are completely new or they are the ones you have studied in the bachelors. It is obvious that if you studied the topics earlier, then, you can prepare them quite well, even in less time. However, if the topics are completely new, then, it will of course take time.

Moreover, every day's schedule will also depend on the months or years you want to give for your preparation. If your preparation time is 1 year, then, the number of hours every day will reduce. Nevertheless, if you want to prepare for this in 6 months, the number of hours will increase. But, here, we are talking of an ideal situation, so, it will not be wrong to say that studying for fewer hours every day for few extra months is much better than studying for a long time every day.

I would like to warn you here that you should not reduce the number of hours thinking that your preparation has been done and that you don't need to study any more. Even if your preparation is done, you shouldn't be lazy about repeating or practicing it. More insights will be added every time you repeat it.

I believe that if you prepare this way, then, you will definitely, be successful. Perhaps, you already know about some of these things. But, if a known fact is proven, then, we start believing it more strongly. All these tips have been proven and these will take you closer to your goal.

I am sure that you have benefitted from whatever has been told to you about the preparation and writing strategy for the mains exam. Although, in the case of human science, no definite facts can be obtained, but, on the basis of past experience, current needs and future possibilities, some conclusions can be derived with which we can use our abilities to the maximum and attain profits. I consider my suggestions to be this valuable.

In the examination hall

There are few points related to the mains exam which hasn't been told before. Although these points are small; they are very important. Just like on the cricket field players need to run for singles and doubles also. They cannot make centuries scoring only in boundaries. Similarly, students cannot be successful without being careful about the small points. Following are few points by being careful about which you can score more marks:

- ☑ The biggest and the most important foundation for success in life is self-confidence. As soon as you get the question paper, you either get too excited or disappointed. These are not the suitable situations for the competitor. You will forget the facts out of your disappointment or you will lose your way out of too much excitement.
- ☑ That is why the most important thing is self-confidence. Whether the question paper is too tough, easy or of medium level, you shouldn't let it affect your self-confidence. There is, obviously, no problem if the question paper is good. However, if the question paper is tough according to you, even then, you should think that you have to do your best in whatever you know. The only important thing is the marks you score. How you get it or why you don't get it, is not important. UPSC has nothing to do with this. For example: a player who can't score much while batting, tries to prevent the other team from scoring more runs during while fielding, the same facility is available to you too. If one paper goes bad,

then, you have the other papers in front of you. You can try to cover up in those papers. Hence, you shouldn't let the bad situations affect your self-confidence.

☑ The second important fact for success is balance of thoughts and opinions. Whenever your opinions are asked in the question paper, you should make sure that there is a balance in your thoughts. You should neither be in favor nor in opposition. You should be balanced and rational in every situation. You should remember that this balance in thoughts has a direct and very deep relationship with self-confidence. Excessive courage or discouragement affects the balance of thoughts.

☑ Before entering the examination hall, you should switch off your mind. That means you should not be unnecessarily worried about the questions which will be asked or the result. It is human nature to worry about the situations which haven't even happened. This is wastage of our mental energy. You shouldn't think- 'what you don't remember', 'what you remember perfectly', 'what kind of questions would be asked', 'what if I don't do well in exams' etc. You should just think that you have to do your best, no matter what kind of paper you get.

☑ You should read the question paper very carefully as soon as you get it. It has been observed that students, generally, try to go through the paper once hurriedly as soon as they get it. Actually their anxious minds try to know how the question paper is. But remember: by doing so, not only do you waste few minutes of your precious time, but also, there is a fast emotional effect on your psychology, which is not good for you.

You should read the question paper as if you have to read it only once. After reading the question paper, you should make a small sign in front of the questions you are going to answer first, then second and which ones at the end. Following are the advantages of this:

☑ You will save your time.

☑ The whole question paper is clear to you.

☑ The strategy of writing the paper will be clear.

☑ You will get an idea on how much time you need to devote for every question.

☑ Your mental and emotional balance will be maintained.

☑ After reading the question paper, you should decide how much time you are going to devote for every question. Many students have said out of their experience that if students don't do this, then, they either end up answering to the questions at the end very lightly or they leave few questions. You should remember that leaving few questions unanswered, just for the sake of answering a particular question very well doesn't profit you in any way. It is always better to attempt all the questions, even if you have to reduce the time devoted to the other questions. You can keep in mind while devoting time to the questions:

☑ You should know how much time it takes to write an answer of 200 words. If you already have an experience of writing the paper, then, you shouldn't be bothered, but, if you don't have such an experience, then, you should practice at home and see how much time you take to write an answer of particular number of words.

- ☑ You should also be clear about the time you take to write an answer of 800-900 words.
- ☑ You shouldn't do the time allotment proportionally according to the number of questions and the time given. Proportionally means that suppose you have 3 hours to answer 5 questions. Here, 'proportionally' means that you should give 36 minutes to every question, but, you shouldn't do this. Rather you should give 40 minutes each to the first 2 questions. You can even give 42-45 minutes to the first question and 40 to the second one, and then, you can reduce these 10 minutes for the remaining questions.
- ☑ You can also be careful about, maybe, a question which is difficult for you out of these 5 questions. It is also possible that you know a question but not properly. In such a situation, it is obvious that you will need less time to answer these questions. You can use this extra time in answering those questions about which you are confident. This will help you in scoring more.
- ☑ It is good for you if you solve the question paper five minutes before. These five minutes should be used to check if any question has been left or not. If you are still left with time, then, you can even revise some answers rapidly.

Once you make the strategy of answering the questions in a particular time, you will realize that there is no pressure on your mind. The situation will be very clear in front of you. You will answer the questions with self-confidence and balance.

This actually is considered a good personality trait. You should inculcate this in yourself for another reason as well. This is tested in the personality test (the interview). Hence, it is advisable that you practice this through model papers.

☑ You should try to answer those questions first which have many blocks. Like it has already been told to you that there are few questions which can be divided into blocks. The more blocks a question can be divided into, the more points can be obtained. For example, there is a question of 50 marks which is divided into 3 parts. It is clear that each block is of 17 marks. If this question had only one block, then, you could have scored maximum 35marks. Since the question is now divided into three blocks, you can very easily score 13 out of 17 for a block, that means, total 13*3= 39 (which is more than the maximum 35 marks you would have scored otherwise).

Another benefit of the questions which are divided into parts is that you are prevented from losing your way for the answer. There is more possibility of answering 'to the point' in such answers. This has a good effect on the examiner.

☑ If a question seems difficult to you or you have to think a lot before writing, that question should be answered towards the end according to the time left, like you generally do in the general study's paper. You should not be worried about answering to this question first as it will have adverse effect on the other questions. I am not talking of the chronology of the questions here, but, the way they should be answered.

☑ You should not ignore the fact that your answer sheet represents your personality in front of the examiner. It has been observed that students are generally careless in regards to their answer sheets. Copy is twisted, dirty, ink is spread, alphabets are written in a shabby way, etc. All this affect the examiner in a negative way. A clean and organized thing appeals to even a dirty and unorganized person. For this, you need the following:

- ✓ Your copy should be very clean.
- ✓ Handwriting should be neat. Alphabets should be written in a way which is comprehensible to the examiner. Good answers generally fail to impress the examiner if they are not written in good handwriting. If your handwriting is bad, the examiner would run away from reading it. That is why you should work on your handwriting and should make it at least comprehensible. This comprehensible handwriting should be at the time of writing fast and not leisurely.
- ✓ You should leave proper margins at the left.
- ✓ If the copy is with lines, you should either write above or below the line. You should maintain one way of writing. It shouldn't be different on different pages. This way your copy appears to be cleaner.
- ✓ You should also try to use the same pen throughout the paper unless the pen stops working. There is

uniformity in your copy which makes your copy better. You shouldn't write or do anything in the copy which shows a negative personality of yours. Your copy should appear organized and clean.

- ✓ You should be careful about making paragraphs while writing. As soon as one point is completed, you should change the paragraph. You should definitely not be worried about the number of lines in a paragraph. Paragraph is related to the thoughts and not the lines. As soon as one thought is completed, the paragraph should be changed. The new paragraph should be started from approximately the middle of the line.
- ✓ While answering, whichever word or line, you think is important and you want the examiner to read carefully, should be underlined.
- ✓ If there is any answer which can be written in both detailed and point wisc manner, then, preference should be given to point wise method. This will help you in presenting your answer in an organized way. The examiner will be able to evaluate you properly as well.

☑ You language should be according to the topic. If it is weak, then you should make it stronger by working on it. Your language should be according to the topic as every topic has a different vocabulary and you should master it.

☑ The last important point is that the first question paper is in the forenoon and the second one is in afternoon in the competitive exams. There is a break of 2 hours in between. It is advisable not to discuss your first paper with anybody during this break. You shouldn't even try to know which questions you have done correctly and which ones incorrectly. You should utilize this time, have light food and revise the main points of the second paper. This will not only help in clearing the topic further, but, also help in maintaining your mental balance.

I believe that by following these advises and solutions, you will reach closer to your goals. God will also help you, provided you help yourself.

Chapter 15

Essay shouldn't be taken lightly

I qualified my civil services exam in 1982 when there was no paper of essay in it. Later, the Commission felt its need since it helps in correct evaluation. In 1992, it was started again and it was for 200 marks, that means, out of total 2000 marks, 200 marks are for essay. The exam format was again changed in 2013, but, essay was continued. It wasn't only continued but was given more weightage. Now the total number of marks of all the papers is 1750, out of which 250 are given to the essay paper. If compared, the marks assigned for the essay paper have been increased from 200 to 250 when the total marks have been reduced to 1750 from previous 2000. The important part to think here is whether it is done all of a sudden or it is a planned strategy.

Nothing is changed suddenly, especially, academically. IAS examination is definitely not a bureaucratic matter, but academic as it is determined by not only different commissions, but, also the contribution of ideas by intellectuals of their time. Now the question which is raised here is why are essays given so much importance?

Why are they important?

Every paper of civil cervices exam has its own template including the general knowledge paper. This decided template provides students with few important points on the basis of which they prepare and honestly, the preparation is done easily as well. For this, we have books, newspapers and magazines. If you notice, you will see that the questions which are asked in the general knowledge paper, are available in written somewhere, whether, you have read it or not or maybe, you read it, but, you didn't give it much importance. It is very clear that the preparation of general knowledge or optional papers has to be much disciplined and the books or methods of preparation are almost same for every student.

However, can we say the same thing about essay? You should pick up and look at the unsolved papers of essay of last 20 years. You would hardly find an essay which was asked twice. Every year, you are presented with new topics. The main point to note here is that none of these essays are available in written. If they are available, it is there only in two people's mind: one, the person who suggested the topic, and second, the person who is going to write the essay.

The content of essay is generally scattered. It will not be wrong to say that the way a honey bee makes honey by sitting on different flowers, in the same way, an essayist writes an essay after studying different types of topics.

Let's see what UPSC needs in regards to this. The Commission has very clearly stated that "they will be expected to keep closely to the subject of the essay, to arrange their ideas in orderly fashion, and to write concisely. Credit will be given for effective and exact expressions."

This can be considered like mathematics to an extent. You cannot memorize mathematics. However, if you know the formula, you can answer any question using it. Essay is also the same, you cannot memorize it, but, if you know how an essay is written, then, you can very easily write. It is, however, more challenging than mathematics. Whosoever knows the mathematics' formula can very easily answer using it and the answer will be more or less the same. In spite of this, can we say that people who know how to write an essay will write it in exactly the same way on the same topic? I don't need to answer this. This is actually the biggest challenge of essay writing, but, at the same time, it is its beauty too.

It is said in English- 'style is the man himself', that means, a person's way of expression shows his personality. This is said for literature writing, but, it also applies to essay writing. The way an author's personality is reflected in his work, in the similar way, an essayist's personality is reflected in his essay. Maybe, you don't realize it, but, the person reading it can make it out. You should consider essay's paper a way by which UPSC is conducting your interview in written. While giving an interview, you are in front of the interviewer, whereas, in an essay, your copy is in front of the examiner.

I have said that your personality is reflected in the essay you write. I know it is hard for you to believe this, but, I would like to tell you few things to make you believe me. This is important because if you don't believe me, then, you will not give due importance to this paper and when you will not give due importance to it, you will not do any justice to it either. By doing this, you will of course, not do any justice to yourself too. So, let's see how it reflects our personality:

☑ You can read, understand, memorize and answer any topic. However, there is nothing of your own in the answer. Maybe a few thoughts here and there, but, all in all it remains borrowed. Nevertheless, whatever you write in an essay is your own. It is possible that knowledge is not yours, but the usage of knowledge is completely yours. Your role, here, is like that weaver who doesn't weave the threads but uses the threads to make clothes. The same way an essay is your creativity, you can also call it your 'fundamental work'.

☑ The essayist's opinion is definitely there, no matter, what the topic of the essay is. A good essay cannot be written without a clear idea of the topic. Unless you have a clear-cut opinion of your own, your thoughts will remain scattered and you won't be able to keep your essay well constructed. Clear concept is the backbone of the essay and it is also directly linked to our life. The essay's topics are chosen in a way in which these points are reflected-whether the topic is related to science and technology or economics or international relations. Hence, it shows the writer's viewpoint towards life.

☑ You can write any topic after memorizing. Every topic has its own language. You memorize that language and that is why that language is not yours. Your language can be evaluated only through an essay as you don't have any other help there. A good and influential language reflects the communication skills of a person and to be an efficient administrator, good communication skills are very important.

☑ Another aspect linked with language is style. Language is the choice of words and the structure of the sentences, whereas style is related to the composition of sentences. This is directly connected to the composition of the essay. Actually, essay is not much affected by language but by style. Style is also a part of communication skills. Sometimes style affects the essay to an extent that you do not care to ask for facts that should otherwise be asked to support the thoughts and opinions of the writer. But remember: until and unless a person has good knowledge of the language, topic, life and society, his style cannot be influential.

☑ There is one more thing which is no less important than the others. That is vividness. Language and style, both are continuously flowing elements like a river. They constantly change. The language and style which are convincing are the ones related to our time. If your essay's language and style are attractive, that is only because you are vividly connected to your present time and society. This is one of the biggest qualities of a person. Even the general knowledge paper checks how alert you are towards your time.

So, these are the reasons why essays are given so much importance. I hope that after reading these facts, your attitude towards essay would have become a little serious.

Your attitude

If essay's paper is deceitful, then, it is persuasive as well. Honestly, since it is the most persuasive paper, it is the most deceitful too. This paper makes me remember that part of Mahabharata when Duryodhan went to the palace made by Pandavas. He sees water in place of floor and floor in place of water. It was only looking at this foolish behavior of Duryodhan that Draupadi comments 'the son of a blind man is also blind'. He was deceived although he believed that 'there was water and the other place was ground'.

I didn't have to give essay's paper, but, being a Hindi literature student and then a professor, I know this topic very well. I have always scored well in essays. You can even say that I have been in love with writing essays. I also won a prize in a national competition for essays in the year 1985. My love for essays became even more prominent when I opted for the career of writing. I am going to share the same experiences of mine.

I am sad to say that I have seen many students who are not very serious about this paper. There are reasons for this. The first is that you are generally given four topics, out of which, you have to write on only one. This makes a student think that it is not a tough job. They are not wrong in thinking this either as the topics which are given don't ask for any specialty in it. They think they can write and it is true that they write as well. I have never met such an unfortunate and stupid student who would say that he was unable to write the essay. Everybody knows language and everybody has some knowledge on the topic (proficiency level may differ though). There is also a possibility of connecting two dots from a totally different context. There is no review required either. They consider this to be like batting in such a situation where there are no fielders on the ground- even no stumps and no wicketkeeper. That means a free flow of runs and no possibility of getting out.

Perhaps, now you have understood why I said, 'this is the most deceitful as well as persuasive paper'. As soon as you become over-confident in regard to anything, you become prone to be deceived by that thing then and there. Same is the case with the essay as well.

You think that this paper is easy which is not wrong. But you fail to understand that 'the easier the work is, the more difficult it is to do it'. It is very easy to draw a curvy line. But, drawing a straight line is the most difficult. You can apply this logic to essay paper as well. If it was such an easy paper, there was no need for UPSC to include it in the most difficult exam of the nation. Am I wrong in saying this?

Let's use Mathematics

The written exam is only for 1750 marks. Out of this, 250 marks are assigned for essay. If we remove these marks, then, the written exam is for 1500 marks. Suppose you score 825 out of 1500, which is 55% and is considered to be a good score in IAS. You have scored these marks on studying the subject. Marks for essay are not included in this score.

The problem with the essay paper is that you can get from minimum 10% to 60% marks. 10% means 25 marks and 60% means 150 marks. Hence, the maximum marks are 150 and minimum are 25. This way the difference between minimum and maximum marks is 125. Let's imagine that you have scored 825 in rest of the exams. Now if you score 20% in essay, then, your total score would be 825+50= 875. Hence, your percentage would be 50 since you have scored 875 out of 1750.

Now let's talk of a student who has scored 50% marks in other papers excluding essay. That means 750 out of 1500. He can score 60% in essay, which is not impossible. Now his total score is 750+150= 900.

Now let's calculate this score. Even after scoring 55% in 6 papers, the first student's total score was 875 since he could score only 20% in essay. On the other hand, the second student got only 50% in 6 papers. But finally, he scores more than the first student by 25 marks since he scores 60% in essay- irrespective of the fact that he was 75 marks behind in the rest of the papers as compared to the first student. It was only by scoring more in essay that he moved ahead of the first student. Just think that if the first student scores 50% rather than 20% in essay, which is not very difficult, then, his total marks would be 950. 950 out of 1750 mean 54.8%. That means selection is definite, that too, with a good rank. My question is how was this difference created? Very clear answer- essay.

Art, not science

Don't make the mistake of taking this calculation of mine as imaginary. This is true and it generally happens with the science students. That is because writing an essay is an art and science students lack the experience of this art. Although it isn't difficult to learn this art. And you can even master it by practicing. The purpose of this chapter is more or less to teach you this art.

I have a batch mate. His daughter has done masters in Sociology from Lady Shri Ram College, New Delhi. After this, she tried to attempt the IAS exam. Unfortunately, she lost all of her attempts except the last one. That girl accidentally met me at the World Book Fair in Pragati Maidan, New Delhi where I went to participate. When she greeted me, I was shocked because I had known her since the time she knew only to cry and could barely speak. Listening to her greetings, it seemed that even today by way of uttering those words she was actually crying. I immediately thought of the 6-months-old girl and I could sense her untold sadness which really troubled me. I called her aside and we sat and started talking in a corner. My wife, son, my batch mate and his wife went to have a look at the books. She told me it was her last attempt at IAS. In May, she has the preliminary examination and the mains exam in October. Before this, she had taken the mains exam twice, the first time she couldn't clear it, the second time, she did clear it but couldn't clear the interview. Since it was her last chance, she became very sensitive.

We talked to each other for about 3 hrs. She told me about her marks of every subject of both the years. It was very clear that she could score well in all the subjects except in essay. She was unable to score more than 40-50 (at that time, it was for 200 marks). I thought if she could get 60 somehow in essay, then, her selection was definite. So I asked her to change the game plan. I wanted her to prepare well for essay now and not much for the other subjects. So I told her how to prepare for essay and gave her my book as well.

I am glad to say that neither did she disappoint her parents nor me. She got 25th rank and now she is an IAS officer. My friend's family got not only an IAS daughter but also an IAS son-in-law. A small weakness of not being able to write a proper essay was one of the major problems in her major success.

So, you shouldn't ignore this part. I am not saying that you should prepare for it on the cost of other parts. If you want to crack IAS, you shouldn't ignore any part of the exam, and especially, the essay. If you ignore this, then you shouldn't expect success. Perhaps, you are not able to reach the 75% mark, but, at least you would be able to score more than what you could with a little more practice and seriousness.

Meaning of essay

Generally, an essay means without any limitation. Something that is free from all the limitations is an essay- sky is the only limit.

Nevertheless, there is another meaning of essay. That is the opposite of the above that is, perfectly bounded- in a well built cage.

I am assuming that you are confused after reading both the meanings since both of them contradict each other. On one hand, it is a free bird and on the other, it is a parrot in the cage. The problem in front of you is which of the above you should take as correct for an essay in order to start your preparation. Don't worry; I will help you solve this problem.

Both the meanings of an essay, which appear to be contradictory, somehow support each other too. The first meaning is related to the contents of the essay, whereas the second one is related to the writing style, expression and its structure. I mean to say an essay can be written on any topic- from nuclear test, God particle and Mars orbiter to environment, poverty, inflation and success in life etc. This can even include topics like agriculture, entertainment, sports, science and even quantum physics. There is no limit to the essay's topic. This way it is free and without boundaries.

However, the freedom of topic doesn't mean that 'anything' can be written. You are given the liberty to write anything related to the topic. But, whatever is written should be somehow related to the topic. It is like a cow which is tied with a nail in a ground with a rope which is 15 meters long. It is free in the sense that it has enough space to roam around. Nonetheless, it is confined within the distance of 15 meters.

The second boundation is that of its composition. An essay doesn't mean anything can be written anytime and anywhere. It has its own structure in which we have to say what we want to say. Hence, we can say an essay has two limitations- one is that of opinions and thoughts and the second is that of its style.

Essay for whom?

The headline of this section has a hidden meaning, which is, 'essay can be written on any topic'. Suppose something has to be written on God Particle. It is clear that it is a topic of science which will be suitable for either scientists or science students and not for the common man. However, when the topic will be written for everybody, then, it will become an essay. An essay is a mode whose reader belongs to the common section. This is a kind of writing which is written for common people. This common man doesn't need specific information like a scientist or a physics student do. Hence, an essay fulfills our need that every topic is for everyone and at the same time, it is not for everyone.

I am discussing this point as it is very important for essay writing. When you write an essay, your role is that of an effective communicator. In order to communicate effectively, you need to know who your target audience is. Only then can you decide what kind of information should be conveyed and in what style. You have to consider the needs and wants and the grasping power of your target audience. Without it, your essay may prove anything but a fancy piece of writing.

General Studies vs. Essay

Being a candidate preparing for IAS, you have to prepare for General Studies- for preliminary exam, mains exam and even for the interview. You must have noticed that few topics (that are given for essays in the essay paper) can be put under the category of general studies. They are directly related to sociology, politics, economics or science and technology. It is natural to have a question in mind- "if essays' topics are related to general studies, then, why is there a separate exam for it?" You will find the answer here itself and I also understand why knowing this answer is so important for you.

There are two things- knowledge and understanding. If you understand the difference in these two, then, you also understand the difference in general studies and essay. A person who has done M.Sc. in agriculture has agriculture related knowledge; however, an illiterate farmer has an understanding of farming. Both are related to agriculture, but, one has theoretical knowledge and the other has empirical knowledge. The person who has knowledge will have to develop it into understanding by doing farming for a few days. You can also look at it this way that there are many roadside mechanics repairing cars and scooters in small towns, but they wouldn't even know how to spell Mechanical Engineering. Despite this, they have sufficient knowledge to mend your vehicle. They do this on the basis of their understanding and not theoretical knowledge. So, an essay is meant for a farmer if it is written about farming. And if it is being written on Electrical Engineering, then it should be for that 'chhotu' who keep busy all the day checking and repairing vehicles in a roadside workshop.

When we study a subject in general we are totally confined to that subject only. This is true for an essay as well. But essay is different in the manner that it can have many sub-topics included in it. When you have to make someone knowledgeable of the topic, you cannot digress from the topic. However, if you want to make somebody understand, you can go to any extent, can give any example to make the concept clear. When a political science professor talks about the basic rights, then, he sticks to that and does not digress. However, when the same person becomes a minister and works hard for the protection of the basic rights of the people and addresses them, then, the facts and the points change. That means knowledge is obtained in the classroom, but, it is applied in the free ground of life.

Hence, it is clear that there is enough scope for analysis in General Studies. You can put forward your point using arguments. However, essays are never analytical. They are informative. You collect the information on the basis of which you come to your decision.

That is why you should be careful and focus on the point that you don't end up writing a General Studies paper instead of an essay. This thin line between these two should be very clear in your mind. If you are able to maintain this psychological discipline, then, you would see that you can transform your knowledge into understanding and can write an effective essay. This will help you become a successful communicator.

I am definitely not saying that there is no relation between General Studies and essay. It is just not possible. There is a definite relation. An essay challenges you to show your talent while understanding this difference. I think my saying, 'your general knowledge is tested in general studies, whereas, the general understanding is tested in an essay', can make this difference clearer.

Informal Style

Suppose you have to speak on 'contribution of science', and that too, in three different places. The topic is the same but the audience is very different. First, you have to speak on this in front of the school children, then in front of a General Assembly, and at last, in front of scientists. How would you speak? I hope you have understood what I am trying to say. Your language and style would be different in front of the school children. It will be different in the General assembly and, of course, very different with the scientists. Your language will be very formal and will have scientific terminology with the scientists. That, actually, would be a scientific language, very different and not at all comprehensible for the common man. However, in the general assembly, you will speak not only about what benefits the common man, but, also, what they can understand. Wherever you feel that they do not understand something, then, you have to make them understand in a different way. You can use examples, some stories or incidents, some amusing things, discuss incidents, etc. Your efforts should be 'to make them understand anyhow'.

This is what I have called, 'informal style'. This is one of the styles which don't have a fixed pattern or a format. But, this doesn't mean that it is deformed. It is said that the topic itself chooses its style. This way your style depends on the topic you are going to write your essay on. This is for sure that you don't have to show 'how knowledgeable I am' in it.

If you learn by heart this meaning of essay, then, for sure, your fear of writing it, if there is any, will be removed. However, it is very important to practice for the same.

The qualities of a good essay

There is nobody who doesn't write an essay, but, there are very few who score well. Why? Because only few people can write a good essay. The question, here is - what is a good essay? I am going to tell you about the same, briefly. Briefly, because whatever has been told to you till now was somehow to clarify what an essay is. If you get to know what an essay is, then, you naturally get to know what a good essay is. After knowing about an essay whatever you write will be good. The problem with most of the people is that they write an essay, but, they don't know what it is.

I am going to talk about those main points, which were not discussed properly before this.

I. **Topic's compatibility :** the major problems which I have seen while checking the copies of the essay writers is that of disorientation. Student just reads the topic and starts writing. He has been taught to write the prelude first, so he starts writing the prelude. Then he gets too absorbed in it to remember the main topic. He gets disoriented. And when he remembers that the essay had to be written on the main topic, it is then, that he starts writing on it. After writing for a while on the topic, again he gets some phrase or word, that he starts describing, and again forgets the main topic. If I am not wrong, this happens with you too.

This is actually a psychological problem. This is not only while writing an essay, but, also while talking, while asking a question and even while answering a question. If you observe this, you would find that I am not wrong. For example, you are writing an essay or having a discussion on 'the current scenario of Indian politics'. Maybe, you start the essay with 'our politics is in bad shape, it has been ruined by corruption'. Now, you leave politics and start talking of corruption and you start talking of its causes, consequences and the solutions for eradicating it. While doing this, you say that 'right to information can help in stopping this practice'. Now you start talking of the 'right to information'. Then, all of a sudden, you remember that the topic was about politics. So, you try to link the 'right to information' with the politicians saying, 'the right to information can help in controlling the corrupt politicians'. This continues for the rest of the essay and you fail to do any justice to the main topic. Also, the structure of your essay gets deranged.

There is definitely freedom to write anything in the essay, but, it is like the definition of freedom in political science that 'my freedom ends when it starts bothering another person'. You should know the difference between 'freedom' and 'impertinence'. This impertinence can be seen in an essay which makes it weaker. This also proves the point that the person writing it is not a mentally strong person. This also shows that the person doesn't have much to write on the topic. Moreover, this further clarifies that the person is not a good communicator. If he is not all this, then, do you think he should be made an IAS?

II. Tight texture : To be very honest, essay is a procedure that tests how expressive you are more than it tests your studies and level of understanding. It is tested by checking how tight and organized the structure of your essay is. That means:

- ☑ How well organized the facts are. It shouldn't be the case that all the points or facts are scattered. It shouldn't be that as and when you remembered the points, you wrote them.
- ☑ How clearly is the essay able to leave its impression on the mind of the reader?
- ☑ To what extent does it influence the reader?

  An essay's structure should be like that of a pyramid. I am sure you must have seen a picture of it. Its base is broad while it starts narrowing towards the top. This is law of nature. Whichever structure is made using this law will be as firm and stable as pyramids. An essay's structure is also like the following:

☑ First, you introduce your point. Although it is like a prelude, but I would like to call it 'introduction'. It is strange to come straight to the point. It is similar to a situation where you invite somebody for lunch and as soon as he enters the house, you ask him, 'shall we serve lunch'? This is awkward. If you, at least, had asked 'how are you?' it would have been better.

Now you can ask how long this introduction should be. I have already discussed the problem of being disoriented while writing a prelude. Introduction means to lay down a foundation of what you want to say. It is not mandatory to write a paragraph of ten lines for this. It can be of three rows and can even be of a sentence. This is based on how long you want your essay to be. In 2013 civil service exam, you were required to write an essay of maximum 2,500 words. In 2014, essay-writing was divided into two parts. Each part carried 4 essays and you had to choose one from each. That means you had to write total two essays which had a word limit of 1000 to 1200 words. You can keep this in mind and give 5 percent of the total words to laying down the foundation of your essay. I feel that no more words should be given to the introduction. If you write an introduction of more than 100-200 words, then, it will prove the point that you don't have much to write on the main topic.

- ☑ Introduction means foundation. You have laid the foundation of your topic; now, you need to build a structure on it. You should explain everything in detail, as expected, in the structure, but you should remember that every point should be linked to the main topic and you shouldn't digress from it. You should always be careful while writing and ensure that you aren't digressing from the topic. It is a psychological disease which tends to continue very cleverly.

Also ensure that you don't give multiple examples or stories to explain a single point. If you do this, you end up repeating yourself which can spoil the structure. The examiner will realizc that you don't have any new point to say and that you are just stretching the same point. This is similar to 'talking nonsense' which I consider the biggest weakness in an essay. You should use the freedom but not to an extent that you end up forgetting the topic.

And this habit of taking freedom and giving unnecessary details will not be of any use once you have established your point and drawn the interest of the reader. Now that has been done, now you have made the reader curious enough, so, you don't need to use this strategy anymore. You should, now, start putting your facts forward.

- ☑ The essay has started moving ahead and has started becoming narrower and sharper. You have started proving your points with examples and other aids. By doing this, the essay automatically becomes sharper and tight.

☑ The last part of the essay would be that of your conclusion. Whatever you want to prove, will come in the last part. Though, it is not necessary to finish the conclusion in a paragraph, it totally depends on the conclusion that how many paragraphs it needs. It is advised to have the number of paragraphs according to the number of conclusions. However, looking at the total structure, it is suggested not to have a long conclusion.

This way the essay's structure is tight and well organized which is considered good.

III. The balance of logic and emotion : some essays are logic driven like, science, technology and economics related. While some are emotion driven, like life philosophy, culture and society related. It is important to note here that any essay can be either logic driven or emotion driven but it cannot be entirely based on logic or emotion. By 'primacy', I mean to say neither of the above is in abundance. That doesn't mean that it will only have either of these. Hence, another biggest challenge while writing an essay is that of maintaining the balance between logic and emotion. Another challenge is how well you can present logic emotionally and an emotion logically in your essay. Let's know how to do this:

☑ Suppose, you have to write an essay on 'the contribution of science and technology in the development of the nation'. According to logic, you should talk about those inventions which have helped in the development of the nation. However, according to emotion, the inventions should be presented in a way that it doesn't appear to be dry science. It's clear that while talking of science in relation to nation's development, you will not only talk of the monetary and security related development, but, also those related to life. As soon as you start talking of life, the emotional factor will automatically be included in it.

☑ The same point is used to include logic while talking emotionally. You should remember that emotion has its own meaning. It has its own science. It is definitely not something which shouldn't be believed. It is not useless and it has its own science called 'psychology'. It has its own discipline called philosophy. If you remove emotions from the society, then, it will be nothing but a group of animals. It is obvious if you include psychology, philosophy, the scientific sociological point, then you are able to successfully instill logic in emotions.

☑ The main point is that you shouldn't talk so logically while writing an essay that you seem to be a lawyer and you shouldn't be over emotional like a saint who just advocates blind faith and gives baseless hopes. Both of these should be intertwined in a way similar to that of a woman who sews a beautiful sweater using two different colors of threads or wool.

IV. Juiciness : I have intentionally used the word 'juiciness' here. An essay is actually a mode which should be enjoyable to the reader. And how you can enjoy a thing unless it has some juice in it. I talked of understanding before this. But, now I am talking of enjoyment. These are actually not contradictory either. Till the time we don't understand a joke, no matter how good it is, we cannot enjoy ourselves. As soon as it is understood by whosoever, it is enjoyed. I cannot enjoy either the classical music or classical singing as I don't understand it. However, I have seen many people closing their eyes and enjoying classical music in Bharat Bhavan, Bhopal. Since they understand it, they enjoy it. Hence, understanding is the first of the most important 'must be' elements that makes a thing enjoyable.

However, this is not everything. Simplicity is definitely the key to understand something. That is why it is suggested that you shouldn't be like an expert while writing an essay. If you mention some heavy facts or you gather a crowd of irrelevant figures from here and there, and if you use heavy and difficult words or long sentences of English or Hindi, then, the simplicity of the essay will not be there. That is why the following things are said:

- ☑ An essay should be directed to common people. Its language should be simple and easy to comprehend.
- ☑ You should not write words that are not so common or taken from Sanskrit.
- ☑ Use of only one language should not be focused on. It is definitely not a problem if you use few words from other languages like Urdu, English

while writing an essay in Hindi. However, this is important that they come naturally and not forcefully. These words should also be the popular ones which other people are aware of. This definitely polishes your language and also improves the way of saying something.

- ☑ You should avoid making complex sentences. They should not be puzzling to the minds of the readers.
- ☑ The purity and use of correct language is very important as far as making your essay enjoyable is concerned. If you write wrong Hindi or English, then, it has a very bad impression on the examiner. As soon as he notices a spelling mistake, the whole impression is spoilt. That is why you shouldn't take writing mistakes lightly. It is not only important for the essay paper, but, also for other papers. You can create that juiciness and enjoyment in your essay if you work hard on your language and use it correctly. I would like to advise you (if you are from Hindi medium) something. There is a book of mine, 'सही हिन्दी सुन्दर हिन्दी'. It is also published from the same publisher as that of the book you are reading at the moment. I feel you should read that book as it will help you a lot in the following manner.

First, your Hindi will become more pure and more correct. It is quite possible that you are used to writing few words and sentences which seem to be right to you, but, are actually incorrect. This happens with everyone. However, you can very easily correct such mistakes.

Secondly, you will learn how to make your language adorable. This will help you not only while writing an essay, but, also throughout your life. You can become a great communicator with this.

Thirdly, use of correct and good Hindi will help you in other papers of IAS too as this is the only medium with you to present your opinions and thoughts in front of the examiner. Even the best of thoughts fail without a good language. On the other hand, even if your thoughts or views are not that strong, they can be made more influential by using an effective language. I don't feel the need to say that you speak during an interview and not write. And while speaking, two things are necessary- your voice and a good command on the language.

An essay's juiciness not only depends on the comprehensibility of the language, but, also on the way you have chosen to put forward your point and the way you have structured it to get that flow in it. It can be called as a meadow river. A meadow river is a river which flows smoothly without any obstacle maintaining a steady pace. There is another kind of rivers that we know as mountain rivers whose water get obstructed by rocks. You have to make your essay a meadow river that flows without any obstacle maintaining a steady pace. The question is how will you do it? I will give you few tips:

- ☑ You get stuck in those topics which you don't know very well. So, you should write only on those topics about which you know very well to avoid having a flow less essay.
- ☑ You also get disoriented at a point where you don't

have enough points, but, you have to write to reach closer to the word limit. Hence, you should be careful while writing anything.

- ☑ You must practice writing an essay. You must look at a house which is being constructed. You will observe that the floor is repeatedly cleaned to get that shine and smoothness. 'Practice to write an essay' is also like this grinding process. The more you practice, the more flow there will be in your writing.
- ☑ You shouldn't just write and forget about that essay. Rather you should analyze it. You should read every essay a number of times and try to make it better.
- ☑ You should see which difficult words can be replaced and which words can be used in a better way in the essay.
- ☑ The difficult sentences can be rephrased to make the essay longer or shorter.
- ☑ You should also look at the chronology of your points. If they are not in an order, you should rearrange the paragraphs.
- ☑ You must have left few points while writing. So, now, you should include the left out points too.
- ☑ After doing all this, you should write the whole essay again and compare it with the first one to see which one is better. I am not giving you any answer here; you have to find that on your own.

Although, I have told you all this, I know this will not benefit you much. This is not because whatever I have told you is not beneficial. You will be benefitted by this only. But, the problem is that nobody does it. I have had a bad experience in this that people ask, listen and even assure that they will do it. Sadly, they don't. Either they find it meaningless or they escape with an excuse of not having enough time to do this. They protect their inertia and laziness with this meaningless excuse. In such a case, nobody can help, not even God. I am telling you this because I know you will also undergo with such a situation. So, I am alerting you in advance.

Preparation of essay

Many students are worried about this, but, not many are seen working on it. The reason behind this is the typical mentality, 'what's there in an essay, we can manage to write it'. Believe me and start making efforts to get rid of this mentality. If your mentality was right, there was no need to include this paper.

There is no doubt in it that an essay cannot be prepared in the same way as General Knowledge and optional papers. However, it is not the case that the preparation cannot be done or it happens on its own. You should keep this thing in mind that nothing happens on its own in life, so much so that even your finger doesn't move on its own. You have to move it. Keeping all these points in mind, I am going to give you few tips which will definitely help you in writing a good essay. And the day it happens, you should believe that you have overcome one of the biggest problems faced in the IAS exams. I am saying this because I personally feel that a person who knows how to write an essay automatically learns how answers of

General Knowledge and optional papers should be written.

i) Study some basic books

I hope you now agree with me when I say that an essay is a reflection of a person's intelligence and personality. If a question of General studies is answered by 100 people, then, we can still find some similarity in terms of contents and style, whereas, it is not possible in an essay. An essay written by 100 people will have quite different content, if not completely different, and the way of writing will be different too. That is why it will not be wrong if I call an essay a reflection of your inner self.

Now the question is what should we do to mold our intelligence and personality in the way it is expected to be by our nation?

Joint preparation: the way we join a gym to keep our body fit and active, in a similar way we should study, think and contemplate to improve our intellectual make-up and moral nature. You have no choice but to do this.

You read some basic books for General Knowledge. Then, you keep updating it with the help of newspapers and magazines. This definitely helps you in essay writing but considering it as everything will be a mistake. I have already told you the main difference between general knowledge and an essay. You have to do this and you should continue doing it too. How should you use this general knowledge in an essay, I will discuss this point later. However, you should remember that the knowledge obtained from General knowledge should be used as raw material in the essay and not as the final product. If general knowledge is like a shop from which vegetables are bought, then, an essay is the procedure of making the vegetable edible after having bought it. On one hand, you do the work of selling the vegetables and on the other hand, you try to make it edible, the work of a cook.

Separate preparation: the essays asked in IAS preparation should be observed very minutely and carefully. No matter what the topic of the essay is, you will find that either of the following facts would be present at the very core:

- ☑ The essay will be related to life or
- ☑ Related to the society. When I say society, it includes the entire nation. Nation is also a part of the society and those aspects are also a part of it that contribute in its development like, economic, social, educational, political, cultural, industrial etc.

This is the actual challenge posed by an essay and this is how it is different from General Knowledge. You cannot do any justice to the facts present at the very core of an essay unless you have a clear and deep social viewpoint and unless you have a criterion to determine it.

Here I have talked of two things- vision or viewpoint and criterion. Where will you get this vision from? Of course by studying, observing, discussing, experience and also by using it. However, you are not that old that you can give more importance to experience and usage. At this moment, the most advantageous solution is studying, which you already are doing. But, maybe you are not able to understand the subjects for essays.

I would like to strongly advise you to study two subjects,

mainly- even if these two subjects are beneficial for the general knowledge and optional papers or not. And anyways you should prepare extra for essay as out of the total marks in writing, 14.5% marks are contributed by essay. Why have you thought that this kind of study is not important for it? This is your misunderstanding. My suggestion is that you should prepare for these two subjects and the preparation should be of the graduation level. These two subjects are- sociology and philosophy.

Now you may be have a question on what kind of books should be studied. I would suggest you to read the books of Indira Gandhi National Open University (IGNOU). But this is not the only suggestion. If you get other books written by other authors, then, you should read them as well.

Why should we study philosophy and sociology?

Now I would tell why I suggested you to study these two subjects. In my opinion (as a teacher, writer, a thinker of life management), sociology creates a view in us and that is the social viewpoint. This is the viewpoint which is realistic. When we understand what constitutes a society and how it changes, it is only then that we can be in a position to decide which things it needs. It is only then that we can deeply understand its problems. Studying sociology helps in preventing our vision from unnecessary aggression and sentimentality.

Talking of philosophy now. It provides us the criterion that we can use to analyze our vision. Philosophy is basically related to life, which is not very different from the society as a society is made by people only. Like people like society. And society, in return, makes the people on the basis of how it has been made. Both of them are inter-dependent.

By studying philosophy, you will be able to understand, even the small issues very deeply. For example, the essay asked was: 'bring the change you want to see in others in yourself first'. You should try to write it. I am honestly telling you that you will be baffled. The topic seems to be very easy and you understand it as well. However, after writing about 400-500 words, you will realize that you have nothing new to write in it. Since you have to write maximum 1200 words, writing 500 words will not be justified, hence, you will keep writing, just for the sake of writing. The amusing part is that you will just repeat what you have already written. That is why I said that you will be baffled and you will keep spinning in the same sphere. And the examiner will get to know this. And it is your bad luck that he will not even help you in this. You will have to help yourself, and studying philosophy will make you capable of helping yourself.

The mentioned essay is general, but, as per philosophy it is a very deep topic. It not only has depth but also different angles of life. For example, its one side is related to psychology, whereas the other is related to that part of sociology which is related to the way we behave with each other. Its third side is that of religion and spirituality where Jesus Christ said, 'you shouldn't behave with others in the manner in which you don't want them to behave with you'. It can even have a fourth financial argument that even the most dishonest businessman wants his employees to be the most honest. This way philosophy will help you to talk about this in detail.

I am unable to decide if you agree with me on these things or not. But, since I agree with these things, I have told you the same too. I believe in these things because I told the same to my students and I am glad to say that I didn't disappoint them.

ii) Studying apart from syllabus

I have already told you to study philosophy and sociology. But this isn't enough. Don't worry, I am not going to ask you to study another subject. I am going to tell you those minute things which will really help you while writing an essay, provided you are careful. Whatever I am going to tell you now is something which you would already be doing. However, you are mistaken in not being alert for these things as you don't know they are important too. It is similar to our life in which we get various opportunities but, we don't realize they are the ones since we are not careful. And that is why we cannot even get hold of them. This way we not only miss the opportunity but also life. You should note the following things:

- ☑ You must be watching movies but only for fun. From now on, you should be a little more careful and watch them even for your essays. I anyway, would like to say 'studying films', rather than 'watching films'. If you start watching films from the perspective of life's philosophy, you would find that the entire meaning of the movie changes. Behind the pictures of the movie, you would see a different side of life. This will make your vision comprehensive towards life and society.

The biggest strength of a movie is its dialogues. You should observe the language being used in movies, which is today's language, a lively one. You should observe the language, words, the way they have been said and also the way the sentences are framed. The words or sentences which seem to be impressive should be noted. Hence, you shouldn't regret wasting your 3 hours and also Rs.200 or think that you could have studied something during this time. Now you should be happy that, 'you bought a book for Rs.200 and that you managed to finish it in 3 hours'.

- ☑ You shouldn't read only those articles in newspapers which you think are important for General Knowledge. You should read every article written on the editorial page. This develops your vision. And if any article is written in form of an essay, then, you should keep a cut-out of it.
- ☑ Similar attitude should be employed with magazines. I will not ask you to read the whole magazine, but, you should at least have a look at it and whatever seems important should be read carefully. This way you can collect information to write essays.
- ☑ You also shouldn't hesitate to listen to the lectures of the scholars in your city. You shouldn't be lazy and think that 2 hours will be wasted. Maybe, the lecture is not that good, but it is impossible that you will not get even one useful sentence. Even if you get one new point or opinion, then your purpose of attending the lecture has been attained. You cannot expect, and it is not necessary either, that the whole of it will be beneficial. Also, it doesn't

matter whether you liked it or not. What actually matters is whether it was useful for you, if yes, to what extent.

☑ You should always listen to and participate in discussions, as and when they happen. So much so that if two people are talking on any topic, then, you should listen to it carefully.

☑ You should also develop a habit of observing and see what and how things are happening. Some or the other incidents happen everywhere. You should see them and try to figure out their reasons. You should also try to analyze and understand them from within. If you can be a part of it and play a role in it, then, you should do that rather than just looking at it.

☑ It is not important to have figures in essays, but, if you are writing an essay on economics, then, the essay will be incomplete without figures. You can even add figures from the sociological viewpoint to make them more impressive and attractive. However, these should be used in the right number just like salt in food. Hence, as and when you get to know new and basic figures, you should note them down.

☑ The same applies to few good sentences. While reading books, magazines, newspapers or while listening to something, whenever you come across good sentences, you should note them down. This will not only help you in essays but other subjects too.

- ☑ I have already asked you to read philosophy. I am saying the same here because I really want to highlight this point. Last 40 years have witnessed a rapid and drastic change in every sphere of life. Since the new scientific developments are bringing evolutionary changes in the society, they are also changing the thinking related to various fields. These schools of thought are of economics, society, culture, media, psychology, art, history and all the other fields that have an impact on the society. You need to know all these thoughts. These will not only provide you with vision but also various criterions which will make your essay writing much better.

On the surface level, these small things seem to be useless. But this is not the case. The development in our thinking and an eye to observe everything comes with this, like the great artist, Michelangelo said, 'perfection is no small thing, but it is made up of small things'.

These are my views on writing an essay. You will also have some views and few can be different from mine. I would welcome your views too. But, it is entirely up to you to create a balance between my views and yours and to create a perfect model.

About writing essays

This is the last stage of writing an essay which is related to your exam's time. This is very important to write a good essay in the examination hall and to score the best of marks.

Although you will use this in the examination hall, but, if you take my advice and practice writing essays then you can use it even during practice. It would be better to practice using the following points:

(a) Take out some points: what is the biggest challenge of writing an essay? It is that you think you can write an essay, but, when you start writing it, then, you cannot. The topic is very easy. You feel like writing as soon as you read the title. You feel that you can write a lot. However, you write a little and you are tired. The same points keep coming to your mind which you have already written. It seems that you don't have many new points-provided you are careful. Otherwise, students think that whatever they are writing has something new in it.

The question is how can we overcome this problem? The solution is: points should be made. You shouldn't start writing the essay immediately. You should read the topic and keep writing the points that keep coming to you. You should make a long list of the main and even the small points. You should also write the examples or the events you are going to talk about. Basically, you should prepare as many points as you can. You should neither rush it nor be lazy in this. You should avoid thinking that, 'I can write this point directly in the essay'. It is confirmed that you will forget it while writing the essay. You must write the points that come to your mind at this point. It is also going to happen that while writing the essay, you may get some new points. This is not a problem and you can include those points too. However, if you get those points right away, you should include them in the list.

This is very important as you have collected all the ingredients to make the final essay.

a. **Classify them :** you must read the points which you have written at least twice or thrice. After that, you should try deciding the way you are going to classify them. That means which categories the points will be divided in. You will get many points which you can classify in one category only. You should, hence, put them in series. You will realize that the map of the whole essay would be very clear in your mind. Suppose you have got 50 points. While classifying them, you will realize that you can have 7-8 different categories. These 7-8 categories are said as an example and not as a rule. This entirely depends on the number of points.

b. **Decide the priority :** after writing and classifying the points, students start writing the essay. They feel they should just copy the raw material on the paper. This way you can include all the points, but, the essay is not structured. I have already told you that essay is not only presenting the points, but, presenting them impressively. For a structured essay, it is very important that you prioritize the points that you have got till now.

   'Deciding the priority' means deciding which point will come first, which one after that and which one at the end. It is obvious that the most important point should be mentioned first and then according to this, the points should be written. You will see that there will be a harmony in the thoughts of your essay. As the harmony develops, the essay will be more structured.

c. **Do rough work :** the best thing with essays is that the time given for writing it is sufficient. Rather it is more than sufficient. Being a good student, you should make sure that you use it to the maximum. That is why you shouldn't be in hurry. You can do your work taking all the time so that you can do it properly and you must do this.

If you instantly start writing the essays, you would find that you have completed it in an hour only. What will you do in the rest of the time? Either you will keep revising them or you will give your copy and go out of the examination hall. Isn't it better to think about the essays first and even create a rough structure for it? You think yourself that the total word limit for two given essays is 2400 words. In other papers, you have to write around 4000 words in 3 hours. Then why have you been given essays of maximum 2400 words which are to be written in the same 3 hours? It is very clear that you utilize your time and only after thinking you write the essay.

I am not asking you to write the whole essay as rough work. However, this is for sure that after deciding the priorities of the points, you must write them separately on a paper. You should see if anything has to be rearranged or not. If you feel that way, then, you should do it. Even after doing the rough work, you should see if any other point can be added to it. There is always a possibility of adding something. As soon as you get something to add, you should note it down in the rough work at the right placc. I feel that at least half of the given time should be used in doing this as it is only by doing this, that you will get the material to create a structured essay.

You should remember to cut the rough work. Never think,

'I will cut the rough work once I write the essay'. It is quite possible that you may forget to cut it. If this happens, then, according to the examination's rule, the examiner will check the part he gets to see first and will cut the latter part. You just need to draw a slanting line. As soon as the work is completed on the rough paper, you should cut it. You will not be affected by it. However, if you forget to draw this line, then, this will affect you a lot. You shouldn't take risks in such matters. Here I would like to inform you that the last page of the answer sheet is meant for rough work.

d. **Start writing the essay :** After doing the rough work, you should close your eyes for 5 minutes and relax your mind and try to set it as per the essay's topic. Just think how you are going to start the essay and then just start it.

- ☑ You should start very slowly and leisurely. You have enough time. You shouldn't be in a hurry. Let the ideas come to your mind slowly. In the beginning, a lot of points will come to your mind simultaneously. But don't panic. This problem would have been more severe, if you hadn't prepared the points.
- ☑ You would find that even after preparing the points, new ideas are coming to your mind. They should be included right away if it is possible to do so, if not, then, you should note them down on the rough paper.
- ☑ While writing the essay, you should go back to the points which you have written and should also see the prioritized points even in the rough work. Now, you should match the essay with the rough work.

That's not a rule, though. If you think the points have to be reorganized, then, that can be done too.

- ☑ An essay is like a flowing river. If you add a lot of sub-titles or a lot of points, then, the flow is disrupted. Hence, it is very important for the flow that you don't add many sub-titles and use them wherever necessary.
- ☑ But yes, if there is any important word, important sentence, or a point, which you think needs a definite attention of the examiner, you should always underline them. The examiner will understand that you think the underlined part is important. This will help you in attaining the purpose and at the same time, it will not reduce the essay's flow either.

e. **Word limit :** I fail to understand how students don't focus on the word limit and end up crossing the word limit even in those questions in which it is very clearly mentioned 'not more than a particular number of words'. This is called breaking the rules and I feel that a person who himself breaks the rules doesn't have the right to make other people follow his orders. This word limit is one of the most important criteria to check your personality and this shouldn't be taken for granted in any case.

You are asked to write two essays with a combined word limit of 2400 words. Students wonder how many pages they should write for these essays. Why should this question even arise? This is a simple math question. You can calculate it by counting how many words you write in a line and how many lines are there on a single sheet of paper. You can multiply the number of lines with the number of words you write in one line. The number that you get is the number of words you write in a page. Now divide 2400 by this number and you will get your answer. I would like to strongly suggest that you shouldn't exceed the word limit. If you do this, then you will definitely be caught. It would be better that you don't write because then there will not be much effect.

f. **Handwriting :** I will not say that a good handwriting is must for becoming an IAS or for scoring more marks, but, I would say that handwriting should be comprehensible and should be such that the examiner doesn't have to really work hard to read and understand it. Good handwriting doesn't mean a beautiful one but is more related to its comprehensibility. When we write very fast, then, it definitely has a very bad effect on the handwriting. However, the good part here is that there is no need of hurrying up for essay. Hence, the extra time can be used to improve your handwriting.

I don't have enough space to include few essays in it. Nonetheless, all the important points needed to write a good essay have been included. If you devote some time using these suggestions for writing an essay while practicing, then, I am sure that you will benefit from this. This will make you an expert in it.

Chapter 16

Compulsory English : A must win

Finally he got selected. Although it was his fifth attempt. In his second attempt, he cleared his pre exams but couldn't clear the mains. In his third and fourth attempts, he cleared even the mains, but, unfortunately, couldn't reach to the interview level. This was not because he didn't score well in mains, but, because his copies weren't checked. Actually, he could have scored almost the same every time in his mains, but, unfortunately, he couldn't qualify in English (compulsory). That is why his mains' copies were never checked. Like it is said, 'practice makes a man perfect', finally he cleared the compulsory English and he became one of my juniors in civil service. After his posting in my city, he came for a casual meeting. He was, of course, feeling proud while telling me his story, but, I could see the pain behind this feeling. He must be thinking, 'if I had a good command over English, I would have cleared the exam in the second or the third attempt only'.

Friends, whether you know or not know English, it is necessary for you to learn English to clear the IAS exams, even if you don't specialize in it. But before you start complaining about it I would like you to think about those talented people who were efficient before 1979, however, their pen's ink dried just because they did not have proficiency in English language and because an option of writing the exam in Hindi was not available to them. You are much better than them. You are much better in this as UPSC made the inclusion of compulsory English marks in the score card, but, this was opposed to and UPSC had to remove it. The current situation is that you will just have to clear the compulsory English and Hindi papers. English paper is of 300 marks and the qualifying marks are only 25%. That means you just have to score 75 marks. A good knowledge of English cannot affect your merit list at least.

Seeking pragmatism

I would like to say something practical here. It is correct that Hindi is our national language. Also, it was the language of freedom movement and is spoken and understood in the whole country. But we have to understand that the anti-English perception rooted deeply in our subconscious has sprouted from our hatred of Britishers who ruled us for such a long time. It was because of them that English and English speakers got an upper hand that time. This hatred and this anti-English perception were perfectly justified for pre-independence era. But this situation should have changed after the independence in 1947. However, because of a specific group, it couldn't be changed. Even after so many years of independence, the facility of studying and teaching English was available only in expensive private schools, because of which, it was not available to the common people and was considered to be only the elite class' language. Eventually, a different category of English speaking people had been formed in the country and they had a monopoly in administration. Also, they developed a separate culture, the upper class mentality, which was very different from the rest of the Indians.

This is one of the major reasons that Hindi speaking people (except some of the Southern and most of the North-Eastern regions) oppose English. There were movements against English as well as Hindi. The movements continued. During this, the democratic powers kept extending. Under democratic decentralization, Gram Panchayats were made stronger. At the same time, media developed and Hindi reached every corner of the nation. The people related to politics also opposed English. The result of which was that Hindi was used more often in administration. Earlier, Hindi couldn't be heard in the administrative departments, but, with time, Hindi was spoken. So much so that even in the big and the important meetings, people who speak Hindi can be found. In the discussions in Lok Sabha and Rajya Sabha, those ministers, from south India, are found trying to speak in Hindi who either know their mother tongue or English. After 1980, even in the administrative academy of Mussorie, the atmosphere has changed a lot. Instead of the probationers wearing suit and tie and having conversations in English, people wearing pajama kurta and slippers and talking in Hindi can be seen and that too in large numbers. The change has happened and I welcome it too. Moreover, I expect the others to welcome it in a positive way even the people who know English very well.

However, I am trying to say something different here. We should not ignore the practical side of opposition against English, no matter how logical and democratic it is. It is not only related to Indian society and administration, but also with the world and also to the technology of modern day communication. That is why I feel that where loving our mother tongue and national language is our religion, at the same time learning other languages is our duty and sometimes compulsion as well. Moreover, learning one more language shows our language related skills. Anyway, every educated person of the country knows two languages, even when the other language is his native language.

In this situation, I feel that we should learn English in the process of learning another language. And anyway, if you become a part of the Indian service and you are given a region as your workplace whose language you don't know, then, you have to learn its language. You cannot administrate effectively in Tamil Nadu using Hindi. Similarly, a Kannada speaking person cannot be a good administrator in Rajasthan without knowing Hindi. So, if you can learn other languages after becoming an IAS, then, why cannot you learn English to become an IAS? If you try to find an answer to this, you will get, 'why not? I can learn and will learn as well'.

Nevertheless, this is a fact as well that the way a village student was unaware of English around the year 1960-70; he is not that unaware today. These days, English schools have been opened in every nook and corner - even if they are private ones. The trend of CBSE schools has increased and most of the students choose English as the medium. Even with the popularity of engineering and management studies, more students are interested in learning English. Most of the students are addicted to computer and they prefer to work on it in English.

Publicity of media has also helped in making English words available to common people. In such a situation, English is not such an alien language that after starting its preparation, you say, 'what is it'?

I would like to add one more point here. People who don't know English are much tensed. They feel that, 'if I learn English, I will definitely become an IAS'. That means the major problem for them is knowledge of English. But, this is their misunderstanding. People who know English very well, do they become IAS on this basis only? Definitely not, you need much more than this. But this is for sure that if you don't know English, then, it is very difficult to become an IAS.

You are going to become an IAS. It is a tough challenge that you have accepted. You will have to really work hard and will have to change everything that you have learnt. This is not easy. However, if you have decided to become an IAS, then you have also decided to do all these difficult things. And when you have decided to do all the difficult work, then, why not accept learning English in this only? Anyway this isn't that difficult. You should accept this challenge and should take a pledge that, 'I can do anything'. Actually, you will need this thinking to be and after becoming an IAS that 'I can do anything'.

Is this difficult?

Now I would come to the point that is English actually difficult? Believe me, it may appear to you that I am a supporter of English, but this is not the case. However I do not agree those people either who say that English should be thrown out of the country. I have already told you that even I didn't know

English, not at all. In such a situation, I should be totally against it. However, should I be against all those things which I don't know and which stand in the way of my success? This is not the right approach. My approach is I should become capable of the thing which is very important for me. I used the same approach and it also helped me.

Something appears to be difficult to us in the beginning because every new thing is difficult. Now you know how to do cycling. But, when you didn't know, then, wasn't it difficult? You decided to learn cycling and worked hard to learn it as well. Now, you can cycle without using both hands. This has happened because of your will and efforts to learn it and of course the continuous practice. So, the logic that can be applied to cycling, can't it be applied to learning English? Hence, the first thing which you need to believe in is 'I can learn it'.

Grammatically, English language is considered to be one of the easiest in the whole world. You know Hindi that is why it seems easy to you, however, if you look at it from a grammatical point of view, then, it is much more difficult than English. You should ask those people who don't know Hindi; they will tell you how difficult it is. The way English paper is too difficult for the person who speaks Hindi, in the same way, Hindi paper is tough for the person who speaks English. However, if both of them start learning, then, the person will learn English earlier than the person who is learning Hindi as it will take more time and more hard work. The second important point, hence, is that you shouldn't think that English is a difficult language. This is how you can maintain a psychological balance with this.

I will discuss later the way you can learn English. Before I tell you this, I would like to tell you why you should learn English. If you understand the value of English language, then, automatically, you will have a positive thinking which is very important for learning English.

Why should English be learnt?

I don't want to give a long lecture on this. I would like to tell you few practical things which you would come across only after becoming an IAS. That is why UPSC has kept a paper of compulsory English. They think that a person, who has this much basic knowledge of English, will be able to improve upon it lately. I am now discussing the ways in which English will be useful to you.

☑ Although UPSC has accepted all the languages mentioned in the constitution as a medium of the paper, this rule is limited only to the paper. After getting selected, you have to undergo training for a period of 1.5-2 years at different training centers related to your service. Even now English is the medium of learning in various training centers. There is hardly any lecture which is given in Hindi. However, this is a fact that the exam which has to be taken after the training has to be given in the same medium that was chosen for the UPSC exam. Nonetheless, the lectures are in English.

If you don't know even this much English, then you have to deal with this problem. I have dealt with this problem. I never understood the class lectures. Then, I found a solution. I had a batch mate who was from

Lucknow and eventually he became a very good friend of mine. I requested him to tell me in brief everything that was told in the lecture. He started doing this. That is why I am warning you in advance.

☑ Anyway, the use of English has reduced in various states. Most of the state meetings are held in Hindi or the regional languages. However, this is not the case in Delhi. The high officials of Union government come from different regions on deputation. This is not possible that everyone would know Hindi. As a result, English is used in most of their meetings. It is not the case that you cannot speak Hindi at all, but, you need sufficient English to understand what other people are saying.

☑ Most of the Union government's work is still done in English. Whatever letters are sent by the Union government to its departments, ministries and states are sent in English. Due to the necessity of the Constitution, sometimes Hindi letters have to be sent too which are translated by the officials of the national language's department.

☑ This is the same situation with the Union government's files. When you get a file there, you can do the noting in Hindi, but, even for this you have to understand the noting which is already written in the file and which is in English.

☑ When you will be at deputation in the Indian government or posted in some region then you will have to go for meetings in other regions. If you go to the North Eastern regions or Southern regions then your work cannot be done without English. The communication will not be possible the way it should be. This will further create problems.

- ☑ The same situation will be in meetings abroad. You will not be able to do anything without English - from airport to government offices, nowhere. The negative effects of not knowing English would be that you will not be sent to the meetings held abroad. Some other reason will be told to you, whereas, the actual reason would be only this.
- ☑ There are different types of trainings even during the service. This also includes the training held outside. You can even go to learn something to other countries for 2-3 years. Government takes the responsibility of bearing this expense for you. However, this wish of learning will not be fulfilled without English.
- ☑ Most of the government's work is now done using computers. There is software for Hindi as well; however, English is used more.
- ☑ If you have to use internet properly, then, it is not possible without English language. Whether you have to watch and listen to some international lectures or find some information from encyclopedia, all this is possible only through English.
- ☑ The political borders of the countries are still intact; however, the financial, social and cultural boundaries have been destroyed. The dream of acquiring international citizenship of great politicians is about to be fulfilled. We have to accept this strong influence of English. We have to accept this fact that just like Hindi is the main language

of communication in the huge and multi-lingual India, English is the main language of communication in this huge and multi-lingual world.

Friends, I am not saying that without English, you will be unsuccessful. You can go up, even higher than you expected. However, this fact cannot be ignored either that by learning English, you can reach higher as there is no limit for attaining success. And, who knows the task of achieving success (without having the benefit of knowing English) that is appearing to be too difficult for you will seem to be much easier after learning English.

The reason for this may be the colonial mentality, but, the literature and knowledge of this language is vast. This language keeps including the literature and knowledge of other languages in its own. So, it is not wrong to say that if you know English, then, you know the world's language.

English paper's pattern (compulsory)

What is called English (compulsory) in UPSC is called General English in school and college. This is not English, but, General English and this should be understood properly. This is not related to English literature but the understanding of English. Hence, good or deep English is not required to qualify it. You should just be able to know sufficient English to understand what the other person is saying on a general topic, and if you want to say something then you can explain it to others. This is how General English is related to language of communication and not literature.

This can be clarified by looking at the unsolved papers of English (compulsory) of civil services. You need two things to solve this paper:

☑ To have the understanding of English

☑ To have the knowledge of English grammar.

There is a little difference in 'understanding' and 'knowledge'. Knowledge is related to grammar. An illiterate person from Hindi region can also speak Hindi. He understands it very well, even if he does not know it. That means neither has he studied grammar nor he speaks as per the grammar rules. He does all this as per his understanding.

There are three questions in the English paper which are related to its 'understanding', or to say comprehension. Following are the three types of questions:

☑ To write an essay in English

☑ To write a summary of the passage in 1/3rd

☑ To answer the questions asked from the passage.

How would you solve these questions? It is very clear that this would be possible only when you have sufficient knowledge of English to read and understand these things and then write them on your own in your words. You will have to write everything on your own in the essay.

However, there is a difference in essay and summarization. That is, to summarize a passage, it is necessary that you understand every part of the passage well and then rewrite it in your own words. However, you don't need to understand anything for writing an essay. You write it on your own and you write only what you can write in English. Hence, an essay becomes an easy task for you. That is why the possibility of score also increases. However, for both these points, you should have a good understanding of English.

The second part of the paper is related to grammar. In this, the analysis of word knowledge is done, that means how well you understand English words and how well you can use them.

Hence, you have to prepare on two levels for the compulsory paper of English- first would be the understanding of English and second would be the grammatical knowledge of English.

Understanding of the English language

I am writing in advance that you would have to start this with your psychological preparation. Keeping this in mind, I have discussed the psychological situations in detail, for the students of Hindi who become anti-English. You will have to get over it. After doing this, your mind will become used to receiving English language. That is how you can even learn it.

It is obvious that the process of learning a language starts with its grammar. I will discuss this later. However, there is another way of learning a language and that is the practical way. This is not related to the 'knowledge' of English but to its 'understanding'. You will have to read grammar for this (compulsory) paper. But, don't forget that a language cannot be learnt just by studying grammar, like, you cannot become a singer, just by, reading a book of music. You have to practice for that. Hence, I am going to discuss few practical points which will automatically help you in developing that practical understanding. If you wish, you can even call it as, 'the practical approach to grammar'. By these suggestions, you will, not only, be able to solve the questions of 250 marks, but also be able to perfectly understand those 50 marks' grammar questions which can fetch you the total marks.

Language is mainly related to two things: environment and usage. We naturally learn the language in whose environment we live. Even if we don't speak, we will at least understand it. You can even write it if you know the spellings.

One is mother tongue, in which our mind thinks fundamentally. You can call it your natural language. The second language is the one we learn. Our mind doesn't accept the learnt language as natural but in a translated way. That means after listening to the learnt language, it translates into the mother tongue and then it makes you understand it. In the same way, before speaking in the learnt language, it thinks in the mother tongue and then translates it into the learnt language. That is why you would see that a person is not as fluent in the learnt language as he is in mother tongue. So much so that the best creations and the natural thinking have been done in the mother tongue of the people.

Hence, the best way to learn English according to me is to be in the English environment somehow. This will not only help you in practicing the listening skills of words, but also will increase the brain's speed of translating.

You can use the following ways to create an English environment for yourself:

☑ English and Hindi news are broadcasted on radio every night. This news is mainly made in English. Then they are translated in Hindi. If you try to listen to the news, you will get irritated as you will fail to understand it. But, you will realize that after 2-3 months, you will start understanding it. This way you can provide your mind with the English environment for at least half an hour every day. You should, definitely, do this even for the preparation of General Knowledge.

☑ You should watch good films in foreign languages. I am not asking you to watch English movies since you will not be able to understand their pronunciation. It would be better to watch such foreign movies in which you have 'sub-titles' in English. You should try to understand it by reading 'sub-titles'. You will also see the pictures which will help you in understanding these 'sub-titles'.

☑ Newspaper is the best medium of knowing the colloquial and the current English. It will provide your mind with the English environment if you can spend at least half an hour everyday with it. However, only reading it is not sufficient, you will have to work harder- if you are really reading the newspaper with the purpose of learning English. While reading the newspaper, you will come across a number of words whose meanings you aren't aware of. You should look for their meanings in the dictionary and write them with their meanings in a diary. You should also keep reading them from time to time. This will help you in building your vocabulary without which you cannot comprehend a language.

☑ You will face one more problem in the beginning. You will understand certain words but you will not be able to understand the meaning of the entire sentence. You can note them down and ask someone the meaning of these sentences. After this, you can jot down the sentences along with the meaning and revise them from time to time.

- ☑ Listen to speeches in English. If your friends speak decent English, ask them to speak to you in English only. You should also try to speak in English even if what you say is incorrect. Do not hesitate. Do not think that in the compulsory English paper you only have to write in English, and not speak in the language. Speaking in English will help train your brain.
- ☑ You may be staying in a place where no one can speak English; if it is so then you should start writing in English. Pick any topic and try to write an essay on it. Form small and easy sentences and write them down.

In the compulsory English exam, you are asked to write an essay of 600 words for 100 marks. You have the freedom to express yourself. So your preparation should include the will to write the best essay you can. You should aim at scoring at least 40 out of these 100 marks.

Knowledge of English Grammar

Questions worth 50 marks are asked from this section. Important thing is that you can score full marks here. You will mostly be asked about usage of words.

There are plenty of books to help you prepare for this. The questions that are asked are of normal level. The sentences are also not too difficult and long like in comprehension. It will not be difficult to understand these if you have prepared (to some extent) for English language. Once you understand these sentences, it becomes easier for you to solve the questions reading the instructions properly.

English grammar is vast so you should focus on basic grammar. This means you should focus on grammar that is used while speaking everyday English. You do not have to study advance level grammar. Focus on the following -

Tenses, Articles, Modules (can, could, must, shall etc), voice, preposition (in, at, for, between etc), either-or, neither-nor, not only, although, Direct and Indirect Speech, Interrogatory sentence, Prefix and suffix, Punctuation etc.

Friends, this paper is for 300 marks and you need to score at least 75 to qualify. You should aim at scoring 40 in the essay. Then you need to score 35 out of 200. I think three questions, comprehensive in nature, which are worth 150 marks, will be the toughest for you. Among these you should focus on questions that are asked from the unseen passage. If you are unable to answer in your own language, find the lines in the passage and alter them a little to write them down as your answer.

I have two very important things to say. First, you will have enough time to solve this paper. Make full use of it. Do not be in a hurry.

The second thing is: if you find the grammatical questions easy, do them first. You can write embellished essays later on. You should do full justice to both of these sections as they are the most scoring in the paper.

Do not leave any question, no matter how tough it seems to you. Write as much as you are able to write. Write whatever you can, even if some of your sentences may not be correct.

I have no doubt about it that, if you follow this strategy, you will be able to qualify the compulsory English exam. My best wishes are with you.

Chapter 17

Compulsory Language (Hindi)

There are two language papers in the main exam of civil services. The English language paper is mandatory for everyone and a student has to score a minimum of 25 percent marks to qualify this exam. The other compulsory paper is a language exam. A student needs to score at least 25 percent marks to qualify it. A student can choose from a variety of languages in this paper. This examination includes all languages including Hindi which has been mentioned in the Schedule eight of the Indian constitution. Students (except those from Northeast) have to choose one from these many languages.

In this chapter, we will discuss the Hindi language. The subject that UPSC calls Hindi (language) is usually known as general Hindi. There is a misconception about general Hindi in the minds of students that it is a very easy subject. This is especially the case with Hindi-speaking students. On the other hand, science and commerce students assume this is very difficult.

Both the beliefs are false. The paper is not so easy that anyone with a working knowledge of Hindi can solve it, but it is not so difficult also that it is beyond the understanding of science students. They both, Hindi-speaking students and students from science and commerce background, actually require a disciplined preparation for compulsory Hindi exam. It is true, however, that Hindi-speaking students would have to prepare for this a little less rigorously than others. Here are some tips to help you with this. But first let us understand what general Hindi is.

What is General Hindi?

We can divide Hindi into two parts -Hindi literature and General Hindi. There is a fixed syllabus for Hindi literature which includes various streams or forms of literature, its history and its authors. Apart from studying this syllabus, a student of Hindi literature is also expected to have a good command over the language. But this language would differ from the language used in daily communication. This will be the language that is used in literature- more adorable and academically strong Hindi.

Another is general Hindi. In general Hindi, students are expected to have a basic understanding of Hindi language. This will neither test your knowledge of Hindi literature nor will it expect from you to have an adorable language at your disposal. Even grammatical knowledge will not be judged. You will not be asked nouns and pronouns and their types. General Hindi is concerned with the practical aspect of Hindi and not the grammatical aspect.

'The practical knowledge of Hindi' means how well you can use the language. It is not tested whether you have a 'literature-friendly' language at your disposal, or if you can use similes and metaphors in order to make your language more impactful or dramatic, or if you can write academically strong

Hindi. Instead, you will be tested for the correctness of your language. Moreover the test is how well you use it to express yourself while communicating with other people.

Structure of the paper

The exam asks you to write an essay of 600 words. The topic of the essay is very easy since the aim of the essay is not to test your knowledge but to examine your style of language and to see if you can express yourself in Hindi.

One question is that of summarising. You have to summarise a long paragraph to one-third of its length. Here, the examiner tests how you understand the language and essence of the paragraph and express it in your own words.

One question is that of comprehension. You are asked at least 5 to 6 questions related to this. If you give correct answers, you can score up to 75 percent marks.

Other questions include antonyms, synonyms, a word having different meanings, one word for the sentence, idioms and phrases, collective nouns, adjectives and sentence correction. These parts test how aware are you of Hindi words and their usage.

Two more questions of General Hindi are left after this - translating Hindi to English and then English to Hindi translation. It has been observed that the paragraph that has to be translated from English to Hindi is very easy. It is more difficult to translate from Hindi to English. If you know little bit of English language it will be easy for you to translate from English to Hindi.

Yes, you will have to work a little hard to translate from Hindi to English. But as you are already preparing for compulsory English paper, you won't need any special preparation for this.

You don't have to worry much about this paper though. This is of 300 marks out of which you require only 25 percent, to say 75 marks. It is not difficult to get these qualifying marks, and you don't require distinction.

Preparation

As I mentioned before the question paper seems very easy at first glance but do not take it very lightly. It is true that it is easy and since the syllabus is little you will need to prepare less for it, but this does not mean that you should not prepare at all.

To improve your vocabulary, you can pick any General Hindi book. Focus on the words that have been used and try to memorize them. Write down the important words separately. Keep revising them. You should vow to make no mistake in this section. If you stay alert, you will succeed in this.

As far as one 600 words' essays is concerned, I have already told you enough about essay writing in the earlier section. You should keep those things in mind. The only difference in this section is that you cannot write much for a brief essay. You have to be to-the-point and as precise as possible. Avoid giving examples. You can call this writing short notes. Remember you are writing for the layman so your subject matter and language should be simple.

As far as this paper is concerned, 'writing less is more'.

Chapter 18

The technique of writing impressive answers

When I was a student, something would trouble me a lot. After leaving the exam hall, students would discuss that the exam went well and they were able to solve most questions. I was among them. However, the results would tell another story. Some would score very less while some scored well. The range of marks extended from 45 to 65 percent. I don't know about others but I used to write the best answers I could and only for the questions that I could write well on. Some people would still score better than me. I would score somewhere between 55 to 60 while they would be between 65 to 70. I was very curious how I could learn their high-scoring technique. I was eventually able to grasp the technique, though it took me a while. But it proved to be a miraculous thing when I was doing my post-graduation in Hindi literature. And I have no hesitation saying that this technique helped me in civil services too.

Friends, on the basis of these very experiences, I will now share some tried and tested ideas with you. I am sure they will be of great use to you.

You cannot deny the fact that the only way our knowledge is assessed, in a written examination, is through the answers we write. Sometimes, even good students who know their subject well are unable to write good answers. On the other hand, some students may not know the subject very well, but their style of writing puts them way ahead of their peers. Therefore, you should know what a good answer is and how to write one. Let us see.

Features of a good answer

I will give you a simple but scientific formula for this. You have been asked a question, and you have given the answer. Now do one thing. Ask yourself - have you got the correct answer to the question that has been asked? Are you satisfied with the answer to the extent that there are no further questions or doubts arising in your mind? If the answer is 'yes', it means your answer is a good answer.

I will now give you some tips on how to write a good answer -

- ☑ Your answer should contain facts. Don't write anything that cannot be justified with logic. Remember, your answer should be backed more by the facts than mere emotions or feelings.
- ☑ Your answer should not be repetitive. The word limit imposed in the civil service exam does not allow you to repeat things in your answer. If you say the same thing more than once it weakens your answer and ruins your impression.
- ☑ Be to-the-point. Focus only on what has been asked. It is better to keep glancing at the question that has been asked while writing down your

answer. This will prevent you from being disoriented.

When I say 'to-the-point' it means you should not mix up different points. Explain each one clearly and separately.

☑ Your answer must be impressive. Unless the examiner is not convinced with your thoughts, unless he considers it to be real, your answer cannot leave any impression. In other words, to write an impressive answer you have to be persuasive. Do not just write anything, use strong content. Smart analysis will render your answer more convincing.

☑ The answer should be well organised, well structured. Facts and thoughts should be arranged in an order. How will you do this? You must have heard the phrase 'food, clothing and shelter' but not 'clothing, shelter and food'. Why is this so? This is about prioritising. Food is most important, then comes clothing and after that shelter. Your answers also should reflect this. You should write your points in accordance with their importance- most important ones should be written first. This will make your answer well organised.

☑ Most questions ask for an analytical answer. Analyse the topics as asked.

Some questions ask you to list down features, merits-demerits, agree or disagree. These questions have two parts which you need to answer separately. Write down the positive points first.

☑ A good answer must be interesting to the reader. If you cut-paste in your answer, it will break the rhythm and make the answer unimpressive to the examiner.

☑ Follow the word limit. It helps keep your answer brief and concise.

☑ Every student has his language and you should try to write in yours. Memorised language renders your answer artificial. With practice, you can develop your own style of writing. It may be boring in the beginning but once you evolve your own unique style of writing, everything will fall into place.

Structure of the answer

What should be the structure of a good and impressive answer? I'm assuming you do know something about this since you are a graduate. I will not talk about this at length here. This is also because if you know what a good answer is and if you are using the above mentioned strategy in your answers, it will automatically have a good structure. In short, the structure of a solid answer has three parts -

(a) Opening remarks

(b) Main content

(c) Conclusion

Opening remarks mean you should not jump directly to the answer; you have to first introduce the background of your answer and the subject even if in just one line. This will prevent your answer from sounding irrelevant. This will also add a rhythm to it and make it look complete.

The most important part of an answer is the middle part also known as the main content. This is the actual answer. I have already told you how to write this.

The last paragraph is the conclusion. It could be a single line or multiple lines. It depends on how much you have to say. Whatever your conclusion is it should be based on the arguments you have given in the main content of the answer. If they both are not related, it will ruin your answer.

Before you write the answer

Students are under so much time pressure in the exam hall that they do not devote enough time and patience to read the questions asked in the paper. What they do is having a speed reading of the questions as soon as they get the paper and start writing the answers hurriedly. The danger is not reading the paper, but reading it in a hurry. It is even more dangerous to read questions quickly and write down answers. And it results in ruining all your hard work till date.

I am now giving you some tips keeping this psychological challenge in mind. You should practice writing answers based on these things. Gradually, they will be transformed into habits and benefit you greatly in the exam hall.

- ☑ Understand the question: students start writing the answer without understanding the question first. They are not writing an answer to the question that was asked but on the topic related to question. Every question is related to some topic but you should know which part it is from. Instead of writing what is asked, you start writing what you know. And it makes all the difference.

☑ Try detecting the shades of the question: is the colour red the same? Is the red of the rising sun, the red of the blood or the red of the rose the same? Of course not. The colour is red, but the shades are different provided you see it with a sharp eye. Your questions demand the same- a sharp eye. Delve deep into the questions and find the shades in them in order to determine what actually the examiner wants to know. You will find them for sure.

Just because your answer is not wrong does not mean that it is right. Have you seen archery? If you hit the innermost circle you score four marks, after this as you move to the outer circles you get three, two and one marks respectively. You will fetch no marks hitting elsewhere. The hit that scored one mark was not wrong but it was not completely correct either. There was scope to get four marks in that and there will be someone who will achieve it. And the one who got one mark will lose. You will be able to hit the innermost circle once you try to find the shades in a question.

☑ Don't miss out on the keywords in the question: Most students do this. They think that 'discuss it', 'analyse it', 'critically criticize it', 'comment on it' etc. are one and the same thing. But this is not the case. These are the words that tell you how you should be writing your answer. Therefore, these keywords must be taken into account before answering a question. I will discuss it in detail on the next page.

☑ See how many parts the question can be broken down to. Divide the question into as many parts as required and then answer each. This way you will prevent yourself of being disoriented and would be able to give all the answers that are being asked for through a particular question.

☑ If you are having trouble answering the question due to some Hindi word or the meaning of a sentence it is better to look at the English translation. Do not risk answering on guess-work.

Importance of keywords

Students, who are taking their preparation seriously, should never forget that the questions asked in the civil service exams are heavily dependent on the keywords present in them. Any question has two parts - one would be a statement and the other would be an analysis. Consider this question -

"Chola architecture has a great place in the development of temple architecture. Discuss."

The question clearly has two parts. The first one is the statement 'Chola architecture has a great place in the development of temple architecture'. It is the backbone of the question which establishes the main part of the question.

The latter part is- 'discuss'. I call it the 'keyword'. There are so many keywords, e.g., elucidate, assess, critically analyse, describe, justify, prove etc.

Usually, students are unable to see the minute differences between these keywords. At university level, this does not pose such a problem, but this will not in IAS exam. These keywords decide the shades of the question and hint at how you have to write your answer.

These two parts of a question are interconnected for sure.

When you have to answer the above mentioned question, you will keep the speciality of Chola architecture as the basis. But students often do the mistake of writing down characteristics of Chola architecture in this answer.

Read the question again. It clearly states two things -

(a) First, 'development of the temple architecture'. Note, you are not being told of architecture as a whole, it's about only temple architecture.

(b) Second, 'great place'. It's importance.

So you have to answer with facts that establish the importance of Chola architecture in the development of temple architecture, not the architecture in the Chola period.

Your answer is not yet complete. You have been asked to discuss it. So you now need to examine this statement carefully and write your views. In this process, you will now give facts in support of the statement but if you have something against it, you will write that down too. Then only will you have a complete answer. Now you understand how the two parts of the question are supporting each other like two tyres of a cart.

Two types of questions

Whether it is the general knowledge paper or an optional paper, the questions in them can be divided into two types-informative and analytical. Informative questions are asked less often (e.g., 20-25% out of total questions) than analytical ones. Consider the following question :

"The rivers of Western Ghats do not form deltas. Why?"

These are college-style questions. You have solved them before but not the analytical ones. This is why civil service exam poses a challenge for you. On the other hand, this exam seems 'as usual' to them who are used to solving analytical questions.

Analytical questions do not directly ask you the reasons, comparisons, characteristics or merits-demerits. They ask you for your own logical reasoning and way of expression. You will only be able to answer these questions if you know the subject very well. Students who memorise fail completely. At least three-fourth of the questions belongs in this category in thc civil service exam. For e.g. -

"Do you agree that starting new sugar mills is trending up in Southern states? Justify your answer."

Try to see the shades of it. This question clearly asks for your opinion. You could agree or disagree with the statement. First you have to lay down your opinion and then give facts to prove it right. This will only be possible if you have sharpened your analytical skills.

I have experienced it on numerous occasions that students get confused with the keywords, or consider all of them to be the same. Keeping this in mind I am going to share some points here which will help you avoid this confusion:

Regarding Keywords

You will find plenty of keywords in the general knowledge and optional papers of civil services. There are many such keywords and the differences between them are so faint that you can get confused. This confusion may lead you to mental exertion. The important things to consider avoiding this confusion and exertion are -

☑ Not all keywords mean different things. Their meaning is the same even if they are used in different contexts. You can consider them to be synonyms. For example, there is an English word- discuss. You will find three Hindi synonyms for it- 'vivechna', 'charcha' and 'alochna'. But you need not bother why these three Hindi words have different meanings. You should consider them as the same.

☑ Same is the case with English. There is a word- 'explain', which stands for, in Hindi, 'vyakhya' and 'vivran'. 'Explain' also means elucidate, elaborate and interpret. So whenever you come across any of these four words you should consider them as the same. But remember, when I say 'consider them as the same', it applies only on civil cervices exam papers. In the dictionaries they have separate meanings and usages. That is why I feel that having knowledge of the fundamental differences among these keywords would be sufficient for you. Fundamentally, there may be three types of differences: First, words that do not ask for interpretation. Such as: characterise, identify, list the differences, compare etc.

Second, words that ask for analysis but not a very deep one. Simple reasoning would work here. Such as: prove, asses, evaluate, criticize and comment. Third, words those ask for a deep analysis. Usually when two analytical words are put together they ask for an in-depth analysis such as critically examine, critically evaluate etc.

☑ The difference between keywords determines how you analyse each answer differently. If you are asked to 'explain', you will list down important points about the topic. When you are asked to 'discuss', you write down your answer in conversational style. When asked to 'analyse', you write step by step after analysing all parts of the question.

So analysis has to be done for sure, but the manner of analysis will differ with keyword to keyword.

I hope that points mentioned above would have cleared lot of doubts you had earlier. Now you will be better able to understand everything I'm going to write about various keywords -

(1) Criticise : It means contemplating the negative and positive aspects of something. You have to give both sides. This word is seldom used in questions asked in civil service.

(2) Critically analyse : This word is often used. When just criticising an answer, you have to touch upon its negatives and positives but when critically criticising, you have to evaluate the merits and demerits in depth. You actually require a deep insight.

(3) Discuss : This is somewhat like critically criticising something as both the aspects are examined. The style of discussing is, however, different. Discussion is conversational style. That's why this word is used so often in day-to-day conversation, e.g., 'let us discuss it' or 'let us talk'. Obviously, you can give a lot of examples in this.

(4) **Elucidate :** This means explaining the meaning of something difficult. You have to explain the meaning and the context of the fact given to you in such a manner that the reader is left with no doubts. For e.g., you cannot understand a poem written in just two lines, so your professor elucidate it for you so that you can understand the whole context and meaning of those two lines. There is another English word for it- 'elaborate'. The literal meaning of 'elaborate' is 'to expand'. This means to explain a thing, written in a compact and complex manner, in great detail so that there is no room for doubts. This requires you to read between the lines. Anyone can read that which is written but you have to read between the lines. So elucidate means to explain the thing which has not been said but is implied.

(5) **Explain :** It is not exactly the same as elucidate. Whereas while elucidating you have to clarify the meaning of difficult sentences, while explaining it is enough to mention important points related to the topic.

(6) **Comments :** You will find another word as its replacement- 'note'. Comment means telling someone something. Comment can be taken as a short or brief article through which we explain something to someone

in detail. It is an art of keeping forward your opinion in brief. While writing a comment, it is better to justify its relevance as well.

(7) **Analysis :** This is similar to a review, but it is done differently. While critically criticising, we take the question as a whole, in analysis we divide it into separate parts. Each part is analysed individually. This way our thoughts get revealed in a step-by-step manner.

(8) **Examine :** This means examining if something has been done in the correct way. It is obvious then that you will have to decide here and also justify your decision. This word demands you to be original.

(9) **Evaluate :** This word is used frequently and is similar to explain, criticise, critically criticise etc. It means examining the negatives and positives of something.

Evaluate could also mean figuring out the value of something. You should do this via examples and if you can prove your point it would be better.

(10) **Assess :** This is similar to evaluate. When asked to assess, we can presuppose a few things. However, they should not be impractical and imaginary.

(11) **Justify :** You have to prove that the given statement is true with the aid of examples and instances. You should give your opinion here. If you disagree with something it would be better to give an appropriate reason for that.

(12) **Prove :** Substantiate can also be used in the place of this word. These words mean give evidence to support something. You have to list down facts and arguments.

(13) **Illustrate :** This means explain with examples. These

could include statistics, events, diagrams etc.

(14) **Describe :** This is a detailed characterisation or 'sketch'. There is no analysis required.

(15) **Identify :** This also does not require a critical approach. You only have to write down the introductory details about someone or something so its identity is clear.

(16) **Features :** This includes writing only important points from a topic. Even among the important points, importance is given to unique features.

(17) **Compare :** Comparison means you highlight the difference as well as the similarities between two things. However, if you are asked to 'contrast' then you only have to emphasise the differences between the two.

(18) **Define :** The most important thing here is the definition of the given term. But you will also have to elaborate a little on the definition so that the reader can grasp the basic thought. You can take it as a 'short write-up'.

Friends, I have tried to explain the meaning of words which are frequently used in the question papers. I may have missed out on some words but you must have understood their meanings by now. So there is no need bothering about them- neither for you nor for me.

But take my words, do not try to memorise the meaning of these words, it will be of no use. Instead, understand the meanings and then practice them. This will help you succeed in the exam.

Chapter 19

Facing the Interview Board

This is a very sensitive stage. After lots of hard work and a long tiring preparation you pass the preliminary exam. Then you work even harder to qualify the mains examination. It is only after qualifying these first two stages that you reach this last stage of civil services examination, where your life is decided - in the sense that if you succeed, your life will bc something else and if you don't, it will be something else. Also in the sense that if the interview goes well, you will be given your choice of service and if not, then it is possible that you succeed but won't get your choice of service. If the latter happens and you still have some attempts left with you and if age is on your side, then once again you will join the struggle from the beginning.

I am not saying that your life will end if you don't succeed in the interview. Life is not so small and meaningless that it is dependent on IAS; if you don't get it then it will be over. Sky is the limit for everyone and there will be thousands and lakhs of opportunities. It's okay for us to choose a single aim at a time. Sometimes we may not be able to fulfil it. But this doesn't mean that you should let go of all the other aims. None of the aims die nor is the path to your aims closed. In fact, if one door closes, thousands will open. This is not to convince you, but to tell you the truth about life, so that by understanding the truth you make yourself stronger. Being strong is the first challenge you have to overcome when preparing yourself for the interview.

I just said that it is a sensitive stage. Think about the cricketer, who has already scored 94 runs. To complete his century he requires only 6 runs. You will notice that he was playing fearlessly before but he is not able to do that now. He is a bit weak now & plays with a lot of caution. He is worried that he will get out and will be unable to score a century. The player's mental state is very sensitive right now and the more sensitive you become towards your goal the chances of failure also increase. Being sensitive turns a person weak. The player will definitely be out while scoring 97-98 runs.

But there are players who are not counting at all. Such players just have two things in mind - they need to score the maximum amount of runs and save themselves from being out. Such a player is totally focused on the game, rather than the result. He is fully aware of the fact that the result is not important, what is important is how he plays. If he plays well then the result will automatically be good. This is true for science, for nature and for life. Lord Krishna is quoted in Bhagwad Gita as saying "Work without focusing on the fruits of your labour, work is your right, the result is not in your hands." So why should be bothered about something that's not in our hands! Instead, we should focus on what is our right- our actions.

My Thought, My Motivation

When you will reach for the interview, something like this will also happen with you. I want you to believe that whatever is happening with you, you are not the only one. It's happening with everyone. It happened with me and all my batch-mates. I have never met anyone yet who would say that something like this never happened with him. Yes it is possible that it happened more with some and less with the others, but happened. That's why the first thing is that you don't need to worry about it. If you are getting very sensitive about it then you need to try and control it and you can do this with the help of the tip given above. Because this kind of sensitivity is not physical and only mental, thus the way to control it should be: mentally. I am just about to tell you in brief what I did to control it.

When I went for the IAS interview, I was teaching in a college. This was my third interview. Before this, I had already given interviews for State Civil Service and PhD. I was still very scared. When I was in the huge hall waiting for my name to be called out, I was not sure whether I would be able to walk till the door of the Interview room. I was so disconcerted and even my handkerchief was all wet from wiping off the sweat from my face. I understood that it's not my cup of tea. But just five minutes before my name was being called, don't know through what divine inspiration a thought transformed in my mind which burnt all the weaknesses inside me and slowly and gradually I gained confidence. Do you want to know what that thought was?

It was a normal thought but very powerful, and true too. I thought, "its okay if I don't get selected, so what? I am a lecturer in a college. Failing this won't take away my lecturer ship. I will just get to know that I am capable of this only. There is nothing to worry about." Friends, it was a small thought, but the impact was big. This one thought, one small thought helped me reach my goal. This was just a psychological thought.

Choose your "Thought"

I want you to choose a thought according to your liking before facing the Interview. If you have a job (no matter what kind of job it is) that can be a thought for you, like it was for me. If you have some attempts left, it can be a support mechanism and you can think that the next success would be better than this one. Another thought which can help you is, "If I don't succeed, then I was not capable enough and people better than me have succeeded. No worries, now whatever I choose to do, I will be so much better in it that I won't have any regrets of failing this."

I want you to believe that this will help you a lot. You have to progress keeping in mind that interview mainly is a psychological process and you need to search for psychological measures. You might have seen gourd, ridge gourd and beans. If they get support of brushwood, they reach the top and then only they are able to bear fine fruits. Or else they have to stretch in the lower ground and therefore are not able to bear such fruits. Just as a vine needs a support to flourish and spread, in the same manner you require psychological support to succeed in the interview. Am I able to make myself clear?

Beware of Misunderstandings

Most of the Examinations have two phases- written and Interview. After a judgment by the court it is now fixed that interview marks cannot be more than 15 percent of the total marks for the written examination. In IAS, the marks obtained in mains examination are the basis for the merit list and the mains examination is of 1750 marks. The marks in general Hindi and general English are removed from the merit list. You are only required to pass them. Thus, keeping these 1750 marks in mind, 275 marks are fixed for the interview.

I caught two misconceptions prevailing among the IAS aspirants. They are:

- ☑ The first misconception is that they think if you score high marks out of 1750, then scoring less in the interview won't matter. They think that out of 275 marks, they will get at least some marks.
- ☑ The second misunderstanding is that they don't focus on the interview. They think of first clearing the mains and then preparing for the interview. Some are in the delusion that many coaching institutes take mock tests and can help them prepare in 2-4 days.

I would like to warn the aspirants about these misunderstandings. I will make my point clear by presenting the following logics to you. Consider them.

My first logic is regarding the first misconception. Exams are held every year and every year, the merit list is set. It is clear that every year the merit list contains a border line above which the aspirant gets selected in IAS and one scoring just below the line gets IPS or others, though they were also focusing on IAS. You can also think as that aspirant, who got IAS as the service and who just sits at the bottom of the list. Had he scored 1 mark less, he wouldn't have got IAS. Likewise, those who couldn't get IAS, had they scored 2-3 more marks, they would have qualified for the service. Now for those who didn't get IAS, if they still have an attempt left, they will again sit for the examination. This will happen every year and someone or the other will come on the border line. But we should leave no stone unturned from our side. This is why you should not take the interview lightly.

Now I come to the second misunderstanding. This misunderstanding is related to the preparation of the interview. Preparing for the interview is a continuous process. You cannot develop the personality of a person in one day. Yes, on the level of your consciousness, you can be alert and comfortable for a while and portray yourself as someone else. For example, when you will go in front of the interview board, you can control your behaviour for that half hour, be humble and show all the required etiquettes- even if in daily life you are an unstable person, a rebel and rude. And most of the students try to do this. They think they will portray themselves to be nice and smart like they do in front of their girlfriends.

But friends, there is a huge difference here. Your girlfriend is naive. She doesn't have many experiences in life, which is why she is not an expert in catching the right things. She doesn't have the eyes, which can take x-ray of your inside. But the people sitting in the interview board have these qualities. Their eyes are like a sonography machine able to see the smallest thing inside you. On your level of consciousness no matter how clever you are, it won't work there. They don't judge you on your consciousness; rather they try to reach your subconscious and unconscious. No person is the same as its conscious mind. He is what is in his subconscious and unconscious mind. Psychology has already proved that our personality seen by others is just 1/6th of our true entity- exactly like an iceberg whose 1/6th portion is seen above water and the rest is not seen due to its existence under water. The interviewer tries to catch that unseen portion.

So you think that you will be able to improve your personality in a couple of days? Do you still believe that you need to work on your personality development after giving your mains examination? Personality is made up of small things which take time. So you need to start its preparation from the very day when the thought of being an IAS enters your mind.

So what to do?

I know if I am saying these things, the question that definitely arises in your mind is "What should I do about it?" Your question is valid and it should arise. Here it's not possible for me to describe it in detail. It itself is an independent topic and also very important. A pleasant personality is not only required for IAS, but in every test of life. The study in management has repeatedly proved that the contribution of one's knowledge to their success in life is merely 15 percent. The rest 85 percent of the contribution is of his personality. So working on it will be very beneficial for you.

Keeping this fact in mind, I have written an Independent book, named -"Personality Development for Students".

Originally it is in Hindi. But its English translation is also available. If you really want your personality to flourish, then you should go through it. This is not a routine guide. For the first time you will be able to know and understand personality. In this book, I have not mentioned the mechanical and theoretical sides of personality rather only the practical side of it. During the year 1987-1997, I was lucky enough to meet and talk to many great personalities of the world, like Nelson Mandela, President of Russia Brejnev, Princess Diana, many noble laureates, actor-actresses and other great personalities. Based on these experiences, I have written down this book. I feel that you should read it and also recommend it to other people - regardless of whether they are preparing for IAS or not. A good personality is needed in every walk of life.

I said that its preparation is a continuous process. Yes, from personality's point of view, it is a continuous and long process, but in the context of knowledge also it is a continuous process. As soon as you start preparing for your initial examination, be cautious that you have also started preparing for the interview. If we look on the basis of topics, then there are three main topics from which questions are asked during the interview. The first is- about your own self. You don't need to work on it differently. Second one is- about the subjects whom you had during your graduation and the subject in which you completed your post graduation. And also the subject, which you took as an optional paper. The third is knowledge of contemporary events, in which most of the questions are based on the present political situation. Together the three subjects, in a way, cover up approximately 75 percent of the questions.

Think yourself that when you start preparing for the initial examination, the third part i.e. general awareness preparation also starts. In a way it is a part of general studies, which occupies the largest part of the interview.

Then as soon as you start preparing for the mains examination, you also prepare for the optional subject in the interview. The questions relating to current affairs asked during the interview, they are more of the subjective types than objective. They are trying to learn your views. As the nature of the questions asked in the mains exam is analytical and elucidative, you prepare for the general knowledge keeping only this in mind. So don't you think this is going to prepare you for the interview also?

Note that the preparation of the interview starts from the beginning. If you keep this in mind, thcn automatically you will be able to look at any issue in detail. Don't stick to the illusion 'I will prepare for it later.' Of course after the mains exam you can choose those important topics, which were the center of discussion for a while. Give importance to such issues. Reshuffle and prove them well and set your thoughts about the issues, so that your answers are clear in your head before facing the interview board.

What is an Interview?

Actually interview is a lively process. While the preliminary examination and mains examination evaluate you indirectly, the interview does a face-to-face screening.

According to me this is not 'interview', but 'inner-view'. A very good word is available in Hindi language for it called 'character examination'. It is the process of judging the inner characteristics of a person. You can either be attracted to a person or be impressed by someone. Personality is not an ability to attract but a great ability to impress people. It is possible that you don't look attractive, but your impact could be great. And just the same way it is also possible that someone might look very attractive, but his impact is null. I have met Nelson Mandela and I can say that he was not at all attractive. But his impact was great. America's former President Abraham Lincoln can even be described as ugly, but his impact was so deep that he is counted among the greatest Presidents. The story of Ashtavakra in India tells the same thing. Ashtavakra's body was disfigured from 8 places. He was short-heighted, black complexioned and you can imagine a person whose body is disfigured in eight parts, how much attractive he can be? However, his personality was so strong that knowledgeable people like Raja Janak called him in his court, to gain knowledge from him.

But don't think that this means an attractive person won't be impressive and the one, who is impressive, won't be attractive. There are some people whom nature has given an amazing combination of both. U G Krishnamurthi, Rajeev Gandhi, music director Naushad and Amitabh Bachhan etc. have been blessed by God. The sole purpose behind saying all this is to make you aware of the real meaning of personality.

Now I will discuss what UPSC wants during the Interview. But I will play just a mediator here. I am just giving you an analysis of what UPSC has mentioned in its syllabus under the heading 'interview test'. UPSC has clearly mentioned that-

- ☑ The object of the interview is to assess the personal suitability of the candidate for a career in public service.
- ☑ The test is intended to judge the mental calibre of a candidate.
- ☑ In broad terms, this is really an assessment of not only his/her intellectual qualities but also social traits and his/her interest in current affairs.
- ☑ Some of the qualities to be judged are mental alertness, critical power of assimilation, clear and logical exposition, balance of judgement, variety and depth of interest, ability for social cohesion and leadership, intellectual and moral integrity.

  There are two other things clearly mentioned in UPSC, which are to be better understood-

- ☑ The candidate will be interviewed by a Board who will have before them a record of his/her career.
- ☑ The aspirant's interview is taken by a Board of competent and unbiased observers.

I would like you to believe that the 'capable board' and 'neutral members' mentioned in UPSC, is hundred percent true. There should be no doubt in your mind regarding this. The board members are capable, experienced and experts in their own areas. When they sit in the board, they feel the responsibility given to them. They consider themselves equivalent to a judge, whose mind is free from any other influence. The character Arjun, in Mahabharata, focuses only on the eye of the bird he has to shoot, likewise, these members concentrate on the aspirant sitting in front of them. They deeply feel the obligation that their decision will give the country an administrator, who will handle the country and society's reigns for a minimum of 30 years (if he is selected at the age of 30 years). Wherever he will be, he will be as a chief executive and he will play an important role while implementing the government policies.

That is why if you get to hear any ill talks about the interview, then according to me you shouldn't discourage yourself by believing such talks. Whatever anyone says, but trust me that there is nothing like that in UPSC. And the truth is that this can never happen, because the system of the interview is made in such a way that no one can do anything knowingly.

Now I will come to the misunderstanding which I have found in many aspirants.

Some aspirants take interview as the only manner of question-answers. They have this wrong concept that they will be asked some questions in the interview, and if they give all the answers in the interview, they will score high and if they are unable to give answers or give a wrong answer, then they will be unsuccessful. Subjugated by the concept, many unsuccessful aspirants complain, "I was asked 20 questions and I gave 18 right answers in them. Even then I was given less marks." The truth is that to evaluate being successful and unsuccessful in the interview in this way is wrong. Interview is a method, in which your knowledge and personality are examined not by the number of answers given, but on the basis of originality of the answers and the style of expression.

UPSC also, in its syllabus for the interview, has clearly

mentioned in other points that the objective of Interview is to evaluate the mental quality of the aspirant.

In paragraph 3, UPSC again clearly states that "The interview test is not intended to be a test either of the specialised or general knowledge of the candidates which has been already tested through their written papers. Candidates are expected to have taken an intelligent interest not only in their special subjects of academic study but also in the events which are happening around them both within and outside their own state or country as well as in modern currents of thought and in new discoveries which should rouse the curiosity of well educated youth."

Friends, think a little what UPSC is saying. On the surface, it looks very simple, but it is very deep, and in true sense it is the essence of interview. It is clearly said that asking you question and the answers given by you, is just a means, because without any means it is not possible to test the internal properties of someone. When in arrange marriage a boy comes to see a girl or when a girl meets a guy, it doesn't happen that they decide whether they want to marry each other just by looking at each other. Yes, it will be decided what you feel after seeing someone (in terms of beauty), but you will get to know about his thoughts and views and approach towards life only after talking. And this is what is done.

Therefore, it is clear that during the interview, a person's looks or appearance or just his knowledge for his subjects is not tested. If it was like this, then only 'good looking' people would have had government jobs. But you might have seen that many normal looking people are seated in high posts. It only means that during their interview, their internal personality was being tested. Literally, the aim of interview is not to test your knowledge. Its evaluation is already done in the initial and mains examination by the department. Its main aim is to judge your overall personality.

What UPSC wants from you, I have already told you in its own words. But I would also like to add some facts, which are however included in the wanted characteristics, but are not that explicit. I am placing them differently here, so that you understand them clearly. I am saying this because I talked to members, who take the interview for IAS. I also had a talk with such students and still do, who came out of the interview. Though I never got a chance to interview someone for IAS, but I have been a member of 'Mock interview board'. Along with it due to my high government posts, I have had many chances of being in the interview boards and heading them. Since I got a chance to judge students many time, so I know what all expectations one has from the students.

Expectations of the Board

1. Confidence

As I have mentioned before, the moments before the interview are very frightening, in which the aspirant is disconcerted. But I would also like to tell you that it all goes away as soon as you face the interview board. It is somewhat like when during winters you are scared of getting in the pool, but once you get in, then you start enjoying.

The board members understand the nervousness in the starting. The challenge here is how and how soon you can overcome your nervousness. It expresses your confidence.

Another medium which introduces your confidence is your way of answering the questions- how clearly and exact answers are you able to give. It can happen that even after giving the right answer the board members held it wrong, cross-questioned you and confused you. By doing this, they are actually testing your confidence in your answer. Keep in mind that this confidence is not only seen in your answers but in your voice too. When your voice is seasoned, you are not rushing and there are no signs of being frightened in your face, so it means that you have full confidence in whatever you are saying.

2. View towards Life

UPSC has used one word - 'intellectual and moral obligation'. What does it mean? Many aspirants are unable to understand it. They believe that intellectual honesty means saying what they know. They think that saying in front of the board members "I want to work for the society, do something for the country, and remove corruption" shows our moral honesty. Actually, to think like that is nothing more than fooling yourself. Here, the board members will not get trapped by your words. They are able to see through this.

In reality the intellectual and moral honesty depends on your point of view towards life. Whenever you are being asked the solution to a problem, and the solution you recommend that time, is based on your point of view towards life. During the discussion, a number of issues come up and a number of situations arise, when directly-indirectly they can glimpse your views on life. It is clearly detected what kind of life you want to live, your notion towards society and individuals, your basis for decision making and evaluating something or someone, your criteria for a solution to a problem, whether you are a liberal thinker or a narrow minded person, how progressive or reactionary views you have, your behaviour towards the poor, Dalits and the underdogs etc. All these talks are rooted in our minds like the smell of a flower is rooted in itself. It cannot be seen. It can only be sniffed. Do you think that you can prepare for all these qualities in a couple of days?

3. Human Qualities

Here human qualities don't mean the qualities of human beings, but means humanity. You all are aware of the qualities of humanity. To help people is a human characteristic. To act with politeness is a quality of humanity and to behave with proper etiquette is also a human quality. It also includes the ability to love and to forgive someone.

Just opposite to this are inhuman characteristics. The pride of being an officer is a cruel attribute. Anger and selfishness comes under this. Neglecting other people's rights or doing them harms, just for the sake of monetary gains, cannot be considered human.

Before you set your mind to be an IAS officer, I think first you need to prepare yourself that you are not going to govern the people but are going to serve them. That's why it is known as 'civil servant' in English. Gone are the days when people used to treat every government official as 'mai-baap' or 'hujoor-sarkaar'. Even if you will have lot of authority, don't ever forget that you are given those rights so that you can complete your obligation, and not so that you misuse it for your own benefit. It is clear that the human qualities required in servant, are the qualities searched for during the interview.

4. Character

You need to take its meaning in a comprehensive way. It has two sides. The first side is related to human qualities, which you are aware of. The second side is related to behaviour. Every society has its own behavioural norms, known as culture. For example, to respect women and aged people is our culture. The second type of behaviour is related to our profession. When you become an IAS officer, you are expected to behave according to your profession. After becoming a college professor the requirements are different and they are different when you become a doctor. Likewise the code of conduct for a businessman is different.

Here I have an advice for you. The list of etiquettes seems unending. In different places and for different occasions, different behaviours have been prescribed. Especially those aspirants who belong to rural background and don't have much exposure, they are personally very gentle, simple and honest, but are not aware of how to behave in a particular place and on certain occasions. As a result of which their personal impression turns out weak.

So for every candidate who really wants to improve his personality, I would advise them to read this book in hindi, titled "Student aur Shishtachar". This book under my guidance and my request has been written by Gautam Masaniya, with a lot of hard work, and is very well written. The book mentions in detail how you are required to behave in which places and on certain occasions. This book has also been printed by the same publisher as this book which you are reading. My advice is that you should read this book and always keep it with you. This is neither a one-time read book nor a book to learn. This is a book of "code of conduct", which should be always lying on your table, so that you can read it from time to time.

Being an educated citizen of a country we are required to behave in a certain way, which is known as 'civilian manners'. It's not related to profession. To respect the other person's dignity, wearing clean clothes, to talk to anyone decently, to stand politely in queues and wait for your turn, to follow the rules and laws of the system and to follow the constitution- all of these come under this type of behaviour. These things are being noticed when you face the interview board.

Keep in mind that to evaluate these qualities you will not be asked any different questions, because the interviewers know that you will give the same made up answers like everyone else. They try to catch these indirectly. I would like you to notice one of the words used in the syllabus under 'interview test' in UPSC. It is written there that the evaluation of the aspirant will be done by a board, which will have "competent and unbiased observers". Notice that 'unbiased members' is not written here instead 'observers' are mentioned. Observer means one who observe. They don't just listen to you but also scan you. They not only observe your facial expressions, but your voice too. Maybe you won't understand it, but all the work is of observation here.

Downside of personality

Now I come in the second part of Personality. Till now

we have discussed the positive sides of our personality which everyone should have. There is another side of our personality- the negative side. This is the side, which we shouldn't have. It's not wrong if we say that there is not a single person, who has all the positive things and not a single negative thing in them. Every person is a mixture of these both sides. The only difference is the balance of positive things and negative things in a person. Another difference is what are your positive aspects and what are the negative aspects. In a way, only after preparing a balance sheet of the two can one evaluate one's personality.

The process of personality development is literally like a flowing river. It never dries up. Never stops. If a person is aware of his personality then there is a continuous struggle between his positive and negative aspects. In this struggle we try to strengthen our existing positive aspects. We also try to build positive aspects of our personality which are not in us and we think should be there.

During this struggle we continuously face negative elements, which we want to get rid of. After dealing with them in different ways we slowly weaken them and eventually eliminate them. The result of this continuous struggle in our life is that in the balance sheet of our personality, the list of positivity keeps on increasing and the list of negativity decreases. And this is where we win.

What do I mean by 'negative aspects'? In general terms, these are aspects of an individual's personality which are neither beneficial for him nor the society, the country or the whole world. These are those demerits of our character and behaviour, which if are present in another person we don't like them. At least some of the demerits are present in everyone's personality. Our biggest challenge is how we remove these demerits with continuous struggle.

I'm listing some demerits that may be present in you and every possible step should be taken to get rid of them.

- ☑ Every person is selfish in some manner. The spirit of selfishness is not evil but there should be no fraud, deception and illegal aspects. An administrator is not expected to be cunning or deceitful, or one who is willing to do another person wrong (up to any extent) so that his own requirements could be met.
- ☑ From a psychological point of view, there are two main types of complex. When a person unnecessarily thinks of himself as best, then it is his superiority complex. But when he unnecessarily undermines himself, then it is his inferiority complex. In superiority complex, you deny the other person's existence, importance and their dignity, while in inferiority complex, you deny your own existence, importance and dignity. The presence of any of the two is not considered appropriate, because both will imbalance our personality. Keep in mind that this is present, to some extent, in everyone, but the challenge is to how you can reduce it and how much you can keep it in control.
- ☑ Everyone wants to see himself as best, courteous and good. This is not wrong. But this turns out to

be wrong when a person is not like this but pretends to be. Thus his whole behaviour, gesture, mode of speech and character everything seems artificial. It is not just the interview board but any experienced person also will be able to spot artificial persons. Don't you feel that doing this is a kind of fraud?

☑ To be a good administrator and even a good social person, it is necessary that you are liberal in your view, be progressive, full of scientific consciousness and humanist. Little thinking and a narrow point of view doesn't make a person large and successful. Our approach towards life should be very open, not rigid. We should be free from all the prejudices based on caste, religion, language or geographical differences. Everyone should be equal in our point of view. Then only will we be able to behave equally with them, especially when, we have some rights given to us by the society and the government.

☑ There is no such person, who is never disappointed in his lifetime. The important thing is not to omit it. The important thing is how soon we can make it go away once it comes. Feeling of hopelessness gives rise to negative thinking towards life. People having authority and responsibilities as big as of a civil servant need to stay positive all the time. They should be like the old character in Earnest Hemingway's novel "An Old Fisherman", who in spite of being terribly battered keeps on thinking 'something will turn up' till the end, meaning something good will happen.

- ☑ I have felt that especially the youth up to 25 years of age are either very emotional or very logical. Those who are very emotional, they seem weak in spite of everything right, and the logical youth despite seemingly strong prove to be too brash and even perverse. The right balance of personality is formed by the two.
- ☑ I have many times seen a feeling of hesitation in most of the people belonging to village, small towns, Hindi medium students and lower middle class and economically weaker sections. The hesitation is ok but now when you are about to become IAS, it is not correct. It will be tough for you to make your subordinates work and lead people. Can you imagine some people are so hesitant that they even hesitate while greeting someone? Clearly how will such people talk to others, how will they attend meetings and how will they keep their point effectively in front of someone?
- ☑ Some people are sycophants. They lack patience. This quality of their personality directly affects their process of decision making. They make decisions on the basis of sycophancy and it is seen that these kinds of decisions are mostly wrong. If the impact of the decision is just on you then it's not a problem. But as an IAS officer, your decision

doesn't affect you as much as it affects the society and the world. Don't you think that in such a case being impatient will be a big demerit?

☑ It is expected from an officer that his views are flexible. If required he is ready to change his views, his decision. Only such people get others' support, and are able to do something. The people who take harsh decisions are known as a dictator and they can never be an impressive and welfare officer. There are certain ways of taking an effective decision prescribed in management books. One of the most important among them emphasizes on listening as much views on a particular topic as possible. The more thoughts you have, the more success you will get to reach the right decision. From this, you will get a lot of raw material for your decision. Since the people will find them so involved in the decision making, they will show enthusiasm for implementing it.

☑ You have cleared the mains examination. Somewhere it is a proof that your language is good. It has fewer impurities and you can clearly put your views in front of other people. But please note that till now you have just put your views in writing and have not spoken them out loud. After becoming an IAS you will have to give your views on most topics verbally. This quality is also tested in the interview. It also means that you need to work on your communication skills. It is what you call "Art of speaking".

The list of the negative aspects which I have mentioned here is not complete in itself, but is necessary. Apart from this, there can be many other demerits inside you that can make you weak directly or indirectly. It's not tough to identify them. In my opinion, you should always be alert towards your behaviour and try to identify them. When you will do this, you will find that psychologically a war has begun against the demerits inside you. Slowly there will be fewer demerits and after a while a new personality will emerge from within. Your newly emerged personality will not be difficult to recognize for you or the others. This will bring clarity in your views. Your behaviour towards others will be filled with harmony and cooperation. The irritability, anger and imbalance will decrease. You will find that slowly you have started building the capability of impressing others. This is the situation where you will score good marks by impressing the members of interview board.

What to do for a Good Personality?

Having read all these things regarding interview, if you are now eager to ask "Then what shall we do for it?", then I appreciate you. Appreciate because if only reading would have been required then the whole of India would have been personified because reading is what everyone does from Ramayana, Geeta, Vedas and Epics to various moral stories. But was it helpful? Remember neither reading, nor listening, nor thinking makes the difference but what makes the difference is doing the work. But yes, reading, listening and thinking are initial steps to action. But nothing is going to happen until you do it. A parrot that recites Ram-Ram the whole day is neither a sage nor a philosopher. So let's talk a bit about it, only a little bit because I don't want this book to transform from the one that helps to make you an IAS to the one that makes you crack an interview. Now if you agree even to some extent to what I have told you about interviews then I personally suggest you three books for further reference in its respect. The first and the second book are written by me and the third one is written by Gautam Masaniya.

1. Students and the
2. Personality Development for students
3. Student aur Shishtachar

Do you wish to know what the biggest hurdle is for IAS aspirants? I am talking about the problem that I have faced while training them for the IAS exams and I feel really bad about it. The problem is that when you tell the students about such books they listen very carefully to it and shake their heads up and down like a very obedient student but as soon as you leave, this thought is overridden by another thought. They think that questions in the exams are not going to come from these books as they are not included in the syllabus for IAS. So they drop the thought of studying such books.

Actually this thought in their mind is not an instantaneous one but the reality is that they never have been encouraged, since the beginning of their school days till college, to read some extra books which were not included in the syllabus. So for them it is a waste of time and sort of burdensome. They just don't want to study and then to overcome the guilt of disobeying their teacher, they search for excuses to establish that such books are not worth reading at all. The thought I was talking about is born out of these excuses only. People with repeated failures are the people obsessed with this kind of attitude. And I do not have any sympathy for them. Now you should know what kind of a person are you?

I would like to make it clear to you that thinking of preparing for the interview in 1-2 months will prove to be destructive for you. It would have been productive for sure had the interview was structured to be mere a medium of knowledge transmission. But the problem is that this is not the case. Interview is not a test of knowledge; it's a test of personality as mentioned by UPSC. And personality can never be changed in a month no matter how much you work hard. It's a continuous process and should be in progress even after you become an IAS. Hence I mentioned previously that you should get on its practice from the day you get this thought of becoming an IAS.

Friends, how to enhance your personality is dependent on two means. One is not in your hand and other is in your hand. From the day a child is conceived, his personality starts forming. From then on various factors and numerous incidents have their due impact on the person and mould its personality in a particular form. Some of these incidents are controllable and rest are not. All in all, I am pointing out towards some important aspects which can (if handled well) strengthen your personality. Major aspects are -

☑ Family background, where we are born. We perceive our values, thinking and language from here. Our physical attributes are dependent on our genes (DNA). We don't have any control in regard of this aspect.

☑ The Environment in which we live, our locality. This has a great impact on our personality and we cannot resist it. Only a few people can stay untouched. The place where we live, the people whom we live with sets the base for our etiquettes, dressing sense, speaking and behaviour. Initially, we do not have much control on it as it is determined by the circumstances of our parents at that time.

☑ Our educational background too plays an important role. When I say 'educational background', it includes what subjects we have studied, which school which university we belong to, and even who have taught us through the years. We can easily make out the difference between a student of engineering and a commerce student.

☑ In our life every second there are some incidents which take place and these incidents can be good as well as bad. It is not necessary that bad incidents have a bad impact on our personality. The science behind this is that incidents are not important, what is important is our reactions to those incidents, means how we take those incidents. Like, if a father is an alcoholic, then there are two clear directions in front of the son. First is he decides to make his life better than his father's by not being alcoholic and the second is he walks in his father's shoes and also starts drinking. It all depends on how you think. This way we can control it as much as we want.

Apart from it, there are number of things which mould our personality. I don't want to go into detail. I just want to say that whatever points we have talked about previously, some of them are passed on to you and rest are given by the incidents that take place in your life. But I don't support the fact that you are a slave to these incidents or the family trades that you are born with. And don't take it as if you don't have control over them so you cannot do anything about it. You may know many people in your life like me who have increased their limits by their will power. I deeply believe that "Our limits are what we set for ourselves." I would like you to trust me on this that it makes no difference whether you are rich or poor, highly nourished or underdeveloped, living in metros or in a remote place, what actually matters is whether you have a strong will to bring positive changes in your personality or not.

Now I will give you some practical tips that you can implement in your behaviour which will make your personality more visible and powerful.

- ☑ Don't be an introvert. Meet different people and talk to them. Instead of meeting the same people daily, meet different people. Interact with them. Try to listen more and speak less. Examine people and find out what are the things that impress you. Note these things and repeat them continuously. In this way you will break your hesitation. Plus, you will start absorbing impressionable traits of others.
- ☑ Whenever you get a chance to speak, don't leave it whether it's a simple conversation or a debate or speech competition or any chance to speak or perform in front of people as it enhances your

confidence.

- ☑ Don't limit your reading to syllabus books only. Try to read literature, not only novels or stories or poems but also society, politics, psychology etc. This will enhance the content you can speak.
- ☑ If there are some good programs -social, cultural, educational- in your locality, village, city etc., participate in them. Watch drama, go to music concerts, and enjoy the dance performances. Pay attention to the comments and the speeches etc. given by others- no matter on what topic they are speaking. Don't hesitate to go for movies either. But remember: you have to 'read' the movies more than 'watching' them. You can learn a lot from movies. Try to grab the knowledge about the culture, the traditions and the values of the background shown in the movie. As far as dialogues are concerned, they provide you with the opportunity to learn the latest language.
- ☑ Search for what is lacking in your behaviour, speaking and thinking. Work on them as these will take time to perfect and the practice to perfection should start from now onwards. For example, if you have pronunciation problem then sort it out, or if your style of sitting and standing is abrupt or you produce sounds while eating and drinking then work on them and rectify them. These kinds of things, no matter how small or negligible they seem to you, their collective influence can make your

personality less effective. Surely our upbringing and tradition plays a vital role in it but the best part is that these can be rectified easily.

- ☑ You are literate and have done your graduation. And being a graduate is not just accumulating a degree. It asks for a special type of thinking, personality and behaviour. But most students are unaware of it. No matter from where you are, what your past was but graduating means now you are a perfect 'gentleman'. You are now expected to know all the disciplines as well as you have all the etiquettes in your nature. Now you cannot give these excuses that I am from a village or I was not aware about it or I am poor. It all may be right but the important fact is that you are a graduate and if you do not have the manners then your graduation is a waste. Therefore, you must take into account all the manners and the etiquettes prescribed for a highly civilized person and start practicing them from today itself.

You should refer to the previously mentioned books for the reference of mannerism and personality development. Now I will talk about the other side of the interview which you will get to know about while sitting in front of the interviewing board. Now I will talk about the following:

- ☑ What is the procedure of interview?
- ☑ What are the commonly asked questions in an interview?
- ☑ How to answer these questions?

☑ How to do the preparations for the interview and what are the chief points that are to be taken care of while sitting in front of the interviewing board?

Basically it's related to the practical side of interview but it does not mean that it's the most important part. Keeping this thing in mind will make you lame. And you cannot win a race if both of your legs do not possess the same strength provided the race is not for handicapped.

So whatever previous conversation regarding personality we have done is not waste, it's very necessary and should be kept in mind. So let's come to the next phase.

How is an Interview conducted?

Mostly the UPSC committee consists of one Head and few other members. These members comprise administrative officers, educationalists, politicians, Justices, and other experienced professionals of their fields. It is decided by the Government of India who should be the members. And then these members happen to be the heads of the various interviewing boards.

For the civil services, every year 5-6 interviewing boards are made and the number of boards is dependent on the number of participants that year in the examination and also on the duration in which these interviewing sessions needs to be completed.

Every Interviewing board generally consists of 4-5 members. Out of this, one member is the member of UPSC committee and that member is the head of the interviewing panel. Rest of the members come from different backgrounds.

They may be senior IAS/IPS, psychologists, experts of their respective fields, prominent personalities from various walks of life etc. Which type of members will a panel constitute of depends on the type of examination. Now since civil services is related to government management and discipline hence Senior IAS and IPS play a major part as the candidate needs to be tested in discipline and managerial skill of government.

To maintain confidentiality, the boards do not know which candidate they are going to interview nor does the candidate know which board is going to be his. Just before the interview a lottery decides which candidate is going to be in which board number. I am disclosing this because candidates usually have a lot of misconceptions or ill thoughts related to the interviewing panels. In modern social scenario candidates have started thinking of corrupt ways as the only means to get selected in an interview. Don't ever think like that. UPSC does its best to maintain its unbiased nature. So if you hear something negative about it you should not believe it to be true, rather consider it as a rumour.

Now starts the real interview procedure :

☑ After the declaration of mains exam results, the selected candidates are asked to be present on the provided date with some necessary documents at the centre that is essentially New Delhi.

☑ After inspection of the certificates and documents, the candidate is provided with the board number in which the interview will be done and asked to wait for his turn sitting in a huge waiting room. When the name of the candidate is called the candidate goes inside and faces the interviewing panel.

☑ Mostly every member of the panel asks questions about a specific trade, like someone will be asking personal questions; the other will be asking questions related to your subjects; someone would be asking questions from general knowledge; someone else may be up for administration related questions etc. But this doesn't mean that members of the board are bound to ask questions from only one trade. They can interfere in between. For example, 'A' has asked a question. You are answering it. Now upon hearing what you are saying, 'B' is feeling an urge to ask a relative question. So he is absolutely free to do that. Then you should deal with that as there is no such set pattern for questioning but generally one question at a time is asked and with the specified segment of the member's specialization.

☑ During the questioning, your personality is inspected and marked. These marks are given by the members on equal margin. After the interview, the individual marks provided by the members are handed over to the board head that sums the marks. Members generally consult each other before deciding upon what marks should be given to you. But the final decision is taken by the board head.

☑ It's generally seen that a board takes 10 interviews a day- 5 in the pre-lunch session, 5 in the post-lunch session. Every candidate is interviewed for 20 to 25 minutes. If the candidate is very nervous still the panel tries to calm him down. They try their best to make him talk to them for at least 12-15 minutes- no matter how poorly he is performing. The duration of the interview increases if the interviewee is interesting and liked by the panel. It cannot be said, however, that the more the duration of the interview, the more marks you get because sometime there can be a discussion related to any topic and this can lead to excess time trap. But it's generally seen that any interview which exceeds 20 minutes then that's a safe place to be at.

For you, it was necessary to know this process of interview so that you don't find yourself in 'all of a sudden' kind of situation and easily accommodate yourself accordingly. The journey is easier if the roads are known.

In front of the Board Members :

☑ When you go for the interview, you won't find the door open to welcome you. The door will be slightly closed and you need to knock 3-4 times and seek permission to enter the room. After the voice of "Yes, come in" is heard, go in. Step inside the room and quietly leave the door in previous state so it seems closed and the sound of door shutting is not produced.

☑ Reaching in, you would find a moderate size room

in a partially decorated situation. You won't find it as grand as big corporate offices. On one side you will find a table surrounded by 4-5 chairs and board members and head will be on those chairs. On the other side of the table you will find a single chair for you. Reach to your chair and wait for the permission to sit. But don't forget to wish and greet the authorities saying 'namaskar, sir' or 'good morning, sir' or 'good afternoon, sir' as soon as you enter the room. Stand beside the chair and wait for the permission for you to sit on the chair.

☑ As soon as the permission is granted, slightly adjust the chair and try not to make irritating sounds. Rapidly running your eyes towards every board member say thanks to everyone at once, get comfortable in your chair and wait for them to start asking questions.

Take care not to sit until the permission is granted. And if while you are standing someone starts asking questions then do not ask to sit, reply while standing. Don't ever take it as a 'devaluation' or 'insult' of yours. Think that 'may be this is a way of inspection and examination of my personality.'

Now they will start asking you questions. Let's look at what types of questions are asked generally.

Interview Questions

Generally there is a feeling of fear and doubt in the minds of candidates related to the types of questions that can be asked in the interview. They feel that since IAS is the biggest examination so questions can be asked from anywhere and anything. Technically this is correct; you can be asked anything as the questions are not from a set syllabus. But it never happens. The panel members know the limits and reach of the candidates very well. They too have been through all this. They know that the candidate in front of them is an average 25 year old student and not an encyclopaedia. So instead of the right to ask anything they only ask what is legitimate to ask and will be right to judge the candidate.

On the basis of this, we can find a set pattern in the type of questions asked in the interview which will help in preparations of the interview. I have another logic that supports this thought of mine. The sole purpose of an interview is to judge your personality. And this can be done only if there is a conversation between you and the interviewer. If you limit your answers to simple 'yes' or 'no', or if you give plain mechanical answers, memorized answers then there will be no possibility of a genuine discussion. And without a genuine discussion, no one can judge who you really are from inside, what kind of thought patterns and values are stored in your subconscious. So it's like a psychologist, who talks to the patient for hours to know what the mental status of the patient is and what is the problem he is facing.

That means a proper interview will only be conducted if it is in discussion mode. So it's quite natural that only those questions will be asked whose replies are expected from you. And if you are unable to answer those questions, there will be no big issue. This will give them a clue to what your level of knowledge is. Now they will ask you questions that would be easier for you. But again I am requesting you not to take it as 'devaluation' of yours. Interviewers have nothing to do with your level of knowledge. Their only concern is your personality which cannot be judged without having a discussion with you. So never lose heart if you go through something like that.

Now I will put forward the types of questions that are asked during interview. These should serve as the basis of your preparation. Normally these kinds of questions are asked:

- ☑ Personal Questions
- ☑ Questions related to Academic background
- ☑ Questions related to your state
- ☑ Questions related to current affairs
- ☑ General reasoning and mental ability related psychometric questions.

1. Personal Questions

The UPSC has clearly stated that before the interview starts the interviewers have a copy of your resume in front of them. But you should never assume that on the basis of that resume, they would have any perceptions or presumptions regarding your talent and skills beforehand. For example, you are a second or third divisioner, have always studied in government schools and your university might not have that much reputation either. Yes, the board knows it all beforehand, but you too should know that this thing does not count in your interview marking. They know that it's not a joke to qualify the written test of IAS examination and by doing that you have proved that you are worthy of selection as an IAS.

So now the question arises that when they have your

resume in front of them then why do they question it? Actually the purpose of it is to know a bit about you beforehand and decide which types of questions are to be done with you and what are your areas of specialization and what should be the direction of the questions. It just briefs them about you. That is the reason board always starts the interview with direct questions related to you only. The reason behind such questioning is to make you normal and calm you down so that the nervousness that a candidate carries is decreased to minimum as that nervousness makes it difficult for the interviewer to accurately judge your personality and hence these personal questions are helpful for the candidate only. It's very clear that these personal questions are very easy and you can easily answer these questions and when you answer these questions you calm down and become more comfortable at the psychological level. The questions which normally fall under it are

- ☑ What is your name?
- ☑ What is the meaning of your name?
- ☑ For which reason is your city known for?
- ☑ Where in the map of India is your city located?
- ☑ What is the name of your university named after?
- ☑ What's your hobby?
- ☑ Why did you pursue this trade in graduation?
- ☑ Why do you want to become an IAS or an IPS?
- ☑ Why do you want to leave your present job? Etc.

These are easy questions but are not asked in this straight manner and when you are answering these questions may be they get to ask more questions from the answers that you gave.

Like if your hobby is playing cricket then they can ask details about cricket. If you are working in some company they may ask about your job and the company. If you wear specs then they can ask about the lenses. If you are wearing a ring they can ask 'do you believe in astrology?' if you say 'yes' then they can start talking about astrology, science, religion and superstition.

Although the questions related to you may seem easy but you need to be well prepared for them and the preparation should start from today only. You should make a list of expected questions that are mainly asked and prepare your answers accordingly. You must be clear and confident about every aspect of yours. This will help you begin on a positive note. And if your interview starts off well you will face the upcoming questions more confidently.

2. Questions related to academic background

By the way, it's also a personality related phase but here following types of questions are asked

- ☑ Subjects taken for graduation.
- ☑ Subject taken for post-graduation.
- ☑ Subject for M-Phil or PhD.
- ☑ Optional subject for mains exam.

For a good number of students, most of these subjects happen to be the same. But there are also those for whom they do not match. Specially engineering and medical students choose arts subjects as their optional paper. My advice to such students is that they should not limit their preparation only to the arts subject chosen as their optional paper. Board can definitely ask questions related to your engineering or medical background and you cannot say that you do not remember this now as you did engineering in so and so years. This is the real test of personality. If the scenario is like that then it means that you take knowledge in a very casual and temporary manner. You studied, used that to gain marks and then forgot it totally. Board's expectation, on the other hand, is that the knowledge that you have accumulated is your lifelong saving and you should protect that.

Although board does not ask very difficult questions related to your subjects as what they want to know is whether you understand your subjects or not. Mostly it is seen that the board shows huge interest in asking the questions related to your subjects that were directly or indirectly into news some time ago. So it's important for the candidates to be updated to day by day news of what's happening in the surrounding and what's related to their subject in latest news.

All in all, whatever subjects you have chosen during graduation and after, you need to revise those before the interview and keep an eye on the important chapters of those subjects as the majority of questions are asked from them only.

3. Questions related to your state

I've seen most of the candidates doing mistakes in this phase of questions. This mistake is committed mostly by those candidates who either live away from their hometown or are out for studies like IAS preparations. These people lack the touch with their states as the newspaper they read are national newspapers and hardly contain news about their state. As a result of that they lack in this phase of knowledge. It's expected from you that you will have information about your state and your information should be on these topics

- ☑ Political scenario of the state.
- ☑ Economic scenario of the state.
- ☑ Important problems of the state.
- ☑ Important earnings of the state.
- ☑ Cultural values and people of the state.

That's why it's necessary that the candidate not only reads a fundamental book related to his state but he should also keep himself updated with the day-to-day happenings. No book is going to keep you updated with day to day happenings so you need to just read newspapers daily. And keep in mind that you not only have to read the news, but you also have to analyse it on your own so that you develop a clear perspective of what is going on in your state.

4. Discussion about Current Affairs

Most of the questions are asked from this section. Current affairs mean knowledge related to domestic and global topics that are in news etc. or famous. I think this section can be of immense help to you as you already have prepared for it well at the time of mains exam. What is even more helpful is that this preparation of yours is of explanatory type. Now you just need to do one thing. Prepare for those affairs that took place between mains exam and the interview. And I think you should keep doing it till the time you either get finally selected or you drop the thought of selection. All in all, to prepare for current affairs should not be a big deal for you.

I would specially like to mention this thing because it has been seen that in an interview mainly the focus is on two topics (current affairs related). Firstly, the political state of the country. Second is any important national or international news that has been a topic of discussion etc. The interview board assumes you are aware of the news and tries to know your personal take on these matters. So you need to be prepared for these from before with your self-opinions.

Here I would like to tell you about an awesome trick to crack this problem as candidates always ask me, "How to make your opinion and to check whether it's right or wrong?" They want a very small but effective answer on it and that is "They should take Indian constitution as the Bible, Geeta, Quran, Guru Granth Sahib and stick with it." That means whatever your opinion is; it should stay correct on the constitutional parameter. I would like to say in front of you that the constitution is the real mentor to you. It is possible that your personal views, on a particular matter, do not match with constitutional constraints. But being an IAS officer you will be expected, when dealing with public matters, to put aside your personal views or stands and do as directed by the constitution. At a personal level, you will be free to support any aspect but publicly you will not be allowed to do so and since you are being interviewed for a public life hence it's expected from you to take the constitution as the code of conduct.

5. Questions related to general mental ability

In this segment you can take the questions as the version of questions of C-SAT examination. Here your subject will not help. Frankly speaking, even knowledge does not come into play here. What comes into play here is the intelligence i.e. how clever you are and how alert. How early and how accurately you understand the situations and take the steps to rectify it. For example, a candidate was asked to assume that "you are a collector of a district and suddenly you are informed that a train accident has just taken place somewhere in your district. Then what will be your initial step towards it?" Now before I tell you the answer of that candidate I would like you to be prepared with your version of the answer. Ready? Then listen, the candidate answered, "I will firstly find whether it was a goods carrier train or a passenger train." And not to mention that he got good marks in that interview.

You cannot prepare a curriculum of these questions. You cannot prepare for them beforehand either. This depends solely on your inner wisdom that what comes out of your mouth. Those who have good reasoning and analyzing skills do respond to situations more accurately and maturely. Else some emotional person would act like "Oh it's an emergency, god knows how many people have died." These people would send medical and rescue teams as soon as possible without understanding the situation. Hence we need to improve our reasoning skills as much as possible. Debating with friends, group discussions and talking on new topics will help in this.

"God is eternity so is his talks"- this means that the structure of questions that I have provided earlier is not the only necessary thing but whatever I have provided is necessary for preparations and you can take it as a demo. But you should not be tensed. If you are able to answer these questions it's well and good but if it's not then you need not to be disheartened. This is not going to harm your chances.

How to prepare for interview

I have previously said that the preparation for interview is not a mechanical process nor is it an accumulation of knowledge. It's mainly the shine of the personality of a person that cannot be developed in a day. It's a continuous process that should remain going eventually after the completion of IAS.

Now since we are talking about the IAS interview so we should specially focus on it. So let's talk about some topics that can be very important for it. Now we need to talk about the things that are necessary in terms of personality for the interview. Here I will reveal some important and practical facts in front of you, which put you at ease and will help you in gaining confidence. Then your interview will surely be better.

- ☑ You should try to reach at least two days before at the place of interview. Communicate with candidates at the interview centre. This helps to know the kind of questions interviewers are asking. In most of the cases it is noticed that, few questions are asked from many students. We get to know the correct and exact answers of these questions by talking to students. Also, we get the information of nature of interview questions. Also, the terror of interview in mind is reduced.

If we go at the centre for interview on the same day, then a different kind of fear and tension grips the mind. If we go there for one or two days before that, then with that environment our mental equilibrium is established. This helps us to balance ourselves.

Some people say that before interview, you should not talk to other students who came for interview because that creates confusion. Thinking that we don't know the answers of these questions, the self-confidence also gets low. But saying this is not the solution of the problem, rather avoidance of the problem. It's more practical that we talk about interview.

- ☑ Success of interview is dependent largely on your ability of expression. If you are able to put your point clearly and impactful, then certainly its effect is good. Therefore candidates should try to improve their communication skills. Select good words. Avoid using lousy and double meaning words. Your sentences should be simple and understandable. Some people have misconception in their mind that members of board get influenced by complex sentences made from difficult words. This is incorrect. Such type of words and sentences make your language artificial.
- ☑ In front of board, your behaviour should be extremely balanced and gentle. Being gentle and humble doesn't mean that even if member says any wrong point, then also you accept that politely. Humbleness means that your way of speaking should be gentle. If you are not agreeing with the point of any member, then contradict it with full politeness, not with rudeness. If you show severity in such opportunities, then it will be the indication

of your imbalanced behaviour.

☑ If you are not in the condition of answering any question, then do not hesitate to show regret for it. Members understand this point that it is not necessary that you answer every question. But this also doesn't mean that you will be relieved by apologizing for not giving answer to very easy questions. This will be regarded as your weakness only. One more thing, if you are not able to answer easy questions, then absolutely do not give wrong answers. You should keep this in mind that the member who is asking you question, knows the answer. If you try to fool him with your cleverness, then he will immediately guess it.

☑ Your answers should not be ambiguous, rather should be completely clear and to the point. You can yourself be trapped by giving ambiguous answers. In such conditions, members can demand clarification from you and you will be trapped unnecessarily. Therefore speaking less is considered ideal rule for interview. One, who speaks more, will have more chances of being caught.

☑ Your answers should be factual, not abstract. Abstract answers are considered as avoidable answers. Like if a member asks you - 'why did you do M.A. from Hindi literature?' then your answer should not be "because I liked it". It will convey the message that you don't have a definite answer. Instead you should try to explain why you are interested in literature. It is natural that you took Hindi literature because of your interest in it. So if you talk about "interest" then it would not be appropriate. It was an opportunity, when you could have influenced members with your answer but you lost that opportunity by giving a small dry answer. Someone has said, "Interview is not taken by the interviewer; it is given by the interviewee." Means if you are a little bit alert and intelligent, then you can give the interview the direction you want and you can bend the course of conversation according to your will. In above example if you answer, "I like Hindi writers, especially Premchand and Jayshankar Prasad very much. My interest is also in writing literature. Therefore I have taken Hindi literature in M.A." then it may be the beginning of new direction of interview from here, because as soon as you will take the name of Premchand and Jayshankar Prasad, likewise any member can again ask questions on it or as soon as you say that your interest is in writing literature, likewise any member can ask what you write, if you have been published etc. Thus it will change the direction of interview. I tried the same thing and fetched the best results.

☑ While speaking, you should pay attention that you are not speaking very fast or in very high or very low voice. Your speed of speaking and pitch of voice must be fully balanced, so members do not have difficulty in understanding your point. While answering do not try to quote other people too much- no matter how prominent and recognized they are. Otherwise this would mean that you do not have something original to say.

☑ Some students have this misconception in their mind that during interview, they should boast about the government and the board members, but this is wrong. Flattering won't ever help you scoring good marks. This might have helped you out in different aspects of life but it will not help during interview. Your answers should be balanced as it should not be seen that you are biased and bent towards some political party etc. In the same way, it should not show that you are favouring some religion, caste, language, culture etc.

☑ Whatever solution to any problem comes from you should be feasible and right as well as it should also fulfil the social and constitutional constraints. Like if you want to stop some communal riots, you cannot say that for one community, the religious rights should be minimized etc. This reply of yours goes against the secular nature of our constitution. Hence your solutions should be such that can be transformed into action. Too much idealistic views can make your solutions impractical and ineffective. Whether it's about your perception in regard of life or it's about solving a problem, you cannot be idealistic on the cost of being highly impractical or unrealistic.

☑ Many of the candidates have this confusion of what to wear. Candidates get themselves new clothes and shoes. They have a dilemma that shall they wear suits or shirt and trousers? They should put up a tie or not? The answers of these depend solely on one's comfort level. But you should be as natural as possible. To me, your clothes should be in accordance with the weather conditions. Wearing a suit and putting up a tie in the month of June might be a bit awkward- but then there is no hard and fast rule that you cannot wear suits in June. Whatever you wear it should be soft and elegant.

☑ Please do not think that the board members are there to challenge you or to make you feel inferior. Rather have this approach of humbleness and generosity for them, only then can you help them assess you correctly.

☑ As soon as you enter the interview room, your evaluation starts. Therefore there should be a reflection of decency in the way you stand, walk and sit. Don't forget to use the words like 'please' and 'thank you' wherever possible. Many students don't do this out of hesitation. Some important directions for doing so is -

1. Ask for permission before entering the room.
2. Greet the members after reaching the interview table.

3. Without the chairman's permission don't sit on your chair.
4. Don't initiate.
5. Don't show emotions to get sympathy of the board members.
6. While talking use expressions like 'as far as I understand', 'I assume that', 'I think so' and 'In my view', to make your language more natural.
7. Don't forget to greet everyone at the end of the interview.
8. Don't look back while going out of the room.
9. Don't forget to close the door behind you - that too slowly.
10. During the interview, don't behave in a way which looks rude, like - biting your nails with your teeth, shaking your leg while sitting, adjusting your hair, wiping your spectacles again and again, poking your nose/ear/teeth etc.
11. Your answers should coincide with your expressions. If the answer is serious then your face should be serious too. Remember that all this should not be made up, but should appear natural.
12. If a member appreciates your answer, don't forget to thank him.
13. Remember, the rule of etiquette is that unless the senior person puts forward his hand for a handshake, till then you also shouldn't try shaking your hands with them. So if the chairman or a member puts his hand forward, then only you put your hand forward and thank them after shaking hands.

Utility of Mock Interview

Normally, many coaching institutes guide the aspirants

for the interview through mock interviews. The logic behind it is that the students get to know about the etiquettes required in front of the interviewer. Along with it, the board members are able to spot minor flaws in the aspirants, which may weaken the impact of their interview.

There are two different approaches about its utility. The first one is definitely in its favour. Here, I remember a statement given by the great cricketer Sachin Tendulkar. During an interview in the year 2005, Sachin Tendulkar said that the day he was supposed to play a match, just the night before it he had already played the game in his mind. It means he already had imagined all the situations which could happen in the ground the next day. This approach of Sachin Tendulkar definitely underlines the utility of a Mock Interview.

Ycs, it's just a sort of rehearsal, but then the candidate gets introduced to the type of atmosphere he has to face during the real interview. This situation is most beneficial to the aspirants, who have never given an interview. It also turns out to be beneficial to the students belonging to rural background and small or medium cities. This is because the students from government schools do not get much opportunity to speak and the focus is not on academics in their environment, where they can bring themselves forward. In such a situation this small opportunity -even if it is not real- somewhere reduces their fear.

To be true I am also in favour of it, provided the people taking the interview are experienced. When I used to guide the students for IAS for two months, I had set a rule. Each day a different student was given the duty to take care of the class. He used to look at all the arrangements of the class, welcome the people and resolve the problem that comes at that time. He was supposed to change the arrangement of the class for the better. Afterwards, he was supposed to tell about his work done in front of the other students. Then the students used to ask questions which he was supposed to answer. He was even asked questions based on his answers. In this way, a significant discussion took place.

I saw, and found out from other students too, and even the students themselves feel a great change inside them from this small practice. Their hesitation breaks and confidence increases. They now have the capacity to answer other people's questions. If they give a wrong answer, they now have the guts to apologize.

Overall, it was a type of methodology for preparing for the interview and my past students after remembering this methodology turn emotional and say, "Sir, it was a turning point in my life."

Here I would like to give you a specific advice. The members of the mock interview board are experienced in regards with their age. Therefore their comments about your etiquettes, way of talking and the effectiveness of your answer will be beneficial for you only. But they have their own limitations too. They may not be experienced in regard of the nature of the questions asked in UPSC. Also, they may be lacking the expertise needed to evaluate the answers given by the candidates facing UPSC's interview board. But then, something is better than nothing.

As far as the discussion thing is concerned, you shouldn't be completely dependent on them. You need to prepare for it in your own way also. And the best way is to read about the experiences of the past candidates and try to understand the types of questions they were being asked. Also, you should think about why those questions were asked- this is even more important.

It's up to you how and up to what extent you get benefitted from mock interviews. If you are planning to go for it just for the sake of following a trend, then I will suggest you not to go for. But if you are keen on observing minute things in order to improve your personality, then this will provide you with a good opportunity.

I want permission to close this chapter now. I believe that after reading this long chapter, you definitely will have a new understanding about the interview. If it's not the case, then mark my words and read this chapter again. I guarantee that you won't be disappointed.

Chapter 20

Benefits of IAS preparation

Most of the young people want to become IAS. And they have all the rights to do this. There is no harm in this wish. However, the truth is that the number of people who actually become IAS can be counted on fingers. Earlier I told you that if you are not able to qualify the IAS examination, so even if you are able to reach the interview, you will not get any job on this basis. The mark sheet of your mains examination will have no value and you will be back to square one. Friends, if you see the hard work of IAS preparation just limited to IAS only, then my talk is 100% true. Otherwise it's nothing more than a half truth. It's a half truth indeed. No matter what the knowledge is, it's never wasted- provided you don't let it go waste. For this I really like two lines by the poet Bashir Badra ji from Bhopal which mean that 'no effort goes waste, and even if you do not achieve your goal, you will get nearer.'

What is this distance which is reduced? If you search for its answer, you can reach the conclusion that 'My IAS preparation won't go waste- if I don't let it waste.' I am not giving you a 'motivational speech' in order to make you feel good. Neither am I on a high tide of emotions. I am making you aware of a real social phenomenon. What is it? For the last 15-20 years, I have been witnessing a different phenomenon of competitive examinations. On the basis of IAS every state conducts its own civil service examination. Under it deputy collector, deputy police officer and other officers are appointed.

I have been seeing an amazing thing that in these state examinations 80-85 percent of the successful students are those who have prepared for the IAS examination earlier i.e. they are preparing for IAS, but also sit in state examinations. If they are not able to succeed there, they succeed here. It is also seen that if many youngsters don't get a job of their liking in IAS they leave it and join state civil services. It is a matter of their personal needs and wants. It is a saying that anyone's feet can fit an elephant's foot. IAS preparation in itself is like an elephant's foot that is so broad and deep that after doing it, it's not necessary to work hard while preparing for other examinations. The state examination's syllabus is not only less than that of civil service, but the level of difficulty is also lower. In such a scenario, the students preparing for IAS are more likely to succeed compared to those who are only preparing for state examinations. This is the first benefit.

Now I will tell you the second benefit. From the year 2011, a new paper of CSAT has been introduced in the preliminary exam. This paper prepares you for other examinations too, in which bank examinations are the main. Its preparation also helps in other examinations. That's why I suggest my students that even if your goal is to be an IAS officer, you also need to sit in other examinations. You can do this by just preparing a bit differently.

The third benefit is that the level of your knowledge increases which ultimately help you in private jobs too and also when you start your own work. I know a lot of people, whose IAS preparations set them apart from their colleagues. Especially, the people working in media have put up a very good performance. There are two main reasons for it. The first is that their general knowledge increases. Second is that their analyzing capability and writing style also improves. Due to which, they very soon secure a special place for themselves.

There is some good news about the private sector too. When a student preparing for IAS goes for a job in a private company, he definitely gives a better performance with the help of his general knowledge. If he had reached the Interview, then this mark sheet leaves a very good impression on the people taking his interview. Almost every literate person is aware of the challenges and problems of an IAS examination. After looking at such candidate he knows that there is something special about him, specially compared to the other people, which came here to give the interview.

Now we come to self-employment. Knowledge is never wasted. It will come in use here. Preparation for IAS starts a habit of hard work in you. This will come in use here. You wanted to become an IAS; it means that you dreamt big. Now IAS has vanished from that dream but your daring to dream big is still there. And it will inspire you to set higher goals in whatever you do.

One failure should never be taken as a failure of your life. You need to try in every way possible so that your dreams don't die. Along with it, there is this also that when you were preparing many other people were also preparing with you. Some of them were selected among them, and others were not, one of which is you. Don't ever forget that those who got selected are your acquaintances, your friends. Don't get jealous of them, behave in a friendly fashion. They will make a new group available to you, whose positive effect will have an impact on your life and also your life-system.

Friends, that's why I believe that the hard work done for a big and tough exam like IAS doesn't ever go waste. When you reach a stage where you think 'Now I wont give IAS examination' then I advise you to read my book - "Failure is also Success". This book will bring a new light and create new energy in your life, which will be bigger and better than IAS.

Other Books of Author

This book provides a new and alternative approach on how to study. The book shares perspectives and techniques which will help the reader gain a better understanding of how thought works and will stimulate the readers brain. And this book even says- Anybody can do it! A tremendous book for students who want to excel beyond what may be, their perceived limits.

₹195/-

Time is the gallant resource that most of us are short of. If managed properly it promises to liberate us, alleviate us and work wonders for us. This book gives an in-depth practical knowledge of time-management through the control of mind and various techniques and discussions. If these are put into practice evolution and emancipation would start from within. This book is an endeavor (from the author) to connect you to your own-self.

₹250/-

This book dwells extensively upon understanding our self and then the methods to improve upon our weaknesses and shortcomings. The subconscious mind or our higher self knows no bounds. It is through understanding its powers and harmonizing it with that of our conscious mind that we develop the perfect blend to achieve success and fulfillment in our lives. A book that provides you with the diagnosis of your own mind and the remedies to your limitations. Doing so, enables you to reach for the skies.

₹150/-

In this day and age, it is not possible to win the competition of life based only on studies. To stay ahead in life, you need to be different and unique. This is exhibited in your personality, which makes you stand out even in a crowd.
Students will get to learn about body language, communication skills, manners and dressing etc. through the book.
This book will eliminate the gap between an average student and an exceptional one. This book is for those students who want to win the race of life and career.

₹195/-